The Politics of Peacebuilding in a Diverse World

This book challenges the understanding of 'difference' in the field of peacebuilding and offers new ways to consider diversity in the context of international interventions.

International peacebuilding as a practice and academic field has always been embroiled in the 'problem' of difference. For mainstream scholars and policy-makers, local views, histories, and cultural codes are often seen as an obstacle on the way to peace. For critical scholars, international interventions have failed because of the very superficial attention given to the needs, values, and experience of the people in post-conflict societies. Yet the current proposals of hybrid peace and emancipation seem to reproduce Eurocentric lenses and problematic binaries. Differently inspired by feminist, post-structuralist, and new materialist perspectives, the authors assembled in this volume give sustained attention to the theorisation and practice of difference. Taken together, these contributions show that differences are always multidimensional, non-essential, and are reflections of broader power and gender inequalities.

This book thus makes a major contribution to the field of critical peacebuilding by revisiting the 'problem' of difference.

This book was originally published as a special issue of the *Journal of Intervention and Statebuilding*.

Xavier Mathieu is a Teaching Associate at Aston University, UK. Previously, he was a Postdoctoral Fellow at the Centre for Global Cooperation Research at the University of Duisburg-Essen, Germany. His research interests include the theory and practice of sovereignty, peacebuilding, civilisational politics, and the theorising of 'difference' in international interventions.

Pol Bargués-Pedreny is a Research Fellow at CIDOB (Barcelona Centre for International Affairs), Spain. He has developed an interest in the intersection of philosophy and international relations. His work critically interrogates international interventions and perspectives on resilience, hybridity, and social critique. He is author of *Deferring Peace in International Statebuilding: Difference, Resilience and Critique* (2018).

The Politics of Peacebuilding in a Diverse World
Difference Exposed

Edited by
Xavier Mathieu and Pol Bargués-Pedreny

LONDON AND NEW YORK

First published 2019
by Routledge
2 Park Square, Milton Park, Abingdon, Oxon, OX14 4RN

and by Routledge
52 Vanderbilt Avenue, New York, NY 10017

Routledge is an imprint of the Taylor & Francis Group, an informa business

© 2019 Taylor & Francis

All rights reserved. No part of this book may be reprinted or reproduced
or utilised in any form or by any electronic, mechanical, or other means,
now known or hereafter invented, including photocopying and recording,
or in any information storage or retrieval system, without permission in
writing from the publishers.

Trademark notice: Product or corporate names may be trademarks or
registered trademarks, and are used only for identification and
explanation without intent to infringe.

British Library Cataloguing in Publication Data
A catalogue record for this book is available from the British Library

ISBN 13: 978-0-367-20974-2

Typeset in Myriad Pro
by RefineCatch Limited, Bungay, Suffolk

Publisher's Note
The publisher accepts responsibility for any inconsistencies that may have
arisen during the conversion of this book from journal articles to book chapters,
namely the inclusion of journal terminology.

Disclaimer
Every effort has been made to contact copyright holders for their permission to
reprint material in this book. The publishers would be grateful to hear from any
copyright holder who is not here acknowledged and will undertake to rectify
any errors or omissions in future editions of this book.

Contents

Citation Information	vii
Notes on Contributors	ix
Introduction – Beyond Silence, Obstacle and Stigma: Revisiting the 'Problem' of Difference in Peacebuilding *Pol Bargués-Pedreny and Xavier Mathieu*	1
1. Embodying Difference: Reading Gender in Women's Memoirs of Humanitarianism *Róisín Read*	18
2. Hybrid Clubs: A Feminist Approach to Peacebuilding in the Democratic Republic of Congo *Maria Martin de Almagro*	37
3. Peace-in-Difference: A Phenomenological Approach to Peace Through Difference *Hartmut Behr*	53
4. Relational and Essential: Theorizing Difference for Peacebuilding *Morgan Brigg*	70
5. The Politics of Difference in Transitional Justice: Genocide and the Construction of Victimhood at the Khmer Rouge Tribunal *Julie Bernath*	85
6. Governing Conflict: The Politics of Scaling Difference *Andreas Hirblinger and Dana M. Landau*	103
7. Old Slogans Ringing Hollow? The Legacy of Social Engineering, Statebuilding and the 'Dilemma of Difference' in (Post-) Soviet Kyrgyzstan *Philipp Lottholz*	123
8. Beyond Relationalism in Peacebuilding *Jonathan Joseph*	143
Index	153

Citation Information

The chapters in this book were originally published in the *Journal of Intervention and Statebuilding*, volume 12, issue 3 (September 2018). When citing this material, please use the original page numbering for each article, as follows:

Introduction
Beyond Silence, Obstacle and Stigma: Revisiting the 'Problem' of Difference in Peacebuilding
Pol Bargués-Pedreny and Xavier Mathieu
Journal of Intervention and Statebuilding, volume 12, issue 3 (September 2018), pp. 283–299

Chapter 1
Embodying Difference: Reading Gender in Women's Memoirs of Humanitarianism
Róisín Read
Journal of Intervention and Statebuilding, volume 12, issue 3 (September 2018), pp. 300–318

Chapter 2
Hybrid Clubs: A Feminist Approach to Peacebuilding in the Democratic Republic of Congo
Maria Martin de Almagro
Journal of Intervention and Statebuilding, volume 12, issue 3 (September 2018),
pp. 319–334

Chapter 3
Peace-in-Difference: A Phenomenological Approach to Peace Through Difference
Hartmut Behr
Journal of Intervention and Statebuilding, volume 12, issue 3 (September 2018), pp. 335–351

Chapter 4
Relational and Essential: Theorizing Difference for Peacebuilding
Morgan Brigg
Journal of Intervention and Statebuilding, volume 12, issue 3 (September 2018),
pp. 352–366

Chapter 5
The Politics of Difference in Transitional Justice: Genocide and the Construction of Victimhood at the Khmer Rouge Tribunal
Julie Bernath
Journal of Intervention and Statebuilding, volume 12, issue 3 (September 2018),
pp. 367–384

Chapter 6

Governing Conflict: The Politics of Scaling Difference
Andreas Hirblinger and Dana M. Landau
Journal of Intervention and Statebuilding, volume 12, issue 3 (September 2018),
pp. 385–404

Chapter 7

*Old Slogans Ringing Hollow? The Legacy of Social Engineering, Statebuilding and the
'Dilemma of Difference' in (Post-) Soviet Kyrgyzstan*
Philipp Lottholz
Journal of Intervention and Statebuilding, volume 12, issue 3 (September 2018),
pp. 405–424

Chapter 8

Beyond Relationalism in Peacebuilding
Jonathan Joseph
Journal of Intervention and Statebuilding, volume 12, issue 3 (September 2018),
pp. 425–434

For any permission-related enquiries please visit:
http://www.tandfonline.com/page/help/permissions

Notes on Contributors

Pol Bargués-Pedreny is a Research Fellow at CIDOB (Barcelona Centre for International Affairs), Spain. He has developed an interest in the intersection of philosophy and international relations. His work critically interrogates international interventions and perspectives on resilience, hybridity, and social critique.

Hartmut Behr is Professor of International Politics at Newcastle University, UK. His research specialises in political theory, sociology of knowledge of IR, politics of difference, political violence, and critical European Studies.

Julie Bernath is a Senior Researcher and Programme Officer in the Dealing with the Past Program at Swisspeace, which is an associate research institute of the University of Basel, Switzerland. Her PhD dissertation examined the resistance to the state-sanctioned transitional justice process in Cambodia.

Morgan Brigg is Associate Professor in the School of Political Science and International Studies at the University of Queensland, Australia. His work examines the politics of cultural difference in conflict resolution, governance, peacebuilding, and international development, by facilitating an exchange between western and indigenous political systems and philosophies.

Andreas Hirblinger is a Researcher at the Centre on Conflict, Development and Peacebuilding (CCDP), Graduate Institute Geneva, Switzerland. His research centres on the politics of knowledge production in peacebuilding. His doctoral research explored how conflicting governing rationalities underpin peace and transition contexts, based on an in-depth case study of the local government reform process in South Sudan.

Jonathan Joseph is Professor of Politics and International Relations at the University of Sheffield, UK, and an Alumni Senior Fellow at the Käte Hamburger Kolleg/Centre for Global Cooperation Research at the University of Duisburg-Essen, Germany. He is an editor of *Review of International Studies*.

Dana M. Landau is a Senior Researcher at Swisspeace, which is an associate research institute of the University of Basel, Switzerland. Her research interests include post-conflict peace- and state-building, particularly in the Western Balkans, as well as minority rights, nationalism, refugee and IDP return, mediation, and inclusive peace process design.

Philipp Lottholz is a Postdoctoral Research Fellow at the DFG Collaborative Research Centre/Transregio 138 "Dynamics of Security" and based at the Institute of Sociology, Justus Liebig University of Giessen, Germany. His PhD thesis analysed community security and peacebuilding practices and their effects on post-liberal statebuilding in

Kyrgyzstan, and was awarded the 2018 Christiane Rajewsky Prize for best work of young scholars by the German Association for Peace and Conflict Studies (AFK e.V.).

Maria Martin de Almagro is a Marie Curie Individual Fellow in the Department of Politics and International Studies at the University of Cambridge, UK, and Assistant Professor in International Affairs at Vesalius College at Vrije Universiteit Brussel, Belgium. Her scientific research interests focus on gender politics, international relations, and critical security studies.

Xavier Mathieu is a Teaching Associate at Aston University, UK. Previously, he was a Postdoctoral Fellow at the Centre for Global Cooperation Research at the University of Duisburg-Essen, Germany. His research interests include the theory and practice of sovereignty, peacebuilding, civilisational politics, and the theorising of 'difference' in international interventions.

Róisín Read is Lecturer in Peace and Conflict Studies at the Humanitarian and Conflict Response Institute at the University of Manchester, UK. Her research explores the politics of international interventions in conflict, with a focus on the dynamics of knowledge production and representation. Her recent research focuses on gender and race in narratives of the humanitarian encounter, as told through memoir and fiction.

Beyond Silence, Obstacle and Stigma: Revisiting the 'Problem' of Difference in Peacebuilding

Pol Bargués-Pedreny and Xavier Mathieu

ABSTRACT

Whereas practitioners and mainstream approaches to intervention are concerned about the inability to manage difference in a way that is conducive to peace, critical scholars worry about the inability to write difference without essentializing 'it' or reproducing and legitimizing power structures. Can we revert the pessimism regarding the possibility to engage with others sensitively and build peace in a diverse world? In this article, we argue that the current miasma of despair regarding international interventions is the result of three successive errors in the process of seeking to build a peace sensitive to the other: silencing, problematizing and stigmatizing difference. After examining these three errors, we outline three analytical starting points that offer a better understanding of difference: multidimensionality, anti-essentialism, and a focus on power struggles. This discussion opens the Special Issue and hopes to stimulate further conversations on the role of difference in peacebuilding by focusing on its conditions of emergence.

Introduction

International peacebuilding as a practice and academic field has always been embroiled in the 'problem' of difference. To put it simply: how can peacebuilding be made to work in a diverse world? How do differences impact the process of peace? Since the late 1990s, socio-cultural differences have been identified both as the origin of conflicts and as essential to build peace (Avruch 1998; Lederach 1997; Miall, Ramsbotham, and Woodhouse 1999). International organizations have gradually paid attention to the informal settings of societies intervened upon as spheres where differences are reproduced and the seeds of war and peace can be found. Even statebuilding frameworks, which tend to focus on the creation of legitimate governmental institutions and market reforms from 'the top-down', have become more willing to adjust to local contexts (Ingram 2010; OECD 2012). In the twenty-first century, it has become a platitude to admit that peace processes that are not led by local actors and respectful of their traditions and mores are doomed to go awry. Yet, among policymakers, there is a widespread pessimism about the possibility to engage with difference successfully so that a context-sensitive peace can be achieved. Sometimes cultural practices and societal codes seem difficult to comprehend to the external gaze, other times they seem incompatible with the aims of building peace.

In the scholarly literature, particularly within critical circles, the consensus is that international interventions have mostly failed because of the very superficial attention given to the needs, values and experience of the people in post-conflict societies (Kappler 2015; Mac Ginty and Firchow 2016; Richmond 2014). For universal liberal norms and international economic and security programmes cannot be transferred in a diverse world without costs and resistance from local traditions, identities and cultures. Critical reappraisals have thus argued for interventions that are respectful of local contexts and histories and connected with the 'everyday'. Yet the limits of this turn to the local have been widely recognized, as the tendency has been to reproduce Eurocentric lenses, dualisms and serve to legitimize unequal international relations (Chandler 2010; Lemay-Hébert and Mathieu 2014; Nadarajah and Rampton 2015; Randazzo 2016). As Meera Sabaratnam has it, even in critical frameworks of peacebuilding difference is often reduced to 'the liberal/local distinction [that] appears to be the *central ontological fulcrum* upon which the rest of the political and ethical problems sit' (Sabaratnam 2017, 29, original emphasis). In sum, whereas practitioners and mainstream approaches worry about the inability to fully 'capture' difference or manage it in a way that is conducive to peace, critical scholars worry about the inability to 'write' difference without essentializing 'it' or reproducing and legitimizing power structures. As difference seems fundamentally elusive, peacebuilding scholars and practitioners increasingly admit that the other cannot be helped and that any peace strategy that attempts to be sensitive to difference is doomed (Bargués-Pedreny 2017). Today critiques (and critiques of the critiques) burgeon while pessimism over peacebuilding spreads. Like the Titan Prometheus, who was punished by Zeus after he attempted to help humanity, practitioners or bold scholars who propose new solutions for peacebuilding are waiting for a critical eagle to eat their eternally regenerated liver.

Despite the centrality of the 'problem' of difference for the peacebuilding literature, the field is still lacking *explicit* theorizations of difference and comprehensive reviews on the way cognate disciplines have dealt with the concept of difference (for exceptions see Brigg [2008] and Behr [2014]). In fact, difference seems to unite different strands of peacebuilding research yet its conceptualization is mostly avoided. Throughout this Special Issue, we argue that a sustained attention to the theorization, emergence and ambiguities of difference can shed light on some of the problems faced by peacebuilding. We propose to look at peacebuilding through the lens of difference to clarify and help solve some of the deadlocks faced by contemporary scholars and practitioners. As such, this Special Issue offers in-depth empirical and conceptual discussions of peacebuilding that do not shy away from discussing difference. The contributions assembled here seek to go beyond the stagnation and impasse that characterize the elusive engagement of the field with the 'problem' of difference. Nevertheless, neither this introduction nor the Special Issue seeks to offer a 'successful' strategy to capture difference and redress peacebuilding. We rather pursue to act like the demigod Hercules who, more modestly, saved Prometheus from the eagle, rather than humanity.

In this introduction to the Special Issue, our objective is twofold. First, we argue that the miasma of despair regarding difference and peace is the result of three successive errors that occur when dealing with difference in international interventions: silencing, problematizing and stigmatizing difference. The first error was common in early peace-building missions where difference was neglected altogether due to a belief in universalist ways of making peace and progress. Difference here had no relevance and no role to play. Later, statebuilding scholars and practitioners conceptualized difference as an obstacle to be assimilated, recognizing for the first time that difference matters and needs to be considered due to its potentially negative impact on peace. Finally, current peacebuilding scholars and practitioners have become more tolerant of other worldviews but in their attempt to integrate difference they stigmatize it by overlooking the conditions of its emergence.

Secondly, after examining these three errors, we highlight the strategies used by the contributions assembled in this Special Issue and outline three analytical starting points that offer a better understanding of difference: multidimensionality, anti-essentialism, and a focus on power relations. First, differences are multidimensional and complex realities are performed differently in different peacebuilding settings, thus casting doubts on the existence of fixed characteristics of societies (and our ability to 'fix' them). Second, and following from the previous point, difference can be understood as vital to life yet as non-essential in nature. This leads to think peacebuilding as a relational process that cannot be brought to an end through deciding what difference is. Instead, rethinking difference as relational highlights the necessary postponement of conclusive settlements. Finally, and because societal and cultural differences reflect broader relations of power, the challenge for peacebuilding is *not* to include more differences (or more convincing and more 'micro' accounts of them) but to reveal the power relations that make differences exists in the first place. We develop these three alternatives by building upon the contributions to this Special Issue and connecting them to the relevant literature.

Avoiding Avruch's two errors: undervaluing or overvaluing cultural difference

The work of Kevin Avruch is useful to frame the dilemma around difference that confronted peacebuilding analysts and policymakers throughout the 1990s and 2000s. As an anthropologist preoccupied with conflict resolution, Avruch (1998) criticized theories and practices of peacebuilding that rendered culture and cultural differences trivial. For him, 'undervaluing culture' is the 'first type of error' in traditional conflict resolution practices. These practices, he explained, tend to focus on rational negotiations between the representatives of disputing parties, as if context, values, traditions, or ethnic differences played no role for participants in a conflict. Initially, thus, Avruch could be read as pointing towards the championing of culture as an important element for understanding conflict and its resolution. However, Avruch does not suggest that we should talk about or emphasize culture unhesitatingly, with no holds barred, when addressing a cultural dispute. There is a 'second type of error' which surfaces in the process of trying to correct the first: the tendency to 'overvalue culture' by 'overestimating its impact on a conflict' (Avruch 2003, 363). Overemphasizing culture is essentially harmful to some parties in a conflict already saturated with cultural animosities because, Avruch (2003, 367) contends, it homogenizes, essentializes and reinforces particular forms of identity while neglecting or delegitimizing others. In this introduction to the Special Issue, we first re-read the history of the field through Avruch's two errors and argue that throughout much of the 1990s peacebuilding scholars and practitioners erred because they generally undervalued culture whereas in the 2000s the tendency was to recognize it but characterize it as an obstacle to peace.[1]

At the end of the Cold War, humanitarian questions attained universal scope and received unprecedented historical attention. In 1988, the UN Peacekeeping Forces received the Nobel Peace Prize for their missions in places such as Cyprus, the Democratic Republic of the Congo or the Middle East, reinvigorating the influence of the UN in international politics. In the following lustrum, the UN deployed 20 new peacekeeping operations – more than in the previous four decades – and expanded the field roles to include complex and multidimensional tasks. The Secretary General, Boutros-Ghali (1992) strengthened the UN capacities to intervene internationally when adding the idea of 'post-conflict peacebuilding' to peace-prevention, peace-making and peacekeeping tasks. Based on the assumption that democracy and economic liberalism would facilitate war–peace transitions anywhere, the United States and other European states multiplied investment in democracy aid. They sponsored organizations facilitating free and fair elections, supervised legislative and judicial reforms and helped with the consolidation of independent media (Carothers 2000). And institutions such as the World Bank or the International Monetary Fund were leading global economic recovery through encouraging free-market structural adjustments in impoverished regions (Williamson 1993).

In these early international peace support interventions, cultural differences were fairly neglected since every society was seen as willing and capable of democratizing in a similar way (Doyle 1986; Fukuyama 1992; Huntington 1991). Differences among societies did certainly exist, but they represented the different stages of a universal and linear progression towards liberal democracy. Universal logics – such as actors interacting rationally in a perfectly calculable world – drove international relations, providing a convincing explanation for the deviations or delays of some local cultures (Lapid and Kratochwil 1996; Valbjørn 2008, 57–59). However, uncomfortable questions soared as peace proved difficult to consolidate in many non-Western countries throughout the 1990s. If democracy and free market were a source of peace and progress, why has some countries in transition to democracy failed to stabilize? Why had liberal multiculturalism been key to manage diversity and promote cultural rights to minorities in most Western states but failed as soon as it was exported elsewhere (Eller 1999; Kymlicka 2001)? Why was it so onerous to expand the liberal democratic zone of peace?

In debates assessing the difficulties of democratization, liberalization and peacebuilding in the aftermath of the civil wars in the non-West, the notion of difference appeared as a *problem* to be considered. The fact that democratization and economic liberalization were successful in the West, but failed to stabilize countries emerging from armed conflict in the non-West led to the perception that non-Western societies possessed specific traits that hindered their progress. Crucially, difference between human beings was expressed by referring to the inward and unconscious attributes of societies – their 'culture' or psychosocial specificities and logics – and it came to be a key explanatory variable for the failure of allegedly universal policy solutions (see, further, Furedi 1998; Malik 1996; Pupavac 2001). International interventions had thus been guilty of the first type of error identified by Avruch: they had ignored the relevance of culture and assumed that each society would transform into a peaceful liberal democracy in a similar way.

The focus on cultural differences thus revealed a feeling of growing disenchantment with universal values and approaches with worldwide pretensions. Scholars increasingly recognized not only that psychosocial factors had decisive effects on conflicts, but also that these could not be overlooked in peace processes (Avruch 1998; Avruch and Black 1991; Lederach 1997; Miall, Ramsbotham, and Woodhouse 1999). International interventions began to evolve from a concern with the formal and political sphere of societies to the regulation of the more informal settings where differences and inequalities among societies were reproduced over time (Chandler 2010). For example, at the end of the 1990s 'civil society' became a key component of programmes of international intervention (World Bank 2006). It was understood as an informal space beyond the state and formal rights, politics and economy, which had to be technically assisted and empowered in order to achieve tolerance and sustainable peace (for a critique, see Belloni 2001; Chandler 2006).

This emphasis on difference was considered a step forward when compared to earlier understandings that had assumed a one-size-fits-all peace model and ignored local histories, knowledge and mores. In moving from strictly military and security dimensions to targeting the broader social and cultural contexts of conflict-affected societies, these peacebuilding processes appeared apt to address the root causes of the problems and to facilitate psychosocial healing and long-term reconciliation (Lederach 1997, 24–35; Miall, Ramsbotham, and Woodhouse 1999, 206–215). Moreover, exhibiting cultural sensitivity in post-war scenarios was motivated by a normative commitment to respect diverse traditions at a time when Western countries were generally favouring multiculturalism, rather than assimilation, in domestic politics (Glazer 1997).

Nevertheless, a new problem appeared in peacebuilding processes when they gave primacy to culture: the emphasis on identities and differences ran the risk of legitimizing belligerent ideas and reproducing frictions and divisions in societies affected by conflict. Often, particularly when deploying essentialist conceptions of identity and culture, which assume that groups are primordial, homogenous and clearly separated by their differences, frameworks of intervention were guilty of legitimizing and replicating ethno-nationalist perspectives and war-antagonisms (Campbell 1998, 88–93; Valbjørn 2008, 64; Vaughan-Williams 2006, 517–518). Thus a second type of error haunted peace interventions in the context of the 'cultural turn': as Avruch had warned, peace practitioners quickly realized that overvaluing culture brings as many problems as it solves.

Through much of the 2000s, internationally led peacebuilding missions sought to find a solution to avoid the two errors: on the one hand, external actors could not ignore the primacy of those psychosocial factors that had influenced the history and development of the countries intervened in; on the other hand, they could not concede too much to local actors and cultures, and fuel the same identities and disagreements that had caused the turmoil. A *tertium quid* was required and took the form of a 'pragmatic tolerance' in which difference is valued insofar as it has a positive role for building peace. Thus peace missions adopted an unstable middle-ground position in which they would respect difference when seen as not obstructing the non-negotiable goals of stability, the rule of law and economic liberalism. Statebuilding frameworks, for example, can be said to be paradigmatic of a position that admitted the importance of culture in societies intervened in but considered it an obstacle that had to be managed, regulated and assimilated through a process of institution-building (Chesterman, Ignatieff, and Thakur 2005;

Fukuyama 2005; Ghani and Lockhart 2008; Paris 2004). In the field of policy practice, the emphasis on strengthening institutions in places as diverse as Afghanistan, East-Timor, Iraq, Kosovo, or Sierra Leone was translated into a top-down strategy to transform the perceptions, beliefs and other socio-cultural pathologies of the people, so that they could learn to iron out their differences without resort to arms. The Weberian state became the fulcrum of peacebuilding processes, against which differences were censured if deviated too much from universal norms (Lemay-Hébert and Mathieu 2014). Even Avruch, who carried the torch of cultural sensitivity, became cautious not to include (and overvalue) some cultural traits when these hindered the goal of solving a conflict (for a critique, see Brigg and Muller 2009).

Statebuilding projects spread, but they did not win the day, as they ended up privileging the position of international agencies and foregrounding external values and models for peace resolution. While they recognized the importance of difference in processes of peacebuilding, they reduced most differences to obstacles to be managed, corrected and overcome so that the rule of law, state institutions and markets could be consolidated. In this sense, they reproduced what Antony Anghie (2005, 4) has called the 'dynamic of difference', that is, 'the endless process of creating a gap between two cultures, demarcating ones as "universal" and civilized and the other as "particular" and uncivilized, and seeking to bridge the gap by developing techniques to normalize the aberrant society'. If the first error had been to neglect those socio-cultural specific attributes that may affect the progress of peacebuilding processes, the second was to consider difference a barrier to the ends of external agencies.

A third error: stigma in the critiques of liberal peace

As liberal peace projects lost impetus (Campbell, Chandler, and Sabaratnam 2011), however, demands for approaches more sensitive to difference bourgeoned. Over the last 10 years peacebuilding scholars have started to explain the poor record of international interventions by highlighting the insufficient or limited attempts at engaging more fully and genuinely with difference in processes of peacebuilding (Björkdahl and Gusic 2015; Lidén, Mac Ginty, and Richmond 2009; Mac Ginty 2015; Mac Ginty and Richmond 2016). This is self-evident in strategies to promote 'local ownership' which have frequently transferred power to the groups that seem to adjust to liberal norms but have disregarded other actors that are less donor-darlings (Lee and Özerdem 2015). As a solution, scholars stress the need to engage more respectfully with 'the local', involving minorities as well as resistant, rural and other marginalized actors (Mac Ginty and Sylva Hamieh 2010; Paffenholz 2014). Next to academic debates, the policy field is slowly evolving, too. There is a growing awareness of the counterproductive effects of policies that are externally imposed and prescriptive. Blueprints now include the necessity of including 'indigenous knowledge systems and practices' and the diverse resources existing locally in order to sustain peace (UNSSC 2010, 72–74; see also, UNDP 2016).

Critical approaches infer that peace needs to be fostered 'from below'; they are thus necessarily more open to 'local-local actors', 'infrapolitical' dimensions and indigenous 'resistance' to foreign interventions (Richmond 2012, 116–127). Some studies propose as a sine qua non condition for consolidating peace the need to investigate at the micro level and develop more detailed and 'anthropological' analyses of local contexts

(Richmond 2018; Schierenbeck 2015). Others suggest developing positive forms of 'hybrid peace' in which 'international' and 'local' actors shape and participate in a localized process of peacebuilding (Mac Ginty and Richmond 2016; Wallis, Jeffery, and Kent 2016; see further, Bargués-Pedreny and Randazzo 2018). In these cases, difference is not understood as 'culture', as culture is often related to reductionism and simplicity, but as the parapraxes, contingencies and twists that make the everyday life of a society unique.

Critical peacebuilding scholars have thus called for renewed attempts to engage with difference beyond the universalist assumptions characteristic of previous approaches. This implies a move beyond the second type of error outlined above: if difference was recognized, it was too quickly turned into a problem to be solved by assimilation. In contrast, critical scholars argue that difference has a role to play in building peace; whether this role is positive or negative depends on the circumstances and should not be judged a priori by external actors or measured against universal standards. These approaches therefore outline a third way to consider difference in the context of peacebuilding: beyond ignorance and problematization (both leading to assimilation), difference is retrieved as indispensable for building peace.

This third way, however, brings in a new type of error that has long been noticed by scholars interested in the question of difference. Using the idea of a 'dilemma of difference' introduced by Minow (1990), the problem facing these recent peacebuilding approaches becomes clear. For Minow, when trying to correct the inequalities suffered by the different person, one can erase and ignore difference in an attempt to equalize actors (a 'solution' that tends to reproduce the hierarchy it was designed to erase) or, conversely, one can try to adapt to the characteristics of the different person. This second option, seemingly more tolerant and effective, necessitates the identification of what difference *is*. Yet as Minow argues difference never exists on its own: it becomes visible (and comes into being) only in relation to specific normative frames and expectations. As feminists have argued, for instance, women are only different insofar as the reference point is and remains men. The different person is identified by opposition to what/who is identical (and thus equal). As a consequence, any attempt at respecting and valuing difference necessitates its identification which in turn can only be achieved by reproducing the normative structures through which the different person was – and therefore remains – stigmatized.

Two consequences follow from this third error: differences are reified and essentialized as inescapable (for a critique, see Sabaratnam 2017; Nadarajah and Rampton 2015), but also, and perhaps more importantly, difference is linked to stigma (as a deviance from the 'normal' that is reproduced by the frames used to identify it). For instance, difference is often associated to 'informal institutions' or 'tradition'; yet these 'characteristics' only become salient through the use and acceptance of a specific normative frame influenced by Western perceptions of the 'normal'. In this frame, difference is identified in relation to what the Self believes *himself* to be. As such, emphasizing difference (even as something to be celebrated or as a space where bottom-up peace initiatives can be designed) does not remove the stigma attached to it insofar as what passes for 'normal' is not questioned nor made explicit.

Despite the fact that critical scholars strived to treat other societies on an equal footing (and refused to prejudge their values and mores in processes of peacebuilding), this third error makes the stated goal of integrating difference for peacebuilding counterproductive. In fact, the possibility of capturing difference 'on its own terms' has been largely acknowledged as unsuccessful or limited by critical scholars themselves.[2] Recent research on peacebuilding has deplored this state of affairs (Sabaratnam 2017; Simons and Zanker 2014; Kappler 2015; Hirblinger and Simons 2015; Paffenholz 2015; Randazzo 2016) but their conclusions seem to continue to give another life to the line of investigation that characterizes critical peacebuilding. Indeed, they often urge – again – to be more sensitive to the particularities, specificities and intricacies of the 'different' societies intervened in. In doing so, they reproduce the logic of a critique that eats itself, first criticizing previous approaches for failing to do justice to difference, and second trying it one more time, foreseeing that this new go will again be insufficient (Bargués-Pedreny 2017). Scholars (and practitioners) are gradually compelled to recognize their limited, temporal, political and thus biased view of difference, while any strategy to international peacebuilding becomes suspect.

In sum, these three errors constrain the capacity of peacebuilding practitioners and scholars to engage with difference on an equal footing. The first error meant the imposition of universalist frameworks by neglecting the particular identities and realities of the actors involved in peacebuilding. Difference was silenced as irrelevant due to the force of universalist convictions. Confronted with the failures of post-war interventions throughout the 1990s, external agencies began to consider the psychosocial spheres of societies intervened in, but only as something in need of correction, management and control (with the ultimate belief that assimilation to the universal model remained a viable strategy). These two errors reflect what Todorov (1982, 58) describes as the characteristic attitudes of the West towards difference: either the Other is assimilated to the Self and her difference goes unnoticed; or her difference is interpreted as inferiority and in need of transformation. The result is assimilation in both cases. Trying to move away from these two errors, current trends in peacebuilding research and practice have sought to reveal difference in its own terms and use it as a basis for building peace. Once again, however, these attempts are limited by their refusal to engage with the conditions that make difference exist in the first place. Despite their generous starting points, the result is the reproduction of the stigma of difference.

Facing these dilemmas and contradictions, how is one to approach difference? The next section tentatively suggests how to move beyond the three common errors repeated in the theory and practice of peacebuilding. Instead of ignoring, problematizing, or asking for more detailed explorations of what difference *is*, we suggest focusing on three dimensions that have so far remained underexplored, idle lands in the field of peacebuilding. While we do not claim to introduce a new comprehensive peacebuilding framework, we maintain that focusing on these three dimensions can help solve some of the problems faced by peacebuilding scholars and practitioners by shedding new light on the issue of difference. In the remainder of this introduction, we propose three ways in which difference can be understood differently: as a multidimensional reality performed in multiple ways and contexts, as a vital yet non-essentializable feature of human cultures, and as linked to power relations. We also explain how these conceptual arguments are used and furthered by the articles of this Special Issue.

Thinking about difference differently in peacebuilding

Performing (multidimensional) identities/differences

Against the desire to reduce differences to objective realities existing 'out there', the feminist and queer literatures offer a useful corrective (Butler 1990, 1993; Parker and Sedgwick 1995). For these approaches, actors perform their identity through discourses and practices. This means that subjects are present and act but that there is no essential actor present before her (self-)enactment: subjects come into being (and enact their own differences) through the reiterated performance of their identity. Expressed differently, it means that the foundations to which discourses and practices of identification refer to in peacebuilding – 'traditions', 'modernity', 'history', 'indigeneity', 'local authenticity', 'international (scientific) expertise' – do not pre-exist their performance. This radical re-conceptualization of identity and difference changes the goals of those interested in peacebuilding: the objective is no longer to discover the 'real' identity of actors – in order to transform them or to adapt peacebuilding to their identity – but to understand how actors react to and enact regimes of identity (sometimes also exceeding them). Read's contribution (2018), for instance, explores how female aid workers struggle to perform the 'authentic' identity that the ideal of 'the field' and of 'humanitarian exceptionalism' require. These women express their feeling of only 'passing' as aid workers and their difficulty when faced with strict and alienating regimes of identity. As such, the capacity of these actors to identify to a dominant framework is ambiguous, rendering them seemly 'out of place'.

Drawing attention to the performativity of difference also means recognizing that differences are situated and depend on time and context. Actors can be 'local' in some situations – when they try to claim legitimacy through 'authenticity' – and 'international' in other contexts where legitimacy and resources derive from an attachment to a constructed position of 'exteriority' and thus 'objectivity' (Kappler 2015). As shown by Martin de Almagro (2018), political movements and organizations involved in peacebuilding can perform their belonging to either sphere depending on their political motivations and the incentives of the context in which they act. What is important is to display the right type of difference at the right moment and place, taking into consideration that peacebuilding processes tend to favour certain subject positions, while constructing others as inappropriate (see, further, Martin de Almagro 2017). Similarly, as Hirblinger and Landau (2018) argue, difference is 'scaled' at the specific level of *one* group membership (thus disregarding the fact that individuals pertain to a variety of different groups). Peacebuilding can thus be read as the attempt to scale difference at the level thought to be most conducive to peace. This selectivity, of course, facilitates the construction of binary identities and 'entails the violence of repressing or ignoring other forms of difference' (Abu-Lughod 1991, 140).

In fact, recognizing the performative aspect of differences also means that identities are inherently multidimensional – even if often reduced to one social category (ethnic, racial, religious, gender, class ...) to the exclusion of other forms of identification. The political processes through which identities and differences are enacted act as a filter: while some characteristics are read as crucial, others are silenced. Recognizing these forgotten dimensions could help us cultivate the points of connection and overlap that exist between supposedly different actors and to cross the boundaries between Self and Other in order to achieve peace:

> Locating difference securely beyond the boundaries of self impedes our capacity to fully acknowledge and affirm others that always live within, or to appreciate and claim selves that exist as part of others beyond those boundaries. (Inayatullah and Blaney 2004, 44)

The idea of multidimensionality is useful in that regard, yet such recognition can be difficult to achieve in a context where the act of othering helps people manage their fears about 'glimpses of dependence and "difference" in themselves' (Minow 1990, 378).

Deferring closure, longing for relational and open-ended interactions

Second, and in order to avoid the three types of errors that have preoccupied the field of peacebuilding in the past two decades, scholars can choose to insist on the irreducible character of identities, thereby refusing to represent them – let alone use them – in order to sustain peace. This position dwells on deconstructive sensitivities that highlight the irresolvable paradoxes implicated in attempts to make justice to difference: on one hand, there is a need for a decision or an action to assist the other; at the same time, any effort to do so will be unsatisfactory (Connolly 2002; Critchley 1992; Derrida 1982). The consequence of confronting these paradoxes is not stasis or utter impotence. Instead, deconstructive logics bring forward an unstable approach that affirms contradictory impulses while avoiding ultimate foundations. Vassilios Paipais (2011, 140) embraces this instability in order to solve the problem of assimilating difference and revitalize critique:

> What is, perhaps, more important than seeking a final overcoming or dismissal of the self/other opposition is to gain the insight that it is the perpetual striving to preserve the tension and ambivalence between self and other that rescues both critique's authority and function.

If the task of solving tensions between identity and difference becomes impossible, it is a never-ending process that is privileged over closure and conclusions.

This is reminiscent of the argument made by David Campbell. Against dominant understandings of international intervention in Bosnia, Campbell (1998, 242) defends 'an ongoing political process of critique and invention that is never satisfied that a lasting solution can or has been reached'. This implies a double injunction of assisting indigenous needs, values and morals, while acknowledging the limits implicated in these tasks. Other authors have underlined the need for an engagement *towards* difference (and not *with* or *of* difference), holding an infinite predisposition to negotiate its constitution (Behr 2014, 140). Taking this argument further, Behr (2018) develops the concept of 'peace-in-difference' in which peace, as much as difference, is never defined of fixed but seen as a permanent process of dialogue which constantly neutralizes essentialist categories and perceptions.

Yet this position is also interrogated in this Special Issue. For not all that is processual and contingent is positive, and that which is discrete and entrenched is negative. It may be that the apparent refusal to identify difference in the context of peacebuilding is not emancipatory, but instead reinforces or aligns with the powers that be. As Orjuela (2008, 248) explains, deconstructing identities is sometimes used as a weapon of

THE POLITICS OF PEACEBUILDING IN A DIVERSE WORLD

domination if it serves to denounce as 'fake' or 'inauthentic' the identity of the marginalized. Moreover, some argue that deconstructive logics applied to identity are restricted to an academic and privileged position constructed above (identity) politics. Indeed, when faced with the necessity of making advances for peace, doing away with identities and differences rarely seems a viable option (as can be seen when choices and distinctions are made in the critical peacebuilding literature).[3] Lottholz (2018) illustrates this point in the context of Kyrgyzstan where the attempts at forging a 'post-identitarian' peacebuilding have neither succeeded at transcending group differences nor at resolving conflict anxieties. Trying to 'solve' the problem of reifying differences by engaging in a never-ending process of blurring them provokes disorientation to practitioners and a deep frustration to local people claiming peace *here* and *now*.

A potential corrective to the limits of deconstruction in post-war settings could lie in a middle-ground as defined by Brigg (2008, 49 and 46): if identity and difference are 'fundamentally important', they should not be understood as implying 'strong boundaries among people' and we should remain 'circumspect about *particular* claims to *have* or *know* culture'. In her contribution to this Special Issue, Martin de Almagro (2018) develops this theme through the concept of 'hybrid clubs' in order to capture difference in a non-essentialist way: actors can perform their 'membership' to a variety of clubs without being essentially attached to them. Their difference is fluid and changing. Similarly, Brigg (2018) theorizes difference as relational and essential at the same time. Indeed, difference is conceptualized as essential to life itself, unavoidable yet not essentialized in a 'substantialist' way. This is not to deny that difference can appear (and be presented) in essentialist terms by the actors themselves. Such a process can happen through 'strategic essentialism' (see for instance Krishna 1993; Inayatullah 2016) where actors naturalize their identities to serve specific purposes. Yet it remains for the scholar to adopt a skeptical perspective by showing how these differences remain politically constructed and reflecting on the worldview and social structures that made them salient in the first place.

Difference as a relation of power

Finally, and building upon this last point, the ontological status of difference can be reconceptualized. Indeed, most peacebuilding research is built on the assumption that difference is empirically discoverable, identifiable and thus 'out there'. This common (mis)conception is shared by the three strands of peacebuilding examined earlier, which assume that difference can be identified in post-conflict societies or that difference is attached to the actors themselves. But as Maynard (2001, 310) writes, 'difference, as an organizing concept, tends to detract from our ability to consider the relationships between things and the possible consequences in terms of domination and control which ensue'.

As a response to this danger, scholars from a diversity of disciplines have shown how difference is a result of (power) relations. For instance, Minow discusses how differences lie *between* people and not *within* them. She argues that 'difference expresses patterns of relationships, social perceptions, and the design of institutions made by some without others in mind' (Minow 1990, 79), instead of essential and discrete characteristics of some people. Similarly, in anthropology, Abu-Lughod (1991, 147) explains that difference 'tends to be a relationship of power'. This means that differences are always the result of political and historical processes emerging from a particular economy of power (Escobar 2008, 203): in each situation, and out of the almost infinity of traits that characterizes every actor, only some are portrayed as differences. All the contributions to this Special Issue deal with these themes by recognizing that the difference of peacebuilding actors is always linked to broader relations of power. Read (2018), for example, explores how female aid workers mobilize their identity to confront the dominant masculine figure of the 'real' aid worker: here, gender comes to play an important role given the importance attributed to masculinity in humanitarianism.

Denying that difference emerges out of relations of power requires the belief that the Self is able to recognize difference and identity outside of culture and power altogether, to abstract *her*self from *her* own culture (Walley 1997). On the contrary, recognizing the importance of power means that attention needs to be paid to the worldview(s) that powerful actors promote. As Brigg (2008, 11) points out, 'Much of what is at stake in the difference challenge relates, in other words, to different versions of truth and reality'. Only through these worldviews does difference emerge (usually as deviance or anomaly). Ignoring or silencing power – as was done in the universalist as well as in some of the recent stigmatizing approaches – is no longer viable. Similarly, identifying differences as problems to be corrected becomes illogical insofar as these differences are created by those seeking to solve them. As Jonathan Joseph (2018) expresses in the final words of this issue, 'a relational approach to difference is more important than ever, but not without an analysis of the social and material relations that contribute to the production of difference'.

The recognition of difference as a relation of power linked to social structures that constrain and enable opens up new studies of thinking about difference and peacebuilding. In particular, the central questions are transformed: one no longer asks who is different and how this may be useful to build peace but rather how difference has been constructed by specific worldviews that are sustained by a particular economy of power. Bernath (2018), for instance, explores the construction of victim identities in Cambodia with reference to the powerful frame of 'genocide' and reveals how specific differences are entrenched in the process. The necessary yet problematic inscription of identities and differences can help solve conflict or reinforce it. More often than not, of course, this economy of power serves to sustain the order of the powerful Self (Behr 2014, 130). This means that identity and difference must be approached with caution as they legitimize some worldviews and social stratifications, whilst neglecting alternatives.

The three paths detailed here and explored by the contributions to this Special Issue represent an attempt to move beyond the three errors that characterize peacebuilding research and practice. By exploring difference conceptually and empirically, the authors provide concrete examples of a different way to approach difference in the context of peacebuilding. They deconstruct and interrogate the way differences come to exist in an attempt to transform current understandings of peacebuilding practices. They seek to open the way for further and more productive discussions on the role of difference in international interventions contexts. More broadly, this Special Issue participates in the discussion about equality in international relations and about the fundamental issue of our need to engage with others on an equal footing. This concern animates our work as scholars and is reflected in the contributions assembled here.

Notes

1. For heuristic reasons, this 'history' of peacebuilding is presented in a linear fashion. In reality, the three errors discussed here have co-existed and still do.
2. Recognitions of the limits of these academic attempts abound and are usually linked to the fact that the local Other cannot be identified as a fixed interlocutor – 'the local' has multiple, contingent and heterogeneous political identities which rely on perceptions and are thus dependent on the subjectivity of the scholar herself. See examples of these recognitions in Wanis-St. John (2013, 363), Mac Ginty (2015, 841–842), Björkdahl and Gusic (2015, 269), Mac Ginty and Firchow (2016), and for a more problem-solving approach recognising the ambiguities of the local see Schaefer (2010).
3. For a recent example of this problem see Visoka and Richmond (2017) and for a critique see Randazzo (2016).

Acknowledgements

The authors wish to thank all the contributors to this Special Issue and the editors of the Journal of Intervention and Statebuilding for their enthusiasm for this project and their dedication to see it succeed.

Disclosure statement

No potential conflict of interest was reported by the authors.

Funding

We are grateful to the Centre for Global Cooperation Research (University of Duisburg-Essen) – and in particular Julia Fleck – for the financial and logistical help provided in organizing the workshop that led to this Special Issue.

References

Abu-Lughod, L. 1991. "Writing Against Culture." In *Recapturing Anthropology: Working in the Present*, edited by R. G. Fox, 137–162. Santa Fe, NM: School of American Research Press.

Anghie, A. 2005. *Imperialism, Sovereignty and the Making of International Law*. Cambridge: Cambridge University Press.

Avruch, Kevin. 1998. *Culture and Conflict Resolution*. Washington, DC: US Institute of Peace Press.

Avruch, Kevin. 2003. "Type I and Type II Errors in Culturally Sensitive Conflict Resolution Practice." *Conflict Resolution Quarterly* 20 (3): 351–371. doi:10.1002/crq.29.

Avruch, Kevin, and Peter W. Black. 1991. "The Culture Question and Conflict Resolution." *Peace & Change* 16 (1): 22–45. doi:10.1111/j.1468-0130.1991.tb00563.x.

Bargués-Pedreny, P. 2017. "Connolly and the Never-Ending Critiques of Liberal Peace: From the Privilege of Difference to Vorarephilia." *Cambridge Review of International Affairs* 30 (2–3): 216–234.

Behr, H. 2014. *Politics of Difference: Epistemologies of Peace*. London: Routledge.

Behr, H. 2018. "Peace-in-Difference: A Phenomenological Approach to Peace Through Difference." *Journal of Intervention and Statebuilding* 12 (3): 335–351. doi:10.1080/17502977.2018.1501980.

Belloni, Roberto. 2001. "Civil Society and Peacebuilding in Bosnia and Herzegovina." *Journal of Peace Research* 38 (2): 163–180. doi:10.1177/0022343301038002003.

Bernath, J. 2018. "The Politics of Difference in Transitional Justice: Genocide and the Construction of Victimhood at the Khmer Rouge Tribunal." *Journal of Intervention and Statebuilding* 12 (3): 367–384. doi:10.1080/17502977.2018.1496645.

Björkdahl, A., and I. Gusic. 2015. "'Global' Norms and 'Local' Agency: Frictional Peacebuilding in Kosovo." *Journal of International Relations and Development* 18 (3): 265–287.

Boutros-Ghali, Boutros. 1992. "An Agenda for Peace: Preventive Diplomacy, Peacemaking and Peace-Keeping." *International Relations* 11 (3): 201–218. doi:10.1177/004711789201100302.

Brigg, M. 2008. *The New Politics of Conflict Resolution Responding to Difference*. Basingstoke: Palgrave Macmillan.

Brigg, M. 2018. "Relational and Essential: Theorizing Difference for Peacebuilding." *Journal of Intervention and Statebuilding* 12 (3): 352–366. doi:10.1080/17502977.2018.1482078.

Brigg, Morgan, and Kate Muller. 2009. "Conceptualising Culture in Conflict Resolution." *Journal of Intercultural Studies* 30 (2): 121–140. doi:10.1080/07256860902766784.

Butler, J. 1990. *Gender Trouble: Feminism and the Subversion of Identity*. New York: Routledge.

Butler, J. 1993. *Bodies That Matter: On the Discursive Limits of "Sex"*. New York: Routledge.

Campbell, David. 1998. *National Deconstruction: Violence, Identity, and Justice in Bosnia*. Minneapolis: University of Minneapolis Press.

Campbell, S., D. Chandler, and M. Sabaratnam. 2011. *A Liberal Peace? The Problems and Practices of Peacebuilding*. London: Zed Books.

Carothers, Thomas. 2000. *The Clinton Record on Democracy Promotion*. Working Papers 16. Washington, DC: Carnegie Endowment for International Peace.

Chandler, David. 2006. *Constructing Global Civil Society: Morality and Power in International Relations*. Basingstoke: Palgrave Macmillan.

Chandler, David. 2010. "Race, Culture and Civil Society: Peacebuilding Discourse and the Understanding of Difference." *Security Dialogue* 41 (4): 369–390.

Chesterman, Simon, Michael Ignatieff, and Ramesh Thakur. 2005. *Making States Work: State Failure and the Crisis of Governance*. Tokyo: United Nations Univeristy Press.

Connolly, William E. 2002. *Identity/Difference: Democratic Negotiations of Political Paradox*. Expanded ed. Minneapolis: University of Minnesota Press.

Critchley S. 1992. The Ethics of Deconstruction: Derrida & Levinas, Edinburgh University Press, 1992.

Derrida, Jacques. 1982. *Margins of Philosophy*. Brighton: Harvester Press.

Doyle, Michael W. 1986. "Liberalism and World Politics." *American Political Science Review* 80 (4): 1151–1169.

Eller, Jack D. 1999. *From Culture to Ethnicity to Conflict: An Anthropological Perspective on International Ethnic Conflict*. Ann Arbor: University of Michigan Press.

Escobar, A. 2008. *Territories of Difference: Place, Movements, Life, Redes*. Durham, NC: Duke University Press.

Fukuyama, Francis. 1992. *The End of History and the Last Man*. New York: Free Press.

Fukuyama, Francis. 2005. *State Building: Governance and World Order in the Twenty-First Century*. London: Profile Books.

Furedi, Frank. 1998. *The Silent War: Imperialism and the Changing Perception of Race*. New Brunswick, NJ: Rutgers Univerity Press.

Ghani, Ashraf, and Clare Lockhart. 2008. *Fixing Failed States: A Framework for Rebuilding a Fractured World*. Oxford: Oxford University Press.

Glazer, Nathan. 1997. *We Are All Multiculturalists Now*. Cambridge, MA: Harvard University Press.

Hirblinger, A., and Dana M. Landau. 2018. "Governing Conflict: The Politics of Scaling Difference." *Journal of Intervention and Statebuilding* 12 (3): 385–404. doi:10.1080/17502977.2018.1496644.

Hirblinger, A. T., and C. Simons. 2015. "The Good, the Bad, and the Powerful: Representations of the 'Local' in Peacebuilding." *Security Dialogue* 46 (5): 422–439.

Huntington, Samuel P. 1991. "Democracy's Third Wave." *Journal of Democracy* 2 (2): 12–34.

Inayatullah, N. 2016. "Gigging on the World Stage: Bossa Nova and Afrobeat After De-Reification." *Contexto Internacional* 38 (2): 523–543.

Inayatullah, N., and D. L. Blaney. 2004. *International Relations and the Problem of Difference*. New York: Routledge.

Ingram, S. 2010. *Statebuilding: Key Concepts and Operational Implications in Two Fragile States: The Case of Sierra Leone and Liberia*. Washington, DC and New York, NY: World Bank and UNDP.

Joseph, Jonathan. 2018. "Beyond Relationalism in Peacebuilding." *Journal of Intervention and Statebuilding* 12 (3): 425–434.

Kappler, S. 2015. "The Dynamic Local: Delocalisation and (Re-)localisation in the Search for Peacebuilding Identity." *Third World Quarterly* 36 (5): 875–889.

Krishna, S. 1993. "Review: The Importance of Being Ironic: A Postcolonial View on Critical International Relations Theory." *Alternatives: Global, Local, Political* 18 (3): 385–417.

Kymlicka, Will. 2001. "Reply and Conclusion." In *Can Liberal Pluralism Be Exported? Western Political Theory and Ethnic Relations in Eastern Europe*, edited by Will Kymlicky and Magda Opalski, 345–414. Oxford: Oxford Univerity Press.

Lapid, Yosef, and Friedrich Kratochwil. 1996. *The Return of Culture and Identity in IR Theory*. Boulder, CO: Lynne Rienner.

Lederach, John P. 1997. *Building Peace: Sustainable Reconciliation in Divided Societies*. Washington, DC: United States Institute of Peace Press.

Lee, S. Y., and A. Özerdem, eds. 2015. *Local Ownership in International Peacebuilding*. London: Routledge.

Lemay-Hébert, N., and X. Mathieu. 2014. "The OECD's Discourse on Fragile States: Expertise and the Normalisation of Knowledge Production." *Third World Quarterly* 35 (2): 232–251.

Lidén, K., R. Mac Ginty, and O. P. Richmond. 2009. "Introduction: Beyond Northern Epistemologies of Peace: Peacebuilding Reconstructed?" *International Peacekeeping* 16 (5): 587–598.

Lottholz, P. 2018. "Old Slogans Ringing Hollow? The Legacy of Social Engineering, Statebuilding and the 'Dilemma of Difference' in (Post-) Soviet Kyrgyzstan." *Journal of Intervention and Statebuilding* 12 (3): 405–424. doi:10.1080/17502977.2018.1507869.

Mac Ginty, R. 2015. "Where is the Local? Critical Localism and Peacebuilding." *Third World Quarterly* 36 (5): 840–856.

Mac Ginty, R., and P. Firchow. 2016. "Top-down and Bottom-up Narratives of Peace and Conflict." *Politics* 36 (3): 308–323.

Mac Ginty, R., and O. P. Richmond. 2016. "The Fallacy of Constructing Hybrid Political Orders: A Reappraisal of the Hybrid Turn in Peacebuilding." *International Peacekeeping* 23 (2): 219–239.

Mac Ginty, R., and C. Sylva Hamieh. 2010. "Made in Lebanon: Local Participation and Indigenous Responses to Development and Post-war Reconstruction." *Civil Wars* 12 (1–2): 47–64.

Malik, Kenan. 1996. *The Meaning of Race: Race, History and Culture in Western Society*. London: MacMillan.

Martin de Almagro, Maria. 2017. "Producing Participants: Gender, Race, Class, and Women, Peace and Security." *Global Society*. doi:10.1080/13600826.2017.1380610.

Martin de Almagro, Maria. 2018. "Hybrid Clubs: A Feminist Approach to Peacebuilding in the Democratic Republic of Congo." *Journal of Intervention and Statebuilding* 12 (3): 319–334. doi:10.1080/17502977.2018.1482125.

Maynard, M. 2001. "'Race', Gender and the Concept of 'Difference' in Feminist Thought." In *Feminism: Critical Concepts in Literary and Cultural Studies. Volume 4: Feminism and the Politics of Difference*, edited by M. Evans, 300–316. London: Routledge.

Miall, Hugh, Oliver Ramsbotham, and Tom Woodhouse. 1999. *Contemporary Conflict Resolution: The Prevention, Management and Transformations of Deadly Conflicts*. Malden, MA: Polity Press.

Minow, M. 1990. *Making all the Difference: Inclusion, Exclusion, and America Law*. Ithaca, NY: Cornell University Press.

Nadarajah, S., and D. Rampton. 2015. "The Limits of Hybridity and the Crisis of Liberal Peace." *Review of International Studies* 41 (1): 49–72.

OECD. 2012. *International Support to Post-Conflict Transition: Rethinking Policy, Changing Practice*. DAC Guidelines and Reference Series. Organisation for Economic Co-operation and Development (OECD). doi:10.1787/9789264168336-en.

Orjuela, C. 2008. *The Identity Politics of Peacebuilding: Civil Society in War-Torn Sri Lanka*. New Delhi: Sage.

Paffenholz, T. 2014. "International Peacebuilding Goes Local: Analysing Lederach's Conflict Transformation Theory and Its Ambivalent Encounter with 20 Years of Practice." *Peacebuilding* 2 (1): 11–27.

Paffenholz, T. 2015. "Unpacking the Local Turn in Peacebuilding: A Critical Assessment Towards an Agenda for Future Research." *Third World Quarterly* 36 (5): 857–874.

Paipais, V. 2011. "Self and Other in Critical International Theory: Assimilation, Incommensurability and the Paradox of Critique." *Review of International Studies* 37 (1): 121–140.

Paris, Roland. 2004. *At War's End: Building Peace After Civil Conflict*. Cambridge: Cambridge University Press.

Parker, A., and E. K. Sedgwick. 1995. "Introduction: Performativity and Performance." In *Performativity and Performance*, edited by A. Parker and E. K. Sedgwick, 1–18. London: Routledge.

Pol Bargués-Pedreny and Elisa Randazzo. 2018. "Hybrid peace revisited: an opportunity for considering self-governance?." *Third World Quarterly* doi:10.1080/01436597.2018.1447849.

Pupavac, Vanessa. 2001. "Therapeutic Governance: Psycho-Social Intervention and Trauma Risk Management." *Disasters* 25 (4): 358–372. doi:10.1111/1467-7717.00184.

Randazzo, Elisa. 2016. "The Paradoxes of the 'Everyday': Scrutinising the Local Turn in Peace Building." *Third World Quarterly* 37 (8): 1351–1370.

Read, Róisín. 2018. "Embodying Difference: Reading Gender in Women's Memoirs of Humanitarianism." *Journal of Intervention and Statebuilding* 12 (3): 300–318. doi:10.1080/17502977.2018.1482079.

Richmond, Oliver P. 2012. "A Pedagogy of Peacebuilding: Infrapolitics, Resistance, and Liberation." *International Political Sociology* 6 (2): 115–31.

Richmond, Oliver P. 2014. "Jekyll or Hyde: What Is Statebuilding Creating? Evidence From the 'Field'." *Cambridge Review of International Affairs* 27 (1): 1–20.

Richmond, Oliver P. 2018. "Rescuing Peacebuilding? Anthropology and Peace Formation." *Global Society* 32 (2): 221–239.

Sabaratnam, M. 2017. *Decolonizing Intervention: International Intervention in Mozambique*. London: Rowman & Littlefield.

Schaefer, Christoph Daniel. 2010. "Local Practices and Normative Frameworks in Peacebuilding." *International Peacekeeping* 17 (4): 499–514.

Schierenbeck, I. 2015. "Beyond the Local Turn Divide: Lessons Learnt, Relearnt and Unlearnt." *Third World Quarterly* 36 (5): 1023–1032.

Simons, C., and F. Zanker. 2014. "Questioning the Local in Peacebuilding." Working Paper of the Priority Programme 1448 of the German Research Foundation (10): Leipzig and Halle.

Todorov, T. 1982. *La conquête de l'Amérique. La question de l'autre*. Paris: Editions du Seuil.

UNDP. 2016. *Local Governance in Fragile and Conflict Affected Settings: Building a Resilient Foundation for Peace and Development. A UNDP How-to Guide*. New York: United Nations Development Programme.

UNSSC. 2010. *Indigenous Peoples and Peacebuilding: A Compilation of Best Practices*. Turin: United Nations System Staff College, Oficina de Promoció de la Pau i dels Drets Humans, Institut Català Internacional per la Pau.

Valbjørn, Morten. 2008. "Before, During and After the Cultural Turn: A 'Baedeker' to IR's Cultural Journey." *International Review of Sociology* 18 (1): 55–82.

Vaughan-Williams, N. 2006. "Towards a Problematisation of the Problematisations That Reduce Northern Ireland to a 'Problem'." *Critical Review of International Social and Political Philosophy* 9 (4): 513–526. doi:10.1080/13698230600941978.

Visoka, G., and O. P. Richmond. 2017. "After Liberal Peace? From Failed State-Building to an Emancipatory Peace in Kosovo." *International Studies Perspectives* 18 (1): 110–129.

Walley, C. J. 1997. "Searching for 'Voices': Feminism, Anthropology, and the Global Debate Over Female Genital Operations." *Cultural Anthropology* 12 (3): 405–438.

Wallis, J., Renee Jeffery, and Lia Kent. 2016. "Political Reconciliation in Timor Leste, Solomon Islands and Bougainville: The Dark Side of Hybridity." *Australian Journal of International Affairs* 70 (2): 159–178.

Wanis-St. John, Anthony. 2013. "Indigenous Peacebuilding." In *Routledge Handbook of Peacebuilding*, edited by Roger Mac Ginty, 360–374. London: Routledge.

Williamson, John. 1993. "Democracy and the 'Washington Consensus'." *World Development* 21. doi:10.1016/0305-750X(93)90046-C.

World Bank. 2006. *Civil Society and Peacebuilding: Potential, Limitations and Critical Factors.* Washington, DC: World Bank.

Embodying Difference: Reading Gender in Women's Memoirs of Humanitarianism

Róisín Read

ABSTRACT
This article explores embodied difference in humanitarianism and peacebuilding by treating women's memoirs as a form of 'flesh witnessing'. It argues that the essays in the anthology *Chasing Misery* are claims to the authority of 'The Field' that also reveal the women's feelings of only 'passing' as aid workers. Three distinct themes are noted: the construction of The Field as a site of embodied authority and the ways in which the essays reinforce and trouble this; the writers feeling different, and separate, from those they work with/for; and the embodied gender presented with reference to imagined 'real' aid workers.

Introduction

Humanity has long been cited as humanitarians' main constituency, yet – despite the obviously gendered nature of the humanity being discussed – the humanitarian sector (including academics) has been slow to make gender a central category of analysis. Gender has been a central aspect of humanitarian programming without key questions being asked about how gendered power relations shape the sector more broadly. As Miriam Ticktin notes, humanitarian discussions of humanity raise a central paradox of feminism in which 'one must emphasise one's difference (as women) in order to claim one's sameness (as equal human beings)' (Ticktin 2011, 250). This manifests in relation to 'debates about whether to include women as equal subjects/objects of humanitarian aid … or whether to single them out as different in order for them to receive critical attention and care' (250). Gender is a key category of difference in humanitarianism and peacebuilding, yet there is a tendency to overlook it in favour of discussions on the differences between the local and the international (for exceptions, see McLeod 2015; Partis-Jennings 2017; Martin de Almagro, 2018). In this article, I seek to explore embodied accounts of difference in humanitarianism by considering *Chasing Misery*, an anthology of essays by female aid workers (Hoppe 2014a). I propose that we can learn about practices of humanitarianism and peacebuilding by taking these accounts seriously, not as objective truth but as examples of 'flesh witnessing' (Harari 2009).

As Duncanson (2013, 57) notes in relation to soldiers, there is something 'particularly revealing about identity' in memoirs, as they are telling 'their story as they want to tell it'. They can tell us about 'which embodied experiences become important', or, more simply, 'whose bodies count' (Dyvik 2016a, 59). However, such accounts are not just revealing in terms of personal identity but also collective identity, as these memoirs shape and are shaped by broader social imaginaries – following Lennon (2015, 1), the 'affectively laden patterns/images/forms, by means of which we experience the world, other people and ourselves' – which affect not only how aid workers and the wider public think about humanitarian aid, but also how they think about the spaces in which humanitarian aid is deployed and the people who receive it.

Humanitarians, especially in conflict-affected areas, increasingly serve as sources of information about the areas they work in and the people they work with; as such, it is important to critically interrogate their experiences and knowledge. The ways in which female aid workers narrate their experiences of the spaces of humanitarianism offer an important contribution to the construction and maintenance of a distinctly humanitarian social imaginary, which highlights the complex and intersecting hierarchies of gender, race, class, nationality, and age that are deeply embedded in humanitarian practices. The 24 essays in the *Chasing Misery* collection (Hoppe 2014a) frequently collapse public–private and work–life binaries in different ways.[1] They address complex, emotional, and fundamentally sensorial experiences, often viscerally. Difference appears in the stories, in relation to colleagues, recipients of aid, parties to conflict, and friends and family 'back home', but it is always embodied – and this embodiment matters, as there is always 'a tension between women's lived bodily experiences and the cultural meanings inscribed on the female body that always mediate those experiences' (Conboy, Medina, and Stanbury 1997, 1).

In order to explore this tension, I read these stories through a double lens of 'flesh witnessing' and 'passing'.[2] In doing so, I address 'difference' in peacebuilding and humanitarianism as a gendered relation of power, highlighting three ways in which the existing norms that define what it means to be an aid worker produce the women as different, such that they 'have to pass as what [they] are assumed not to be' (Ahmed 2017, 115). As such, women must perform their identity – i.e. try to pass – as aid workers because the legitimacy of their claim to this identity is in question (120). In drawing attention to the ways in which these identities are performed, it is possible to see how the norms which establish difference are both reinforced and contested. I begin this article by arguing that women's narratives of their experiences are claims to the authority of 'The Field'. Following this, I highlight the ways in which the writers produce themselves as different, and separate, from both the populations they are there to assist and their own communities 'back home'. Finally, I show how the essays also reveal that many of the women experience a sense of 'being inadequate to the identity' of aid worker (Ahmed 1999, 96). In taking the essays of female aid workers as a starting point, I hope to highlight the ways in which difference is always embodied and is imbued with meanings, regardless of the degree to which there is conscious awareness of these meanings. Before outlining the approach I take to reading the women's essays, the next section briefly introduces the anthology under examination.

Chasing Misery

Published in 2014, *Chasing Misery: An Anthology of Essays by Women in Humanitarian Responses* is edited by a team, whose lead editor Kelsey Hoppe is an aid worker with both humanitarian and development experience in a range of countries. She states on the book's website that she developed the idea for the anthology 'as a way to give a platform to women's perspectives and voices in the work they do as well as to help people better understand what humanitarian aid is'.[3] The anthology contains 24 essays written by 21 different women[4] from a variety of different backgrounds[5] who have worked in humanitarianism in different roles and capacities.

The editor, Kelsey Hoppe, is explicit in her belief that women have distinct insights to offer: 'women's voices, perspectives and narratives on aid work are unique and deserve their own space', in part because of their ability 'to explore the greys, the "inbetween-ness", to reflect on the questions about being human' (Hoppe 2014d, 12). The book starts from the assumption that women have a different perspective on the world – presumably, different from that of men. Feminism has long been interested in situated knowledge (Haraway 1988), and the book poses interesting questions about the liminality of women in humanitarianism and peacebuilding (for more on the liminality of women in peacebuilding, see Partis-Jennings 2017, 418). For endeavours which claim gender as a central policy and programming expertise, surprisingly little attention has been paid to the ways in which their everyday humanitarian practices are gendered – and given the feminist underpinnings of the 'local' and 'experiential' turns, this oversight seems even more stark.

Difference, embodiment and passing

Feminist approaches to international relations have, in recent years, highlighted the need for bodies to be brought inside 'the frame of international relations' (Wilcox 2015). This literature has tended to focus on the ways in which war needs to be understood as an embodied experience by 'centralizing people's experiences' (Dyvik 2016a, 56). I argue that extending this lens to peacebuilding and humanitarianism is a key move, as these activities are deeply embedded in conflict and, thus, are a key site of investigation for more fully understanding the lived experiences of conflicts and their aftermaths. There has in recent years been an experiential turn in the study of peacebuilding; however, much of this literature leaves the feminist origins of the move to the 'everyday' implicit, and the analyses remain at the abstract level rather than presenting specific lived experiences which engender embodied analysis – although the work of Laura McLeod, Hannah Partis-Jennings, and Maria Martin de Almagro are exceptions (McLeod 2015; Partis-Jennings 2017; Martin de Almagro 2017, 2018). As Christine Sylvester notes, our experiences of war – and I would argue interventions in war – are *experienced through the body*, so we must look at the body as a unit of analysis (Sylvester 2013, 5). International aid workers in conflict settings have interesting and distinct experiences of war; they occupy a strange liminal position – in the conflict but ostensibly not part of it, at risk but also protected from violence. The lived experiences of these tensions can perhaps offer us insights into the broader dynamics of conflict and the interventions which seek to end or ameliorate it.

Just as Duncanson (2009), Welland (2015), and Dyvik (2016a, 2016b) have looked to military memoirs to study the gendered performances at the heart of recent and contemporary conflicts, I argue that humanitarian memoirs can help us to explore the embodied racialized and gendered experiences of aid in conflict. I do not however suggest that these memoirs can be seen unproblematically as 'true accounts'; rather, following Duncanson

(2013, 57), I believe that there is 'something particularly revealing about identity' in people's personal narratives, which tell 'their story as they want to tell it'. There seems to be a pervasive belief that there is something about being in these conflict spaces that is impossible to convey to those who have not lived it: 'it is experienced by those who practice it as a bracketed space, one in which only a few have access to, at once a manifestation of life at its most real and its direct counterpart' (Dyvik, 2016a, 57). Yet, paradoxically, it is an elusive or illusory endeavour, as the 'reality' of the experience can never be fully articulated.

As Catherine Baker suggests, writing about embodiment is necessarily an act of both compression and translation, 'reducing the sensory complexity of someone else's physical experience, or even one's own, into written language that someone else will understand through sight or sound' (Baker 2016, 120). Yuval Noah Harari offers a way of thinking about this problematic through the notion of 'flesh witnessing', a phrase drawn from the observation of a French soldier from the First World War that one 'who has not understood *with his flesh* cannot talk to you about it [the experience of war]' (quoted in Harari 2009, 215).

This notion of flesh witnessing is especially intriguing in thinking about the humanitarian field, as the idea of 'witnessing' and 'speaking out' has a controversial history in humanitarian aid interventions (e.g. Givoni 2011). In contrasting flesh witnessing with eye witnessing, Harari (2009) notes the different kind of authority associated with each. With eye witnessing, authority comes from the notion that you can observe 'facts' that can be verified, which relies on the mastery of a field of information that humanitarians rarely have more than partial access to. Flesh witnessing, on the other hand, offers a more 'novel authority ... which is based not on the observation of facts but on having undergone personal experience' (Harari 2009, 217). Harari notes that flesh witness accounts *seem* to be interested in conveying experiences, but because they do not believe that these experiences can be conveyed to those who have not shared them, 'by definition, they cannot succeed in this' (221). Instead, 'flesh witness narratives are mainly an exercise in authority' (222). As (Dyvik 2016a, 58) notes of military memoirs, they seem to convey the notion that 'you don't know what it's like' even while still attempting to explain – and as such, what they establish is their authority as a witness.

Humanitarian memoirs are not only important for what they reveal about specific humanitarian experiences but also for how they frame a broader social imaginary of what humanitarianism is. As Dyvik (2016a, 58) notes, military memoirs are more than individual stories: 'these texts participate in the writing of war. They help frame what we think war is'. Similarly, humanitarian memoirs participate in the writing of humanitarianism and help frame what we think humanitarianism is. At the beginning of the 2000s, David Rieff critiqued the portrayal of humanitarianism which relies on a 'familiar morality play of victims in need and aid workers who stand ready to help if their passage can be secured and their safety maintained' (Rieff 2002, 87). This remains a common (and deeply gendered) trope in humanitarian imagery.

Michel Agier notes: '[t]he humanitarian world is based upon the fiction of humanity as an identity' (Agier 2010, 32). This identity draws legitimacy from a mythologized humanitarian history and legacy in which 'humanitarian exceptionalism' is entrenched in a particular reading of international humanitarian law (Fast 2014). However, as Ticktin (2011) notes in relation to humanitarian efforts to address sexual violence, the 'human' upon which humanitarians have built their identity is gendered and racialized. She argues that the expansion of the humanitarian mission to include gender-based violence 'has inadvertently opened up space for confrontation with politically significant forms of difference and inequality' (Ticktin 2011, 262). I argue that humanitarian memoirs, as a form of 'flesh witnessing' (Harari 2009), offer an interesting way of thinking about difference as embodied.

When difference appears in discussions on peacebuilding, the most common difference cited is between the local and the international, as Lisa Smirl explores in relation to liminality in humanitarian memoirs (Smirl 2012). This binary is so embedded within the peacebuilding literature that a subfield of literature has emerged to explore how it can be broken down through notions of hybridity (e.g. Mac Ginty 2010; Mac Ginty and Richmond 2015). Concurrently, in discussions of aid worker security particularly, there is recognition of the existence of a 'humanitarian exceptionalism' (Fast 2014) whereby the 'expat' aid worker's status is rendered as something distinct from military or civilian, reinforced by their distinct security practices (Duffield 2010). The 'local turn' in peacebuilding has sought to challenge the dominance of international knowledge both in the academic literature and in practice, yet in doing so has reinforced the distinction between local and international (Randazzo 2016).

As Bargués-Pedreny and Mathieu note, within this hybridity literature

> differences are reified and essentialized as inescapable, but also, and perhaps more importantly, difference is linked to stigma (as a deviance from the 'norm' that is reproduced by the frames used to identify it) … emphasizing difference (even as something to be celebrated, a space to cultivate bottom-up peace initiatives) does not remove the stigma attached to it insofar as the 'norm' is neither questioned nor displaced. (Bargués-Pedreny and Mathieu, 2018, 289)

Turning to a different reading of hybridity, Sara Ahmed talks of hybridization in the context of racial identity, as a rejection of the notion that two racial identities 'can be distinguishable in space and time: hybridisation as the very temporality of *passing through and between identity itself without origin or arrival*' (Ahmed 1999, 88, emphasis added). Bargués-Pedreny and Mathieu (2018) suggest that we need to pay greater attention to the power relations that produce differences which then are presented as already existing, calling for us to see 'how differences lie *between* people and not *within* them'. Passing offers a useful way of thinking about difference in this way, as it involves social differentiation which looks at structural rather than essential difference and invites the 're-opening or re-staging of a fractured history of identifications' (Ahmed 1999, 93).

Building on Ahmed's (1999, 93) consideration of passing – which explores passing in relation to racial and sexual identity – it is only 'ambiguous exceptional bodies' whose difference is remarked upon. In the discourse on peacebuilding, aid workers are generally presented as exceptional 'international' bodies, in contrast to the often homogenized 'local'. Yet, there is also a tendency to treat this exceptional category –the international aid worker – as homogenous, with the implication that one's status as 'aid worker' overwrites all other kinds of difference, from gender and class to race, nationality, and religion. This is partly a consequence of the tendency to study humanitarianism as a disembodied organizational practice.

Partis-Jennings' (2017, 418) discussion of the 'third sex' – 'hybrid bodies, which were marked as both female and foreign, both vulnerable and powerful' – highlights how a focus on gender and embodied affective experiences troubles the notion that 'international' actors can be seen as a collective category. In this article, insisting on humanitarianism as an embodied practice allows for the differences between those international aid workers to be interrogated, and the implications of the power relations which produce these differences to be questioned. While the focus here is on embodied difference as narrated by the 'flesh witness' accounts, there is also a need to consider, as Joseph (2018, 432) warns, 'the underlying social structures that, in a sense, make experience and performance possible as well as imposing constraints on it'.

As this section outlines, the notion of flesh witnessing offers a way of reading the accounts presented in *Chasing Misery* as the establishment of these women's authority to write on humanitarianism. However, at the same time as conveying the authority of 'The Field', the essays can also be read through the lens of passing. Just as Ahmed (1999) suggests that passing is both an 'act of moving through space' and 'a set of cultural and embodied practices', in the essays, the women are 'passing through' the places they write about as well as 'passing' as aid workers by embodying a set of practices which encourages the reader to view them as such. Likewise, just as they do not come to inhabit the places they pass through, as we will see, they also do not come to fully inhabit the identity of 'aid worker'; rather, their 'passing' as aid workers is troubled by their identity as women.

These stories seem to serve to reinforce the identity politics of aid. This is a politics – as Melissa Philips states in her essay 'Real Women in Aid Work: Must we Be Either Angelina Jolie or Mother Theresa?' – in which there are only a limited number of dominant interpretive schema for aid workers: either saints and saviours or 'missionary, mad, or misfit' (Philips 2014, 27). In these schema, the common assumption is that the aid worker is male. These stories, then, occupy an uneasy position, conveying the sense in which women experience exclusion from the aid worker identity while also speaking with the authority granted to them by their 'flesh witnessing' as aid workers. It is with this notion of these accounts from *Chasing Misery* conveying authority that my analysis begins.

The authority of 'The Field'

As highlighted above, viewing these essays through the lens of flesh witnessing establishes the authority of their authors to speak for the humanitarian experience. One of the key ways in which this manifests in the story is through reference to 'The Field'. As Helen Seeger observes in her essay 'The Field: The Ever Receding Vanishing Point', there is an authenticity that comes through discomfort in this sector; recognition of the aid worker is 'directly proportional to how authentically grubby, sweaty, sunburnt and sleep deprived he or she is' (Seeger 2014, 31). This hierarchy operates, Seeger adds, through aid workers' 'proximity to a mythical place called "The Field"', as she sardonically charts her elusive and ongoing search across deployments and projects for this place called 'The Field', which always seems to be 'somewhere else, just down the road' (31).

This view echoes the work of Lisa Smirl, who refers to The Field as a liminal space in which 'spaces of work and play blend into one', totally collapsing any distinction between public and private (Smirl 2012, 237). As Richmond, Kappler, and Björkdahl

(2015, 24) argue, The Field is used extensively in peacebuilding, development, and research to 'label a discursive and geographical space different from their own'. This difference is essential to the construction of the discursive frame of The Field; Richmond, Kappler, and Björkdahl suggest that the most obvious link is agrarian – fields farmed by peasants – but I suggest, in humanitarian and peacebuilding settings, that the use of this phrase owes more to a military context, as it is usually accompanied by the terminology, security protocols, and style of 'deployment' (as discussed in more detail below).

The imagined space of The Field, then, is the site of *authentic* flesh witnessing – and just as this can never truly convey the experience of aid work, the frame of The Field discursively replicates this distance and Othering, as it is a space which can never truly be reached. Borrowing Seeger's words, '[t]he field is in [insert dustier place], where Aid Workers are Aid Workers' (2014, 32). Sheehan (2014) explicitly refers to Darfur, her Field, as 'No Place'. The Field is a 'bracketed space' of the kind that Dyvik (2016a, 57) notes as being inaccessible and filled with life at its most real due to the risk of death. It is especially inaccessible to *international* aid workers, as Seeger (2014) suggests, due to security concerns. However, this only seems to make it a more desirable location, supporting Roth's (2015, 140) analysis of aid as voluntary risk-taking or 'work that requires negotiating the edge'.

Other essays in the collection comment on features of The Field, one of the most common and recurring of which is the 4×4 or sports utility vehicle (SUV). As Smirl (2008, 2015, 2016), Duffield (2010, 2012) and others (Abdelnour and Saeed 2014; Autesserre 2014; Donovan 2015; Redfield 2016; Scott-Smith 2013) highlight, the physical spaces and material practices of aid work in recent years have functioned to create further distance between the international aid workers and the populations of the countries they are resident in. The SUV is the main mode of accessing The Field while also representing the distance from it. As Mia Ali, in her essay 'Built to Carry Thirteen', powerfully puts it, 'I'm too busy helping beneficiaries to help the people by the side of the road' (Ali 2014, 52). She highlights the distancing effect of being in a 4×4, separated (both physically and emotionally) from those populations she is there to assist.

Donovan (2015, 740) also addresses this issue, suggesting that 'the functionality of the 4×4 allows those with access to move about more fluidly' (to pass through) while also rendering the aid worker 'as more secure – even more dangerous – as the vehicle hurtles through the bush'. While some of the essays draw attention to the relative security and mobility that 4×4s provide the passenger – Tracy O'Heir in her essay 'Beating the Odds' notes the absence of safety felt when the promised non-governmental organization (NGO) 4×4 does not arrive to pick her up (O'Heir 2014, 73–4) – in the main, the experiences of the women in relation to the security and danger of the 4×4 are much more ambiguous, troubling the dominant narrative of 'bunkerization' (e.g. Duffield 2010).

Rachael Hubbard flips this idea of the vehicle as a site of security as she recounts 'the day I almost died on the Great North Road' (Hubbard 2014, 152). The Land Rover in her story is a space of 'torture' (151), as she is loaded into the vehicle (which is prone to breaking down) feverish with malaria. In this moment she questions the profession: 'Is this what it meant to serve mankind? Watching children starve, watching babies die, fever, exhaustion, and fighting to breathe?' (157); but, ultimately, she concludes that the experience has 'much to offer and much to teach' (159). Ruth Townley begins her essay, 'Holding Their Stories', in a Toyota Hilux, 'hurtling down a claustrophobic dirt road' with her seat belt unbuckled because her driver has explained that the extra time it takes to 'takes to unbuckle can make the difference between life and death', the present danger of ambush clear as they pass by the remains of another of her NGO's vehicles (Townley 2014, 127).

Mac Ginty (2017) explores the value of 4×4s to the conflict in Darfur, and Hoppe (2014c) picks up this theme as she recounts the 'Gereida incident' from her time in Darfur, in her essay 'I Know What Fear Tastes Like'. The incident sticks in her mind because of the 'brutality against [the] NGOs themselves' (210), during the night when a rebel group attacked an NGO compound, stole vehicles and communications equipment, and attacked Sudansese staff (211). She recalls another 'incident' in which a driver had been killed, staff had gone missing, and 'vehicles had been torched' (213–14), again countering the prevalent discourse that the ever-present 4×4 is a site of security for aid workers; the flesh witnessing of these women challenges the unproblematic notion that for those international actors involved in intervention, 'exclusive transport links into an archipelago of protected international space' (Duffield 2010, 71).

Carmen Sheehan – in her essay 'No Place', which is also about Darfur – draws attention to another danger experienced in relation to the 4×4: that of the roadblock or checkpoint, which also features in Kirsten Hagon's essay, 'There Is No Rape in Darfur' (Sheehan 2014; Hagon 2014). Sheehan (2014, 234–5) describes being stopped at a checkpoint shortly before curfew, her inner monologue – courtesy of her training – highlighting a very specific fear borne from the previous week's security briefing about the attempted rape of a female driver at a checkpoint after dark. She collapses mind–body and internal–external distinctions, immersing the reader in both the physical and mental manifestations of her fear simultaneously, alongside the description of her interactions at the checkpoint: 'Willing the motor not to die, I backed gently out into the road and glanced in the rear view mirror. If the firing squad in the road kept it together I would be free' (237). This highlights the way in which gender impacts feelings of security, a key theme of Partis-Jennings' (2017) work on gendered (in)security in Afghanistan.

The distance which the women report feeling in The Field is not simply physical, represented by the separation caused by the 4×4, or in the material difference in the lives of international aid workers. It is also an emotional distance, as Lucy O'Donoghue makes apparent in her essay, 'Relationships: At the Heart of, Well, Everything'. She compares the 'years of a transitory lifestyle' of the international aid worker to 'the relative stability that … local staff often have through their communities and families' (O'Donoghue 2014, 84). Again we see that these women are simply passing through, their difference both allowing them this privilege and creating distance. She highlights this 'vacuum' as a 'lack' experienced by international aid workers (85). Interestingly, she suggests a need for the building of relationships – in order to reduce the 'gaping chasm of otherness found between expatriate and national staff' – through a recognition of the embodied humanness of the Other: 'being human, recognising our need to give ourselves in relationship and in community' (85). This is not a vision of an idealized local community, but a recognition that the local staff 'rarely [get] the opportunity to compartmentalise their lives' (85). In contrast, in the bracketed, liminal space of The Field, international aid workers are 'thoroughly unmoored' not only from the communities they are there to assist but also from their own communities back home, and – in some cases – their own emotions (80).

The nomadic lifestyle of the international aid worker is a key narrative through which difference is produced. O'Donoghue notes how 'bizarre' it must appear to local staff that 'we, the expatriates, would forfeit our own *natural* environment and longstanding relationships to insert ourselves, usefully or otherwise, into their relatively insecure world' (2014, 81, emphasis added). Through the notion of the 'natural' environment being other than The Field, the difference of the international aid worker is reproduced. Yet, common to many humanitarian memoirs is the trope of alienation from 'home', both while in The Field and especially once returning to 'normal' life.

This paradox at once produces The Field as exceptional but also as real in a way in which ordinary life is not. It is a place that people need to return to in order to feel fully alive, a sentiment conveyed by Emilie J. Greenhalgh in her essay, 'Answers Found in Harm's Way: From Congo to Afghanistan':

> I had not been able to find a balance between the fascination of the crisis, the romance of the humanitarian work, and the blatant desire of a twenty-something woman to have fun and not simply revel in chasing the misery the world dishes out every goddamn day. (Greenhalgh 2014, 178)

'Chasing Misery' is also the title of one of Kelsey Hoppe's essays, which picks up this theme of the desire to experience – as much as possible – the thrill and romance of The Field. Sacrificing comfort and relationships, as explored further below, in pursuit of this nebulous idea of authenticity – of 'real' aid work – comes up in Hoppe's essay:

> We parade through life dressed in immortality. Traipsing around places where it is likely that we will be shot or drowned or kidnapped or beheaded by people who believe things a little too much. Trying our immortality on for size, like new clothes, seeing if it fits. It never does. Immortality never fits anyone. (Hoppe 2014b, 21)

Again, there is a recurring sense of the illusiveness of the authenticity of the experience which is being sought. The metaphor of clothes[6] and their fit resonates with Ahmed's (2017, 125) comments on institutional passing: 'an institution is like an old garment. It acquires the shape of those who tend to wear it; it becomes easier to wear if you have that shape'. Even as these women's experiences of The Field allow them to speak with authority, there is a sense of alienation from the identity they are trying (and failing) to inhabit. It does not quite fit them, and they do not quite fit in it; The Field is always elsewhere, but this only serves to make the search for it more insistent. Thinking about this through the lens of passing highlights the ways in which the women in their essays simultaneously recognize the problematic authority of The Field and also reproduce it; as Robinson (1994, 735) suggests, '[t]he limited subversion of the pass always requires the terms of the system be intact'.

This section has sought to explore the locus of authentic experience, as told in the essays of *Chasing Misery* (Hoppe 2014a). As a bracketed space to which others do not have access, The Field serves as a space of authenticity of which only flesh witnesses can speak. However, the narratives offered in the collection both reproduce and trouble this notion, highlighting the ways in which this space is always out of reach. Indeed, this elusive quality is no doubt part of its appeal. They also highlight the 'inbetweenness' of occupying this space, 'unmoored' from relationships which give meaning (O'Donoghue 2014, 80; Older 2014, 300), thus fostering a search for meaning through 'chasing misery'. The next section picks up on this notion of 'inbetweenness' and explores the ways in which race and gender appear in the women's narratives and can reinforce and trouble notions of 'humanitarian exceptionalism' (Fast 2014).

'Muzungus', gender, and humanitarian exceptionalism

In the previous section, I noted that the limited subversion of the essays in the book challenges the dominant humanitarian narratives, but ultimately ends up also reproducing them. The essays challenge, reflect on, and reproduce the humanitarian system. Humanitarian memoirs are not only important for what they reveal about the humanitarian experience and imaginary, but also for how they frame for a broader social imaginary what humanitarianism is.

In her essay, 'Of Pastries, Loss and Pride', Kati Woronka notes the divide between international aid workers and 'beneficiaries' (Woronka 2014) – the optimistic name that 'we aid workers call the people we help' (Seeger 2014, 32). Woronka describes this feeling of divide, noting in particular the generalizing names that come to define them in different places: 'I felt a terrible divide between expatriates, including myself, and the people we were there to serve. There was always a name for us: Malae in East Timor, Blancs in Haiti, Khawaja in Darfur' (2014, 118–19). Miranda Gaanderse, in her essay 'Send in the Clown', notes of her experience working with unaccompanied minors in Uganda the 'personal victory that they now call by name rather than "Muzungu"' Gaanderse's (2014, 144).

Yet, some of the authors also fall into this trap, referring to themselves as 'expatriates' (O'Donoghue 2014; Woronka 2014) or 'expats' (Feldacker 2014; Greenhalgh 2014), explicitly placing themselves into an 'us' group which is contrasted with the 'them' of the intervention zone. As Woronka (2014, 119) suggests, this grouping seems 'somehow inevitable: to the people we came to serve, we weren't individuals. We were foreign objects. And, no doubt, our hosts figured we felt the same about them. Maybe we did'. As Smirl argues, it is in the everyday practices of The Field and 'their accompanying spaces (the offices, compounds, workshops, projects) that the categories of local and international are (re)produced despite rhetorical commitments to move beyond them' (2012, 230).

This separation, as mentioned above, operates on more than one level, as the lifestyle of aid workers is accompanied by a sense of separation from both home and those with them in The Field. Just as there is 'always a name for us' (Woronka 2014, 118), the writers produce this same difference from 'nameless and faceless beneficiaries' (O'Donoghue 2014, 85). However, some also try to disrupt its Othering power: 'Doctors, lawyers and academics. Artists, musicians and poets. These were the "beneficiaries"' (Woronka 2014, 118). Seeger (2014, 34) highlights and satirizes the use of generic terms like 'beneficiaries' and 'the community leaders' to render difference, noting that they are remote from the aid worker party scene and must surely 'not have such a strong affection for the Black Eyed Peas'. The subtext: they are not like 'us'.

As Miranda Bryant tells us in her essay, 'From New Orleans to South Sudan: How I Healed by Moving to a War-Torn Country', the distancing effect of working in The Field overseas can be easier, as there is an emotional distance which comes with the ability to withdraw; aid workers 'can buffer themselves from the pain of their beneficiaries' experience by virtue of understanding that, theoretically, they can board a plane and leave the disaster when they so choose' (Bryant 2014, 43). Here it is interesting to note Bryant's assertion that aid workers are buffered from the pain of the experiences, while other stories make clear that the difference and separation from the people occupying the spaces in which they work is much deeper and more entrenched.

A number of the essays note the lack of understanding from 'locals' (both staff and otherwise) who question the lifestyle choice of being an 'expat' aid worker (e.g. O'Donoghue 2014, 82). Here gender seems to play an especially important role, particularly in terms of the impact of the lifestyle on relationships. In 'Home Is Where the Hard Is', Caryl Feldacker describes the end of her 'unsalvageable' engagement while in Malawi (Feldacker 2014, 261); a recurring theme in the essay is the way in which she feels the engagement 'legitimised our partnership and gave me additional credibility' (263) in the context of the religious conservatism of Malawi. The contrast in lifestyle between the motherhood of the 'beneficiaries' – repeatedly referenced across the essays – and the decision on the part of the female aid workers to live 'unmoored' lives is a key source of difference, although only rarely explicitly addressed: 'I regretted that I had never been married or even been in a serious relationship' (Woronka 2014, 178).

Romantic relationships (and the lack of them) are a common theme running through a number of the essays, as well as the relationship (or lack of) between the writers and their colleagues and 'beneficiaries'. Reflecting on her own unwillingness to follow her partner to Vancouver, Kelsey Hoppe considers that the difficulty of connecting to someone else romantically may be part of what inspires her to chase misery:

> We are not the sort of people who go places for other people. We are not people who need others to come and be where we are. This is what makes us so interesting. This is what makes us think we are in love with each other when we are not. We are in love with ourselves. We are in love with the idea of ourselves. It is actually a mad grasping fit of jealousy that we mistake as love when we see our lives being lived by another. (Hoppe 2014b, 23)

The idea of seeing 'our lives being lived by another' picks up on a theme explored in the passing literature, that of 'in-group' recognition: that is recognition from the group one has passed from (Robinson 1994). The stories in the anthology perform this function, the women's recognition of each other's passing as aid workers validating their own passing, as well as their claims to authority. In this way, similar to Sue-Ellen Case's observation of the butch–femme aesthetic, 'a strategy of appearances replaces a claim to truth' (Case 1988, 70).

Lucy O'Donoghue's description of aid workers who have 'thoroughly unmoored themselves' and seem 'adrift from any community, at home or on mission' (O'Donoghue's 2014, 80) is an interesting counterpoint to Roberta Romano's 'The Subtle Thread' (Romano 2014), which addresses a growing sense of questioning that is also found in Greenhalgh's (2014, 171) contribution: 'The romance had left almost the instant I arrived, quickly replaced with the feeling of futility that we all tried to forget while commiserating at the local expat bars'. Smirl (2012, 239) also observes this phenomena in the humanitarian memoirs she analyses: 'they begin to realise that they are all in a state of ineffectual limbo, where none of their efforts have any impact'.

As this article shows, across these essays we see that the female aid worker is always Other, even in her own account – different, and separated, both from those populations she is attempting to assist and from her life 'back home', searching for the authenticity of experience in The Field, and the clarity and validation which its dangers and risks can provide. The next section explores the sense in which these women experience the difference of being female in a profession in which 'most of these stereotypes rest on the assumption that aid workers are male' (Philips 2014, 26).

Passing as an aid worker

The essays discussed in this article do not exist in a vacuum. There are broader discourses and narratives on which the writers draw and to which the writers contribute; social imaginaries of the humanitarian sector are already present (e.g. Dechaine 2002; Repo and Yrjölä 2011). In thinking about the embodied experience of female aid workers, it is necessary to explore how bodies become intelligible in relation to these broader discourses and structures. As mentioned earlier, Philips (2014) highlights the common assumption that the aid worker is male. The women in the essays confirm this sense of only 'passing' as aid workers in relation to the 'real' (male) aid workers – a sense of being out of place as women is linked in the essays to notions of their newness, inexperience, and lack (or not) of toughness.

Philips (2014, 25) communicates this through the story of her experience at Nairobi's Jomo Kenyatta airport, where she thought she 'had ended [her] aid career before it even began' because of an alarm clock which 'looked suspiciously like handcuffs' on the security X-ray machine. It was not the situation but Philips' reaction to it which caused the problem: 'I was surrounded by other conflict-weary, khaki-wearing aid workers who were mostly men and I feared I had committed a fatal error [crying] that highlighted both my newness and my gender' (25). For Philips, her gender was a deficiency in relation to humanitarian work that was on a par with her lack of experience. It was not simply the fact of her gender, but the physical manifestation of this in her tears and near hysteria. She had failed to pass in this instance, and the manner of her failure highlights that this 'sense of being inadequate to the identity one assumes (either consciously or unconsciously) involves phantasies about who is the real or authentic subject' (Ahmed 1999, 96).

In the essays, we repeatedly see fantasies about what authenticates a 'real' aid worker. Again, difference is produced for the women in their stories through juxtaposing their extraordinary lives to the lives of those around them, as well as to the more experienced, more 'real' aid workers. Gaanderse (2014, 137) tackles this as she describes finding herself to be 'the girl from headquarters who was bringing a whole household with her to a refugee settlement', subject to the 'mocking stares and incredulous glances – especially from local male colleagues'. She recalls believing: 'I am tougher than they think' (137). The issue of 'toughness' as a norm or standard of what makes a 'real' aid worker is echoed by O'Donoghue (2014, 79) when she describes the persona that she tried to embody; it was 'a fusion of ruthless efficiency and hakuna matata, and it felt like the result was one scratchy, cynical, impatient bitch'. This strategy of passing is common, 'a technique of the self' (Ahmed 1999, 101) in which the passer adopts elements of the identity she is trying to pass as, thus projecting a particular bodily image. In describing these women's attempts to adopt the identity of aid worker, the stories reveal the fetish of the aid worker identity. The women do the work of identifying the elements of the identity which reveal difference from their own; in 'desiring to capture an identity … [i]t takes time and knowledge to see the difference that one may desire (or need) to become' (98).

Seeger (2014, 31) highlights an important aspect of the notion of 'realness' in relation to aid work: its relationship to a specific aesthetic of dustiness and dirt. She notes the 'professional suicide' of a stylish haircut which a 'real' aid worker would not have time for. The spectre of 'real' (masculine) aid workers haunts many of the stories.[7] For Philips (2014, 25) it is the khaki-wearing (male) veteran aid workers at the airport, who seem to share much in common with Romano's (2014, 201) Austrian 'security guy that wears trousers full of pockets and you are sure he keeps knives and compasses in some of them'. Seeger (2014, 32) speaks of the 'infamous [Russian] helicopter pilots about whom every veteran aid worker seems to have a story'. For Roberson (2014, 62) it is the 'big, burly South African and Zimbabwean ex-military men' from the landmine NGO, 'who knew how to drink and have more fun than anyone else' she had ever met. And for Greenhalgh (2014, 173) it is the 'World Food Programme (WPF) guys', who tolerated the presence of female aid workers, 'using it as a chance to gossip and flirt'.

As Ahmed (2017, 122) notes of passing, 'it can be uncomfortable' to not be able to embody established norms, and the discomfort of the failure to pass can also be found in the essays, often made visible by the specific forms of discomfort experienced by the female aid workers. This theme is also explored in Partis-Jennings' account of the gendered security practices of peacebuilding in Afghanistan, in which many highlight 'restriction, harassment or self-enforced security measures based on gender' (2017, 418). Greenhalgh (2014, 172) supplements the general discomfort of The Field with the particular discomfort of being a woman there, recounting the 'unfriendly locals who catcalled', while Gaanderse (2014, 138–9) describes the awkwardness of the showers being situated next to the contingent of Ugandan police officers who were there for her protection: 'I began to wonder whether stripping down in the dark next to a group of half-drunk, undressed, male police officers was really such a good idea'.

A similar issue is observed by Ali (2014, 51), who is hungry and thirsty but conscious of a practical problem: 'what goes in must come out, and there's no privacy for a woman at the side of these roads'. Ali's dilemma is compounded by the threat of landmines away from the road, where privacy could be found. My intent here is not to claim that women have it worse, but to draw attention to the specific and embodied differences which alter how they experience The Field, and to suggest that we need to ask more about these differences and the effects they have on practices of peacebuilding and humanitarianism.

As Philips' (2014) story of her airport experience highlights, women's apparent propensity for tears marks them as different. Hoppe (2014d, 12) notes in the preface to the book: 'women are more apt to cry, or at least admit to crying', framing this as 'often the only appropriate response' to human suffering. Yet, it is often the personal miseries in the essays which lead to tears: Philips at the airport; Woronka (2014) falling out with a colleague; Gaanderse (2014, 135) 'the crying aid worker', emotional at leaving; and Hoppe (2014c, 220) when she is relieved to see a colleague during a difficult time.

The juxtaposition between tears as the appropriate response to human misery and the actual instances of their own crying detailed by the women reflects a concern, discussed in the preface to *Chasing Misery*, that telling the aid workers' stories 'detracts from the stories of those [they] have gone to help or those who are "truly" suffering' (Hoppe 2014d, 11–12). The goal of the book is to stand in solidarity with those who are 'truly' suffering: 'tell

THE POLITICS OF PEACEBUILDING IN A DIVERSE WORLD 31

your story through my story' (12). These stories present a community in which crying is affirmed as an 'appropriate' response and in doing so they also affirm their authors' membership of a community of female aid workers. This affords them a collective voice through which they can challenge the assumed superiority of the masculinity and 'maleness' of the aid worker identity from the position of authority that their experience of The Field grants them.

Concluding thoughts: Women as flesh witnesses in humanitarianism

This article explores what we can learn about embodied difference in humanitarianism and peacebuilding by taking seriously women's memoirs as a form of 'flesh witnessing' (Harari 2009). This focus on humanitarian memoirs – representing 'their story as they want to tell it' (Duncanson 2013, 57) – builds on the important feminist research already conducted on military memoirs, (especially Dyvik 2016a, 2016b; see also Duncanson 2009; Welland 2015), embodiment in peace and conflict studies (Partis-Jennings 2017; Sylvester 2013; Wilcox 2015), and liminality in humanitarian memoirs (Smirl 2012). Drawing on the notion of 'flesh witnessing', I have argued that the essays in *Chasing Misery* (Hoppe 2014a) simultaneously speak with the authority of The Field and reveal the sense in which the women feel they are only 'passing' as aid workers.

I have focused on three main themes of difference, beginning with an examination of the construction of The Field as a site of embodied authority and the ways in which the women's essays reinforce and trouble this notion. The ways in which the women highlight feeling different, and separate, from the people they work with and for were then explored via their use of generalizing terminology and the effect of this feeling of difference on the possibility of forming genuine relationships, which in turn are also foregrounded as a site of difference that is very much connected to the identity of the aid worker 'chasing misery'. Finally, I investigated the ways in which embodied gender causes the women to note their difference from the imagined aid worker, revealing the sense in which they feel that they were only passing as aid workers. The fragility of the imagined identity itself is thus revealed in the collective narration of their experiences as female aid workers.

This article makes an original contribution to the literature on humanitarianism and peacebuilding by drawing on the under-researched humanitarian memoir. In doing so it highlights the curious absence of analyses of humanitarian aid which take gender seriously as a category of analysis, rather than simply a programming area. In highlighting female aid workers' narratives of their own distinct experiences, it foregrounds embodied experience as key to the consideration of the complex power structures and relationships in humanitarianism and peacebuilding. The tendency to view the distinction between international and local as the primary category of difference in humanitarianism and peacebuilding obscures the complex and intersecting hierarchies of gender, race, class, nationality, and age which are deeply embedded in humanitarian practices. Although the focus here is on how gender difference is narrated by female aid workers, further analyses of this kind can reveal important insights about these other categories of difference.

As a final point, I want to note that these memoirs must be viewed as both shaping and being shaped by broader social imaginaries. Explorers' travel writing has 'produced the rest of the world' for European audiences since the 1700s (Pratt 2008, 5) because 'it functions to introduce "us" to the Other. This equally affords us a way of knowing our-selves' (Heron 2007, 3). Memoirs of humanitarianism and peacebuilding perform the same function, introducing humanitarian spaces to Northern audiences in order to reas-sure them that 'Northern countries have a special role to play in alleviating the woes of the poor global others' (Heron 2007, 5). Yet, while the essays in *Chasing Misery* (Hoppe 2014a) perform this function – and are firmly embedded in global structures and relation-ships of power – this analysis demonstrates the ways in which these women also trouble these discourses simply by recognizing them at work. By focusing on gender as a site of difference, the women present a community that affords them a collective voice through which they can challenge dominant tropes of aid from the position of authority that their experience of The Field grants them. In doing so, they trouble the dominant narrative of noble aid workers by recognizing the paradox of self-fulfilment they receive from their apparent altruism – as Kelsey Hoppe puts it: 'We are in love with ourselves. We are in love with the idea of ourselves' (Hoppe 2014b, 23). The book seeks to stand in solidarity with those 'truly' suffering – 'tell your story through my story' (Hoppe 2014d, 12) – yet cannot escape from the dynamics of difference and Othering which plague the humani-tarian system.

Notes

1. The book also features photographic contributions, but these are not included in the present analysis as they are not examples of aid workers narrating their own experiences. The photo-graphs are not of the contributor women themselves but rather of those they are 'aiding'.
2. I want to thank Xavier Mathieu for his extremely helpful suggestion to explore this literature.
3. http://www.chasingmisery.net/editors/. Accessed 4 April 2018.
4. Kelsey Hoppe contributes three essays to the collection, including the introduction, and Helen Seeger contributes two.
5. Although not all authors choose to share their nationality, most who do are from the United Kingdom (UK), Europe, Australia, New Zealand, and the United States (US).
6. Although here the clothes are a metaphor, Maria Martin de Almagro (2018) explores the ways in which clothes are used in performances of hybrid peacebuilding identities (see also Partis-Jennings 2017, 419).
7. For more on hauntings and masculinity, see Welland (2013).

Acknowledgements

I would like to thank the editors of this special issue, Pol Bargués-Pedreny and Xavier Mathieu, for the opportunity to be part of such a rewarding collaboration, as well as the other contributors to the workshop from which this special issue came – especially Nicolas Lemay-Hébert. I thank the two anonymous reviewers for their helpful and generous suggestions, in particular the recommen-dation to engage with the work of Hannah Partis-Jennings. whom I would also like thank. The idea for this piece came from my participation in a workshop organized by Laura McLeod and Maria O'Reilly in 2016 on feminist interventions in critical peacebuilding, and I thank them for the inspiration.

Disclosure statement

No potential conflict of interest was reported by the authors.

References

Abdelnour, Samer, and Akbar M. Saeed. 2014. 'Technologizing Humanitarian Space: Darfur Advocacy and the Rape-Stove Panacea.' *International Political Sociology* 8 (2): 145–163. http://doi.org/10.1111/ips.12049.

Agier, Michel. 2010. 'Humanity as an Identity and Its Political Effects (A Note on Camps and Humanitarian Government).' *Humanity: An International Journal of Human Rights, Humanitarianism, and Development* 1 (1): 29–45. http://doi.org/10.1353/hum.2010.0005.

Ahmed, Sara. 1999. '"She'll Wake Up One of These Days and Find She's Turned into a Nigger": Passing through Hybridity.' *Theory, Culture & Society* 16 (2): 87–106. http://doi.org/10.1177/02632769922050566.

Ahmed, Sara. 2017. *Living a Feminist Life*. London: Duke University Press.

Ali, Mia. 2014. 'Built to Carry Thirteen.' In *Chasing Misery: An Anthology of Essays by Women in Humanitarian Responses*, edited by Kelsey Hoppe, 51–60. North Charleston, SC: CreateSpace.

Autesserre, Séverine. 2014. *Peaceland: Conflict Resolution and the Everyday Politics of International Intervention*. Cambridge: Cambridge University Press.

Baker, Catherine. 2016. 'Writing about Embodiment as an Act of Translation.' *Critical Military Studies* 2 (1–2): 120–124. http://doi.org/10.1080/23337486.2016.1139314.

Bargués-Pedreny, Pol and Xavier Mathieu. 2018. '"Beyond Silence, Obstacle and Stigma: Revisiting the 'Problem' of Difference in Peacebuilding"', *Journal of Intervention and Statebuilding* 12 (3): 283–299.

Bryant, Miranda. 2014. 'From New Orleans to South Sudan: How I Healed by Moving to a War-Torn Country.' In *Chasing Misery: An Anthology of Essays by Women in Humanitarian Responses*, edited by Kelsey Hoppe, 41–46. North Charleston, SC: CreateSpace.

Case, Sue-Ellen. 1988. 'Towards a Butch-Femme Aesthetic.' *Discourses* 11 (1): 55–73. http://www.jstor.org/stable/41389108.

Conboy, Kate, Nadia Medina, and Sarah Stanbury. 1997. 'Introduction.' In *Writing on the Body: Female Embodiment and Feminist Theory*, edited by Katie Conboy, Nadia Medina, and Sarah Stanbury, 1–12. New York: Columbia University Press.

Dechaine, D. Robert. 2002. 'Humanitarian Space and the Social Imaginary: *Médecins sans frontières*/Doctors Without Borders and the Rhetoric of Global Community.' *Journal of Communication Inquiry* 26 (4): 354–369. http://doi.org/10.1177/019685902236896.

Donovan, Kevin P. 2015. 'Infrastructuring Aid: Materializing Humanitarianism in Northern Kenya.' *Environment and Planning D: Society and Space* 33 (4): 732–748. http://doi.org/10.1177/0263775815598107.

Duffield, Mark. 2010. 'Risk-Management and the Fortified Aid Compound: Everyday Life in Post-Interventionary Society.' *Journal of Intervention and Statebuilding* 4 (4): 453–474. https://doi.org/10.1080/17502971003700993.

Duffield, Mark. 2012. 'Challenging Environments: Danger, Resilience and the Aid Industry.' *Security Dialogue* 43 (5): 475–492. https://doi.org/10.1177/0967010612457975.

Duncanson, Claire. 2009. 'Forces for Good? Narratives of Military Masculinity in Peacekeeping Operations.' *International Feminist Journal of Politics* 11 (1): 63–80. http://doi.org/10.1080/14616740802567808.

Duncanson, Claire (2013). *Forces for Good? Military Masculinities and Peacebuilding in Afghanistan and Iraq*. Basingstoke: Palgrave Macmillan.

Dyvik, Synne L. 2016a. 'Of Bats and Bodies: Methods for Reading and Writing Embodiment.' *Critical Military Studies* 2 (1–2): 56–69. https://doi.org/10.1080/23337486.2016.1184471.

Dyvik, Synne L. 2016b. '"Valhalla Rising": Gender, Embodiment and Experience in Military Memoirs.' *Security Dialogue* 47 (2): 133–150. http://doi.org/10.1177/0967010615615730.

Fast, Larissa. 2014. *Aid in Danger: The Perils and Promise of Humanitarianism*. Philadelphia: University of Pennsylvania Press.

Feldacker, Caryl. 2014. 'Home Is Where the Hard Is.' In *Chasing Misery: An Anthology of Essays by Women in Humanitarian Responses*, edited by Kelsey Hoppe, 261–273. North Charleston, SC: CreateSpace.

Gaanderse, Miranda. 2014. 'Send in the Clown.' In *Chasing Misery: An Anthology of Essays by Women in Humanitarian Responses*, edited by Kelsey Hoppe, 135–148. North Charleston, SC: CreateSpace.

Givoni, M. 2011. 'Beyond the Humanitarian/Political Divide: Witnessing and the Making of Humanitarian Ethics.' *Journal of Human Rights* 10 (1): 55–75. http://doi.org/10.1080/14754835.2011.546235.

Greenhalgh, Emilie J. 2014. 'Answers Found in Harm's Way: From Congo to Afghanistan.' In *Chasing Misery: An Anthology of Essays by Women in Humanitarian Responses*, edited by Kelsey Hoppe, 167–180. North Charleston, SC: CreateSpace.

Hagon, Kirsten. 2014. 'There Is No Rape in Darfur.' In *Chasing Misery: An Anthology of Essays by Women in Humanitarian Responses*, edited by Kelsey Hoppe, 241–254. North Charleston, SC: CreateSpace.

Harari, Yuval Noah 2009. 'Scholars, Eyewitnesses, and Flesh-Witnesses of War: A Tense Relationship.' *Partial Answers: Journal of Literature and the History of Ideas* 7 (2): 213–228. https://doi.org/10.1353/pan.0.0147.

Haraway, Donna. 1988. 'Situated Knowledges: The Science Question in Feminism and the Privilege of Partial Perspective.' *Feminist Studies* 14: 575–99.

Heron, Barbara. 2007. *Desire for Development: Whiteness, Gender and the Helping Imperative*. Ontario: Wilfrid Laurier University Press.

Hoppe, Kelsey, ed. 2014a. *Chasing Misery: An Anthology of Essays by Women in Humanitarian Responses*. North Charleston, SC: CreateSpace.

Hoppe, Kelsey. 2014b. 'Chasing Misery.' In *Chasing Misery: An Anthology of Essays by Women in Humanitarian Responses*, edited by Kelsey Hoppe, 21–24. North Charleston, SC: CreateSpace.

Hoppe, Kelsey. 2014c. 'I Know What Fear Tastes Like.' In *Chasing Misery: An Anthology of Essays by Women in Humanitarian Responses*, edited by Kelsey Hoppe, 210–220. North Charleston, SC: CreateSpace.

Hoppe, Kelsey. 2014d. 'Preface.' In *Chasing Misery: An Anthology of Essays by Women in Humanitarian Responses*, edited by Kelsey Hoppe, 11–15. North Charleston, SC: CreateSpace.

Hubbard, Rachael. 2014. 'The Great North Road.' In *Chasing Misery: An Anthology of Essays by Women in Humanitarian Responses*, edited by Kelsey Hoppe, 151–158. North Charleston, SC: CreateSpace.

Joseph, Jonathan. 2018. "Beyond Relationalism in Peacebuilding." *Journal of Intervention and Statebuilding* 12 (3): 425–434.

Lennon, Kathleen. 2015. 'Imagination and The Imaginary'. Abingdon: Routledge.

Mac Ginty, Roger. 2010. 'Hybrid Peace: The Interaction between Top-Down and Bottom-Up Peace.' *Security Dialogue* 41 (4): 391–412. http://doi.org/10.1177/0967010610374312.

Mac Ginty, Roger. 2017. 'A Material Turn in International Relations: The 4 × 4, Intervention and Resistance.' *Review of International Studies* 43 (5): 855–874. http://doi.org/10.1017/S0260210517000146.

Mac Ginty, Roger, and Oliver Richmond. 2015. 'The Fallacy of Constructing Hybrid Political Orders: A Reappraisal of the Hybrid Turn in Peacebuilding.' *International Peacekeeping* 3312: 1–21. http://doi.org/10.1080/13533312.2015.1099440.

Martin de Almagro, Maria. 2017. 'Producing Participants: Gender, Race, Class, and Women, Peace and Security.' *Global Society*. Advance online publication. https://doi.org/10.1080/13600826.2017.1380610.

Martin de Almagro, Maria. 2018. 'Hybrid clubs: a feminist approach to peacebuilding in the Democratic Republic of Congo.' *Journal of Intervention and Statebuilding* 12 (3): 319–334. https://doi.org/10.1080/17502977.2018.14821251380610.

McLeod, Laura. 2015. 'A Feminist Approach to Hybridity: Understanding Local and International Interactions in Producing Post-Conflict Gender Security.' *Journal of Intervention and Statebuilding* 9 (1): 48–69. http://doi.org/10.1080/17502977.2014.980112.

O'Donoghue, Lucy. 2014. 'Relationships: At the Heart of, Well, Everything.' In *Chasing Misery: An Anthology of Essays by Women in Humanitarian Responses*, edited by Kelsey Hoppe, 79–85. North Charleston, SC: CreateSpace.

O'Heir, Tracy. 2014. 'Beating the Odds.' In *Chasing Misery: An Anthology of Essays by Women in Humanitarian Responses*, edited by Kelsey Hoppe, 71–78. North Charleston, SC: CreateSpace.

Older, Malka. 2014. 'Accepting Thanks.' In *Chasing Misery: An Anthology of Essays by Women in Humanitarian Responses*, edited by Kelsey Hoppe, 295–301. North Charleston, SC: CreateSpace.

Partis-Jennings, Hannah. 2017. 'The (In)Security of Gender in Afghanistan's Peacebuilding Project: Hybridity and Affect.' *International Feminist Journal of Politics* 19 (4): 411–425. https://doi.org/10.1080/14616742.2017.1279418.

Philips, Melissa. 2014. 'Real Women in Aid Work: Must We Be Either Angelina Jolie or Mother Theresa?' In *Chasing Misery: An Anthology of Essays by Women in Humanitarian Responses*, edited by Kelsey Hoppe, 25–29. North Charleston, SC: CreateSpace.

Pratt, Mary Louise. 2008. *Imperial Eyes: Travel Writing and Transculturation*. 2nd ed. Abingdon: Routledge.

Randazzo, Elisa. 2016. 'The Paradoxes of the 'Everyday': Scrutinising The Local Turn in Peace Building.' *Third World Quarterly* 37 (2): 1351–1370. http://doi.org/10.1080/01436597.2015.1120154.

Redfield, Peter. 2016. 'Fluid Technologies: The Bush Pump, the LifeStraw® and Microworlds of Humanitarian Design.' *Social Studies of Science* 46 (2): 159–183. http://doi.org/10.1177/0306312715620061.

Repo, Jemima, and Riina Yrjölä. 2011. 'The Gender Politics of Celebrity Humanitarianism in Africa.' *International Feminist Journal of Politics* 13 (1): 44–62. http://doi.org/10.1080/14616742.2011.534661.

Richmond, Oliver, Stefanie Kappler, and Annika Björkdahl. 2015. 'The "Field" in the Age of Intervention: Power, Legitimacy, and Authority Versus the "Local".' *Millennium – Journal of International Studies* 44 (1): 23–44. http://doi.org/10.1177/0305829815594871.

Rieff, David. 2002. *A Bed for the Night: Humanitarianism in Crisis*. London: Vintage.

Roberson, Steph. 2014. 'Falling Down.' In *Chasing Misery: An Anthology of Essays by Women in Humanitarian Responses*, edited by Kelsey Hoppe, 61–69. North Charleston, SC: CreateSpace.

Robinson, Amy. 1994. 'It Takes One to Know One: Passing and Communities of Common Interest.' *Critical Inquiry* 20 (4): 715–736. https://doi.org/10.1086/448734.

Romano, Roberta. 2014. 'The Subtle Thread.' In *Chasing Misery: An Anthology of Essays by Women in Humanitarian Responses*, edited by Kelsey Hoppe, 199–207. North Charleston, SC: CreateSpace.

Roth, Silke. 2015. 'Aid Work as Edgework – Voluntary Risk-Taking and Security in Humanitarian Assistance, Development and Human Rights Work.' *Journal of Risk Research* 18 (2): 139–155. http://doi.org/10.1080/13669877.2013.875934.

Scott-Smith, Tom. 2013. 'The Fetishism of Humanitarian Objects and the Management of Malnutrition in Emergencies.' *Third World Quarterly* 34 (5): 913–928. http://doi.org/10.1080/01436597.2013.800749.

Seeger, Helen. 2014. 'The Field: The Ever Receding Vanishing Point.' In *Chasing Misery: An Anthology of Essays by Women in Humanitarian Responses*, edited by Kelsey Hoppe, 31–35. North Charleston, SC: CreateSpace.

Sheehan, Carmen. 2014. 'No Place.' In *Chasing Misery: An Anthology of Essays by Women in Humanitarian Responses*, edited by Kelsey Hoppe, 226–240. North Charleston, SC: CreateSpace.

Smirl, Lisa. 2008. 'Building The Other, Constructing Ourselves: Spatial Dimensions of International Humanitarian Response.' *International Political Sociology* 2 (3): 236–253. https://doi.org/10.1111/j.1749-5687.2008.00047.x.

Smirl, Lisa. 2012. 'The State We Are(n't) in: Liminal Subjectivity in Aid Worker Biographies.' In *Statebuilding and State Formation: The Political Sociology of Intervention*, edited by Berit Bliessman de Guevara, 230–245. London: Routledge.

Smirl, Lisa. 2015. *Spaces of Aid: How Cars, Compounds and Hotels Shape Humanitarianism*. London: Zed Books.

Smirl, Lisa. 2016. '"Not Welcome at the Holiday Inn": How a Sarajevan Hotel Influenced Geo-Politics.' *Journal of Intervention and Statebuilding* 10 (1): 32–55. http://doi.org/10.1080/17502977.2015.1137398.

Sylvester, Christine. 2013. *War as Experience: Contributions From International Relations and Feminist Analysis*. Abingdon: Routledge.

Ticktin, Miriam. 2011. 'The Gendered Human of Humanitarianism: Medicalising and Politicising Sexual Violence.' *Gender and History* 23 (2): 250–265. http://doi.org/10.1111/j.1468-0424.2011.01637.x.

Townley, Ruth. 2014. 'Holding Their Stories.' In *Chasing Misery: An Anthology of Essays by Women in Humanitarian Responses*, edited by Kelsey Hoppe, 127–134. North Charleston, SC: CreateSpace.

Welland, Julia. 2013. 'Militarised Violences, Basic Training, and the Myths of Asexuality and Discipline.' *Review of International Studies* 39 (4): 881–902. http://doi.org/10.1017/S0260210512000605.

Welland, Julia. 2015. 'Liberal Warriors and the Violent Colonial Logics of "Partnering and Advising".' *International Feminist Journal of Politics* 17 (2): 289–307. http://doi.org/10.1080/14616742.2014.890775.

Wilcox, Lauren B. 2015. *Bodies of Violence: Theorizing Embodied Subjects in International Relations*. Oxford: Oxford University Press.

Woronka, Kati. 2014. 'Of Pastries, Loss, and Pride.' In *Chasing Misery: An Anthology of Essays by Women in Humanitarian Responses*, edited by Kelsey Hoppe, 115–122. North Charleston, SC: CreateSpace.

Hybrid Clubs: A Feminist Approach to Peacebuilding in the Democratic Republic of Congo

Maria Martin de Almagro

ABSTRACT

Critical approaches to peacebuilding have achieved a local turn wherein alienated indigenous experiences are the cornerstone of emancipatory practices – yet this emancipation of the 'different' risks perpetuating the discrimination and normalization of the challenged liberal peace. Using the case study of a feminist campaign to elect more women in the Democratic Republic of Congo (DRC), this article's feminist approach to critical peacebuilding utilizes storytelling to develop a conceptual grid that reveals the complexities of the politics of difference, and proposes the concept of the 'hybrid club' as a cluster of local and international actors coalescing to develop peacebuilding initiatives.

Introduction

We had been talking for about an hour, sitting on the front porch of her father's house. Clementine tells me that she lives in Goma but is in Kinshasa this week because the women's organization that she founded is part of the 'Rien sans les femmes [Nothing without the Women]' (RSLF) campaign. They have a whole programme of advocacy activities planned for the next few days in the capital. The campaign, formed by international non-governmental organizations (NGOs) and national women's organizations, is seeking to put more women in electoral seats in the Democratic Republic of Congo (DRC). Clementine studied law, but she says she is no lawyer; her friends say she is not like a 'normal' Congolese woman – and indeed, her role as the leader of a Congolese women's organization has attracted the attention of both international donors and researchers such as myself. As I am about to leave, I ask if I can take a picture. She pauses to think for a moment, then agrees – but only on the condition that she can change her clothes. I patiently wait on the porch. When she returns, she is adorned with a piece of cloth that reads 'Nothing without the Women'. I am curious. 'Why did you want to change clothes?' I ask. 'Because out there', she replies, 'this is who I am – one of the leaders of the movement. Isn't this the reason why you interviewed me in the first place?'

Clementine feels the need to represent a certain collective and perform in front of the camera for her international audience.[1] She is conscious of the fact that the international community has assigned her a role and a series of attributes that go hand in hand with being a local woman of colour in charge of a women's organization in the DRC. This also means that she is part of a group of 'locals' in important positions who are equipped with the necessary skills to strategically make the most of this differentiation. She belongs to what Spivak named a floating zone of elite subalternity (Spivak, in Landy and MacLean 1996). Actors in this zone of elite subalternity naturalize their identity and difference in what constitutes 'a strategic use of positivist essentialism in a scrupulously visible political interest' (Spivak [1985] 1996, 214). 'Strategic essentialism' supposes that members of groups, although being highly differentiated internally, engage in the process of homogenizing their public image in order to portray a common identity as a means of achieving certain objectives. In order to illustrate this strategic essentialism, I propose the concept of the 'hybrid club' as a cluster of local and international actors that join forces to develop a series of peacebuilding and development initiatives. This club can be considered as a diagnostic site for studying complex processes of differentiation and identification in post-conflict settings.

I argue that, first, the hybrid club constitutes a space where difference is crafted and performed through the sharing of knowledge and practices with – and *only* with – its members. What makes the club 'hybrid' is not the diversity of the passports of its members but rather the fact that the performance of difference is deployed strategically as belonging to the local – and therefore 'authentic' – sphere, while also being part of the international sphere through promoting and valuing the notions of democracy, human rights, and civic identity. *Strategic* then borders on *pragmatic*, because it presents a definition of a certain political practice. Second, the hybrid club is also a space where actors build individual and collective identities through which they can make political claims. In other words, these identities intersect with the ways in which the club articulates and represents peacebuilding, development, and security. Ultimately, the club restricts access to competing modes of thought about what peacebuilding is, what development should take place, and who should be in charge of implementing it, as these modes of thought are heavily dependent on the collective identity that is developed.

This article focuses on the creation and strengthening of a national women's movement as a hybrid peace performance, recognizing that an initiative by two international NGOs instigated a process of collective identification and positionality. From the beginning of the 2000s critical approaches have been used to great effect to push practitioners to discover local knowledge in conflict-affected societies and interrogate the normative universality assumptions of liberal peacebuilding (Autesserre 2014; Mac Ginty 2010; Richmond 2011; Tadjbakhsh 2011). From the World Bank to the smallest international NGO, practitioners have engaged in a 'post-liberal' or 'hybrid' peace approach in which local and international peacebuilding actors 'coalesce and conflict to different extents on different issues to produce a fusion peace' (Mac Ginty 2010, 397). Nevertheless, hybrid peace works have been censured for reproducing the liberal and binary schemes that they were meant to overcome, failing to properly engage with 'difference' (Bargués-Pedreny and Mathieu, 2018; Heathershaw 2013; Millar, Van Der Lijn, and Verkoren 2013; Rampton and Nadarajah 2017; Randazzo 2016; Sabaratnam 2013; Wolff and Zimmermann 2016). In other words, hybrid peace works seem to have forgotten that identities are multidimensional, and that the dichotomy between the international and the local is often arbitrary, as is the perceived internal coherence of the categories.

In this article, first, I unpack how to engage more generously with 'difference' by using a feminist relational approach to critical peacebuilding (McLeod 2015; Read, 2018). A relational approach takes dynamic and ever-changing relationships amongst agents as the appropriate unit of analysis, as opposed to structural accounts that focus on social stratification embedded in social structure (Joseph, 2018). Agents acquire meaning through and are constituted by their transactions, connections, and relations with other actors that are developing a peacebuilding and development initiative. In turn, these transactions and connections are constituted not only by the formal rules and processes deployed in peacebuilding and development initiatives, but also by their informal and mundane practices. Second, I use storytelling in order to grasp not how the international understands alterity but rather how alterity identifies itself with and embraces international interventions, as well as how it differentiates itself from them (Daigle 2016). Some authors distinguish between a story and a narrative, the former denoting the 'tale' told by an individual and the latter uncovering the means of enquiry (Roberts 2002, 177). I use both terms almost interchangeably in order to offer an entry point for hybrid peace scholarship to study peacebuilding and the 'different' as a gendered, embodied, spatial experience. I argue that this can give us hints on how the politics of difference work. More specifically, I propose two theoretical and analytical points: feminist methodologies can provide more complex understandings beyond the essentialist dichotomy of local vs international; and feminist peacebuilding approaches analyse power, dominance, and resistance from a relational perspective by investigating the collective experiences of those at the margins – namely, at the intersections of gender, race, and class hierarchies and exclusions.

Focusing on data that is not often collected in international relations – data derived from participant observation and biographical interviews – I capture varied meanings of difference as experience in everyday peacebuilding practices and discourses. The article draws mainly on data gathered from my observation of an advocacy campaign conducted in May 2017 in Kinshasa, DRC on the reform of the electoral law in order to incorporate gender concerns. I documented this campaign using detailed field notes, photographs, and informal conversations with participants, activists, and audience members. I also conducted 13 semi-structured interviews with women who took part in the campaign, and I draw on data gathered from over six years of research and several months of fieldwork on gender and peacebuilding processes in the Great Lakes area, and in particular in Burundi, Rwanda, and the DRC.

The conceptual grid used allows for the interpretation of relationality in a holistic way. Knowledge is interpreted in its context, and the scholar can reflect upon her own positionality while 'reading between the lines of everyday practices' (Wallis and Richmond 2017, 8) and how this positionality influences her interpretation of knowledge (Daigle 2016; Enloe 2010). Consequently, this research has been conducted with an awareness of the positionality and ontological assumptions of my own embodied experience of being a Western feminist researcher from a Belgian university – the ex-colonial power and one of the first donors to the DRC in terms of monetary income. That is to say, in choosing the stories and voices that are not mine but for which I will select words that inevitably interpret them, I am already pointing to what I consider to be difference and commonality. The body of this article is organized as follows. The first section offers a proposal for a feminist relational understanding of difference and presents a conceptual grid of three elements –

embodiment, experience, and space – through which the politics of difference can be grasped, accessed, and understood. The second section explores the different stories about women and peacebuilding developed on and about the DRC. The third section illustrates the preceding set of theoretical arguments through an analysis of the case of the RSLF women's movement. The article then ends with some concluding reflections on the potential of a feminist relational perspective for unpacking the possibilities and limits of the politics of difference in peacebuilding.

Telling stories of experience, embodiment, and spatiality

In this section, I offer a feminist relational approach to studying the politics of difference. I suggest that difference might best be characterized as an assemblage of relations which draws together diverse experiences of space and spatialization, embodiment and becoming, and conduct and social practices. First, I postulate that understanding the process of hybrid peacebuilding from a relational perspective can move the local turn away from a default understanding of difference or alterity as a fixed label. The idea is that the meaning of difference is acquired and evolves through the relationship between local and international actors in peacebuilding and development initiatives. This dynamic process also demonstrates slippage and interaction between the different and the common, as sometimes they are both so enmeshed that treating them as exclusive, fixed entities makes little sense. Second, I use the concepts of embodiment, experience, and spatiality as a frame which helps us to examine individual stories that illustrate how power relations shape the politics of difference and produce subordination, domination, and resistance.

Individual stories are key to a relational perspective to peacebuilding, as they are 'a primary way by which we make sense of the world around us, produce meanings, articulate intentions, and legitimize actions' (Wibben 2010, 2). Stories are therefore sites where power is exercised, and where 'the personal and the collective deviate' (Wibben 2010, 2). Stories make sense of embodied experiences, and are therefore subjective. Stories narrate personal experiences about war, peace, and security from everyday perspectives (Holland and Solomon 2014; Read, 2018; Vaughan-Williams and Stevens 2016). Additionally, using storytelling as a method gives scholars the opportunity to pay greater attention to interpretive praxis (Wallis and Richmond 2017) and to step out of the binary division between personal and political (Enloe 2014; McLeod 2015).

Storytelling is therefore 'a means of illuminating lived and embodied experiences' (Daigle 2016, 30) that constitute and are constituted by the politics of difference in peacebuilding. Although individually performed, stories are always intersubjective and relational, as they are used to make sense of *experience* that goes beyond the individual *embodied* event in a particular *space*. To be sure, studying personal experiences and their (re)production through individual stories can be problematic because it relies on the 'fragility of human memory' (Woodward and Jenkings 2012, 120). In addition, and as Joseph (2018) points out, there is a risk of privileging narrated experience 'over the context within which difference occurs' and treating it 'as though it were unmediated by wider relations, institutions and processes' (Basham 2013, 8). Therefore, the stories herein should be read as part of a set of 'processes of identity production', as testimony on the 'discursive nature of experience and on the politics of its construction' (Scott 1992,

37), and as facilitating the (re)presentation of that which is 'unstructured, contingent and difficult' (Daigle 2016, 25).

Embodiment

A number of feminist scholars have challenged taking a disembodied approach towards knowledge production (Butler 1999; Dyvik 2016; Enloe 2014; Gatens 1996; Haraway 1988; McLeod 2015; Moon 1997; Young 1980). In particular, these scholars criticize the body versus mind hierarchical dichotomy which puts the mind over the body as a site of knowledge production, and which also associates mind with rationality and body with passion, then rationality with masculinity and passion with femininity, as this series of associations effectively subordinates the feminine to the masculine (Grosz 1994; Prokhomik 1999). Bodies indeed produce and are productive of race, class, and sexual configurations of power and knowledge and should therefore be 'directly involved in the political field' (Foucault 1991, 25). However, although this turn to experience and embodiment is prominent in the literature on war and international relations (Parashar 2013; Sylvester 2013; Wilcox 2015), this is not the case in the literature on peacebuilding (Read, 2018), a field that is still seen from an essentially technical perspective, as though matters of war and peace can be easily separated and put into two different boxes.

Experience

Experience is connected to embodiment, as stories about embodied and emotional experiences enable us to understand how peacebuilding practices are simultaneously creations of, and creative of, identities and differences (McLeod 2015). What is more, 'experience is not something that happens to the self, but experience becomes the self – it is that through which identity is forged' (Nordstrom 1997, 185). Although hybridity takes very seriously everyday local experiences and practices (Richmond 2010), the diversity of the personal experiences of the international is not examined (McLeod 2015, 6). It is as though there are no individuals in the international sphere whose everyday practices and logics can shape the meaning of peacebuilding and development initiatives. Therefore, if we are to understand better the power relations shaping knowledge production negotiation between local and international actors, we need to analyse the diversity of personal experiences of both – local and international– in their everyday practices.

Spatiality

Through the concept of spatiality, this article stresses the contingency, precariousness, and instability of identity. This is done by paying special attention to the different places in which actors in post-conflict contexts are constituted by a multiplicity of positions that do not respond to the binary local–international (McLeod 2015). This understanding resonates with the ideas of Henri Lefebvre on space as being socially and meaningfully produced in stories and implicated in embodied social practices at sites where the structures of the national and the international are both reproduced and challenged (Lefebvre 1991, 33). Therefore, while being grounded in materiality, spaces are social constructs produced through and by embodied experiences and practices. Although it is true that the local turn has caused a shift from state-centric analysis to the study of local dynamics, it has prompted little examination of the ways in which local spaces become meaningful in terms of being produced by identities and memories.

In sum, there is no difference before its performance. Difference and commonness come into existence through the relational process of identity (re)production. But identities are not 'out there' – thus, differences are not inherent to one person or group. Instead, these (individual and collective) identities are born out of embodied experience. Once born, these identities are deployed and open up new spaces in which new relations between groups conforming to collective identities are formed. These new relations, in turn, produce new embodied experience. By focusing on embodied experience and post-war spatialities, I try to challenge hegemonic narratives and capture the intricate ways in which difference is regulated in the stories told in and about peacebuilding. In doing so, this article focuses on the ways in which storytelling both talks about other bodies and collectivizes bodily experience, in particular spaces, recognizing that peacebuilding and development projects are relational encounters in which the different is produced, retained, or discarded.

Differentiating gender narratives, resisting peacebuilding initiatives

International narratives about women in the DRC have propagated a bad reputation when it comes to gender equality and justice (Eriksson Baaz and Stern 2013; Holmes 2013, 2015). For example, in a speech by the United Nations (UN) Special Representative of the Secretary-General on Sexual Violence in conflict at the time, Margot Wallstrom, the eastern part of the DRC was labelled 'the rape capital of the world', where sexual violence is perpetrated in a war driven by conflict minerals (Wallstrom 2010). What is more, these narratives have been stabilized by popular culture through documentaries such as *The Greatest Silence: Rape in the Congo* (2007) and *The Man Who Mends Women* (2015) portraying women in the Congo as victims of sexual violence and other atrocities. Eastern Congolese female bodies are thus stripped of any political agency and associated in this narrative with the experience of sexual violence during conflict. This fits very well with the main narrative of the UN Security Council (UNSC), which understands the gendered body as female, and as being a passive body that needs to be protected from violence (McLeod 2015, 12). For example, the 2006 Security, Stabilization and Development Pact put in motion by the International Conference of the Great Lakes Region understands gender as a transversal issue, but gender disappears completely in the 2013 Framework for Peace, Security and Cooperation for the Democratic Republic of Congo and Region, wherein gender as a power relation is substituted for a meagre mention of 'women's empowerment'. What is more, different declarations by heads of state in the region related to the issue – the Goma declaration on the eradication of sexual violence and the eradication of impunity in the Great Lakes region, and the Kampala declaration on sexual and gender-based violence (SGBV) in 2011 – have focused on sexual violence. The Stabilization and Reconstruction Plan in Eastern DRC (2009) concentrates on SGBV, as does the 2010 national action plan for the implementation of UNSC Resolution 1325, which urges the UN and its member states to ensure women's participation and involvement in decision-making in peace and security matters, and to mainstream gender in all areas of peacebuilding. The resolution has been very much criticized for putting an accent on the protection of women from SGBV in conflict and for equating gender with women (Martin de Almagro 2017). This is important because although these plans and frameworks are national and regional mechanisms, they are supported and funded by the United Nations Organization Stabilization Mission in the Democratic Republic of the Congo (MONUSCO) under the framework of the Women, Peace, and Security Agenda.

It is with the idea of countering this narrative in mind that the RSLF campaign was developed, under the hybrid initiative of the international NGOs International Alert and Kvinna till Kvinna and several women's organizations in eastern Congo.[2] The two international NGOs invited 30 leaders of Congolese civil-society organizations to a workshop in March 2015 to reflect on how to promote the political participation and representation of Congolese women in the country because 'the National Action Plan on UNSCR1325 focuses too much on SGBV'.[3] The result of the workshop was the launch of the RSLF campaign, which constitutes one of the rare occasions where female activists from North and South Kivu and female activists from Kishasa joined forces. It had two aims: firstly to advocate for the enactment of the Parity Law that would recognize the importance of women's participation in governmental structures and more broadly in all aspects of public life, and secondly to request the revision of electoral law to require the inclusion of women in all electoral lists. The campaign managed to collect more than 200,000 signatures from individuals around the country, and in May 2015 it submitted its petition and signatures to the President of the National Assembly. The petition asked that Article 13.4 of the electoral law be revised to require that all future electoral lists would respect the principle of parity between men and women. Marches were organized at the same time in Bukavu, Uvira, and Goma in order to gather popular support for the campaign. More than 6000 people joined the march in Bukavu, and these marches were an essential mechanism for setting up the counter-narrative of women as passive victims, since they constitute a visual performance of female bodies actively protesting and occupying public spaces. Although the Parity Law was passed in August 2015, the movement has kept on growing since and now incorporates more than 160 women rights organizations.

During the last week of May 2017, representatives of the movement from Goma and Bukavu flew to Kinshasa to join forces with the capital's representatives in order to carry out a week of advocacy activities and present their detailed report on the successes and shortcomings of the recently passed Parity Law.[4] Throughout the advocacy activities, rather than focusing on women's fundamental rights or on women as victims through a rights-based approach, the master narrative was that parity in decision-making institutions is good for sustainable development and peace. It is worth highlighting here that this master narrative is framed in opposition to the earlier dominant narrative while still playing with some of the keywords that appeal to donors. The idea is that making political institutions accessible to women is a condition sine qua non for a successful bottom-up approach to peace. The advocates of the initiative aim to create a new space for women to voice their experiences and become political subjects instead of being mere beneficiaries of peacebuilding processes. The organizers explained that peacebuilding projects which include gender are normally directed at protecting women yet fail to challenge the structures of the state that have disempowered them and made them vulnerable to violence in the first place.[5]

This framing marks the first determinant of difference by which the international approach to implementing the Women, Peace, and Security agenda based on women's rights – which has previously been embraced as the standard – is actively being countered, in this case by a coalition of international and Congolese women's organizations engaged in resisting the agenda of the UN and the DRC government. The women I interviewed, all of whom belong to activist organizations, indicated that they had become active in political resistance because they saw no other way out.[6] These women were fed up with the international narrative which seemed to simply have forgotten that women in the DRC had mobilized for peace during the inter-Congolese dialogue in 2001 that put an end to the Second Congo War:

> We were a group of African women leaders that were taken to a training in Sweden. The first thing they do is to show us a film on Liberian women as peacemakers and a second one on Congolese women raped as a result of war. But we were also in Sun City, we also participated to the inter-Congolese dialogue, we are also here, fighting.[7]

The violence experienced by their female bodies did not depoliticize them, but rather provided a collective story for mobilization. The life stories of these activists not only ensure them a subject position but also provide counter-narratives to the dominant international narrative through which alternative forms of peace can be proposed: 'We have not documented to the world the story of the fight of the Congolese woman. There is a story of the women victims, but not of women peacebuilders. And I can say today that we have fought a lot'.[8]

Telling their story as a sustainable peace narrative provides a way to establish 'a political identity from which to make claims' (Stern 2005, 116). Moreover, it also offers a counter-narrative to the international idea that there is not a women's movement in DRC with a clear leader and joint efforts.[9] The RSLF movement represents one of the most important hybrid alternatives to the official line of implementation of UNSC Resolution 1325 in the DRC and its national action plan. The next section shows how the construction of a hybrid club constitutes a political strategy for selling a story in the peacebuilding market.

Clubbing in the DRC: It is not always the Other who is the Different

Having discussed the particular emphasis on political participation and the seemingly contradictory stories on embodied experiences of victimhood, I now move on to discuss the ways in which the local women elites, who are part of the women's organizations, conceptualize difference through particular sensory regimes. An intricate web of individual and collective identities results in power relations being determined not only by whether or not an actor is associated with and/or associates herself with the 'local' or the 'international', but also by interpersonal relations between actors at the local and international levels. These power relations, in turn, regulate who can and cannot participate in a certain hybrid peace initiative.

From the perspective of several women's groups in the DRC, it is not only that some of the local actors are more connected to international actors for different reasons such as funding, language, and geographical situation, but also that clusters of local actors and organizations are more connected to particular international actors and institutions, forming what I call 'hybrid clubs'.[10] Several interviewees attributed the difficulties of having a strong and united women's movement to club divisions: 'if you work with one women's organization, you need to work with members of that organization's club. And you have to be very conscious of which organizations are part of this club and which are not'.[11]

Performing embodied sameness and difference

The RSLF movement is one of these hybrid clubs. Resistance to the implementation of a certain approach to the Women, Peace, and Security agenda is one element of determining difference, effectively positioning itself against other 'hybrid' projects on gender and peacebuilding. Additionally, it is also a way of reinforcing group identity. Several other sensorial strategies are implemented by the movement to reinforce group identification. One of the most telling practices of embodied identification and differentiation is dress. On 24 May 2017, four women belonging to the RSLF were in charge of presenting a report for the movement on the challenges of the Parity Law to the international donors, at the residence of the Swedish ambassador. Sweden had funded the 'Tushikiri Wote [Let's Participate!]' project through which the movement was funded, and all the women – the representatives of the international NGOs included – arrived at the residence of the Swedish ambassador wearing dresses made of cloth that read 'RSLF'. If these dresses provide a trait of unity amongst members of the hybrid movement, it is the introductory remarks of one of the international NGO representatives about how the 'equal participation of women and men in politics is vital for sustainable peace' that make the RSLF different from the rest of the hybrid initiatives on gender.

However, this identification is not fixed, but variable, and some differences are created depending on the spaces in which they are performed. For example, whereas the 'locals' and 'internationals' dressed uniformly in an effort to show the international community present at the Swedish ambassador's residence that a hybrid initiative telling a story of women as peacebuilders is worth funding, the internationals and locals dressed differently for the movement's presentation to members of parliament the following day. Indeed, the visual element that was used to identify 'sameness' one day was used to identify 'difference' the next; this time it was only the local women – and the newly appointed Minister of Gender – who wore the RSLF clothes and spoke about sustainable peace. As requested by the Congolese members of the campaign, the members of the international NGOs sat at the back of the room, did not speak at any time during the event, and wore different clothes in an attempt to prove to parliamentarians that this was not a hybrid initiative but a truly Congolese one. The way in which listening to and seeing difference is called into being lies in everyday, seemingly trivial details that make bodies intelligible with reference to clubs. But however trivial these may seem, and contrary to what we might think, these are performed in a very much conscious attempt – remember Clementine's insistence on wearing the RSLF clothes for the picture – to shape the politics of difference.

When sensorial strategies are no longer needed to perform club membership, alterity is felt in another way. For example, the distribution of space and distance amongst individuals who are part of the same movement is striking; before the event at the residence of the Swedish ambassador started, clusters of staff from international NGOs asked one another how their children were doing and when they were going on holiday, while the Congolese women also gathered in groups of three or four to chat informally. The ordering of 'different' bodies in the same space was also very telling during an informal preparatory meeting conducted the previous day at the headquarters of one of the international NGOs. The oval table distributed the bodies in two opposite spaces: two representatives of the international NGOs were seated on the left side of the oval table, while on the right side – the one farthest away from the door – six female Congolese members of the RSLF prepared for the week of activities ahead. This distribution of the physical space is vital because it also demarcates the distribution of tasks in the movement: the direction, coordination, and even cheerleading comes from the international side – but the final decisions are taken on the local side of the table. Nevertheless, there are also differences amongst the locals; the two women from eastern Congo sat together, their bodies touching one another, even though one had come from Goma and the other from Bukavu. They were the ones who were away from home and whose bodies had directly experienced conflict. They came to the meeting dressed in traditional clothing, portraying a clear visual difference from the Kinshasa-based activists, who attended wearing Western attire.

The making of 'difference' happens through the complex performances of individual and collective bodies. Wearing a particular item of clothing, occupying a certain space, speaking or staying silent – these are all parts of the production of commonness and difference that goes beyond geographical spaces and skin colour, and simultaneously makes individuals part of the same club. As the women in the movement actively and consciously rescript their identity, they present certain markers – wearing or not wearing traditional dresses, for example – as primordial. Yet, at the same time, 'they also assign certain social/political meaning to them within the particular historical context' in which they are situated (Stern 2005, 103). Differentiation therefore constitutes a strategic approach to reaching political aims, namely getting funding from the international community or convincing members of parliament of the need to reform the electoral law.

The international is (also) a personal experience

Differentiated narratives and embodied experiences regulate the politics of difference in hybrid clubs. These clubs therefore seem to be very much coordinated and orchestrated by local elites who work with a diversity of donors and international partners on the implementation of hybrid peacebuilding initiatives. What is striking then is that, without exception, all the donors that I interviewed pointed to the fact that the women's organizations in the DRC are scattered, and that previous attempts to work with them have not delivered good results. In this section I argue that past attempts to work with a coherent movement have failed precisely because practising a 'politics of difference' has served to differentiate women's organizations from others and make them stand out in the over-crowded peacebuilding market. These women's organizations are therefore very much wary of sharing their space, narratives, and international partners with the others. The selling point and main narrative of 'differentiation' of the RSLF plays precisely on leaving the differences among members aside in order to create a 'coherent, non-partisan and inter-generational movement' that can transform the story of the everyday realities of women in eastern Congo as victims.[12] As the peacebuilding market in the DRC has started to experience donor fatigue due to the lack of results from engaging with women's organizations, presenting a completely different narrative based on unification seems particularly canny.

The personal stories narrated by my interviewees reveal a clash between clubs – that is, between those organizations supported by UN Women, mainly from Kinshasa, and those who are supported by the international partners of the RSLF. When conducting interviews, it was very clear that women from different clubs experience the international in very diverse ways. One interviewee expressed her confusion about the division: 'We don't understand why UN Women has not joined the efforts. Maybe they had other priorities'.[13] Another expressed her perception of how some organizations give far less local ownership than they claim:

> And here Alert has played the game of local ownership in order to make people feel responsible for their actions and their future, while at the same time doing a close follow-up. However, with other partners you feel that it is very different, they are simply too present and, in a way, that it is almost them who do all the process. I can give you the example of [name of organization], that is a national dialogue framework with representatives in different parts of the country. Every time [this organization] is mentioned, you realize that they follow a project-by-project strategy. For instance, UN Women has just funded one of their projects and all they do is project, project, project, but it is not the women themselves who take the future into their own hands.[14]

It appears from these two quotes that the clubs are led by international partners who have different approaches to what local ownership constitutes and the kind of activities that should be carried out. I therefore decided to talk to the representative of the national dialogue framework in order to explore these differences in more detail. On paper, this national framework funded by UN Women is also part of the RSLF movement. However, in reality, they have never attended any RSLF activities. The representative was upset that women from the east had come to Kinshasa in what she considered an attempt to steal her funding and partners: 'why do they have to fly women from the other side of the country to do advocacy? They can do advocacy directed towards local politicians there and we will do our part here'.[15]

For their part, the international donors had never heard of the RSLF, with the exception of those who had attended the presentation at the Swedish ambassador's residence. Instead, they were very much aware of Café Genre – UN Women's new project. Every two months, a conference is organized at which ambassadors share best practices with the international community and the Ministry of Gender, as well as with civil-society organizations. The aim is to raise awareness and build a network of women in Kinshasa which then distributes information to provincial branches on how the knowledge shared during Café Genre will be 'communicated to those women who cannot read and write'.[16] The fact that the most recent Café Genre conference at the time had been held on the topic of SGBV was very telling, as it served to reinforce the narrative of women as victims. Several of my interviewees from the international community and local women's organizations indicated that this is an event through which UN Women seeks visibility, but that there is no real work behind it. When I asked a local staff member of UN Women whether or not her organization was aware of the RSLF movement and had any synergy with it, she simply shook her head. This is all the more surprising given that, minutes before, she had spoken about her previous personal experiences as the lead researcher for eastern Congo for a project on women's participation in the Great Lakes region. She had been hired specifically for her knowledge on the subject.

The international women involved in the RLSF campaign made clear how they are 'different' from the abstract idea of the international and its institutions operating in the DRC, as they are 'tired and frustrated' from seeing 'incompetent people' or 'people that simply do not care' overseeing the cause of gender in international and national institutions.[17] One of the interviewees deplored the fact that the RSLF has contacted UN Women on several occasions yet received no response.[18] They do not like the fact that 'international organizations fund once, twice, and three times the same national federation of women's organizations, but they have no idea of what they are funding'.[19] The personal experiences of this failure to engage with difference might therefore be due to the politics of hybrid clubs, where funders within the club stick to working with their members, even though inter-club collaboration has been sought. In this case, collaboration between UN Women and the RSLF has not so far been achieved. Certainly, the differentiation strategies between these clubs lie in their disparate understandings of local women's experiences and their opposing narratives – women as victims on the one hand and women as policymakers and political figures on the other – which seem to be irreconcilable.

Using the conceptual toolbox of experience, body, and space to analyse the politics of difference reveals firstly that 'difference' is not to be understood as being between the local and the international but rather between 'hybrid clubs' which portray a certain narrative on gender and peacebuilding, and secondly that these clubs are composed of individuals with complex identities who have chosen to perform sameness or difference according to their particular goals and spatiotemporal circumstances. Looking at 'difference' from a relational perspective enables us to see that it is not always the international actors that seek compliance and the local actors that resist, ignore, or adapt to peace interventions, and/or offer alternative forms of peacemaking.

Concluding remarks: Implications for the (hybrid) politics of difference

My point of departure was that the concept of 'hybrid clubs' can help us to emphasize the non-essential character of difference and study how actors can simultaneously belong to different clubs without being essentially attached to them, while also strategically performing a collective identity. Difference is performative and relational; it is created through encounters and actions in peacebuilding practice (such as the table in the middle of the meeting) and therefore does not exist in a vacuum, independent from the actions of the diversity of agents which take part in peacebuilding and development initiatives. As Laura McLeod claims, 'realizing the diversity of local and international allows a deeper consideration of what knowledge counts and why it matters, and the ways in which certain knowledge is privileged' (McLeod 2015, 14–15). I demonstrate this affirmation by showing not only the diversity of local(s) and international(s), but also how one can be both at the same time in different spaces. In other words, identities are neither essential nor static phenomena. The case of the RSLF shows that identities shift and slide, and that even if a marker of identity is the same (local Congolese women), its meaning differs depending on the context of the encounter between individuals belonging to what previous hybrid approaches have qualified as the sphere of either the 'local' or the 'international'.

I have argued that the value of using a feminist approach to understanding the politics of difference is twofold. First, feminist methodologies based on storytelling can provide more complex understandings of the essentialist dichotomy of local vs international in order to make visible blind spots such as the 'hybrid clubs' identified in this article. Listening to the stories of the embodied experiences of the local elite shows how they walk a fine line of identity–difference that is subtle and shifting, depending on the configuration of power relations in a particular geographical and temporal space. This analysis has brought forth female activists in the DRC as resourceful, agential subjects who know how to play the politics of difference which hybrid peace brings about. Second, feminist approaches analyse power, dominance, and resistance from a relational perspective, thus demonstrating how the local(s) and the international(s) are multiple, and how the dynamics of power and privilege have important implications for who is considered different and in what context. Ultimately, paying attention to individual and collective experiences of hybrid peacebuilding reveals the organizing politics of difference that arrange not only who is incorporated into peacebuilding interventions, but also how this incorporation is negotiated, resisted, or validated through everyday micro-politics.

This micro approach may be considered by some to be banal in terms of its relevance to better understanding the politics of difference in hybrid peace. In response to this view, I claim that there are two points to be made. First, I argue that attending to micropolitics and its manifestations through a relational approach is a crucial undertaking if we are to better understand how identity–difference is created during peacebuilding interventions without essentializing one or the other. The ordinary instances of differentiation depicted in this article were employed by individuals and groups to gain better access to resources, improve work performance, and/or denounce having been left behind. At the same time, they all constitute embodied experiences that transform identities and differences in a peacebuilding and development initiative – and in doing so, these experiences defy problematic assumptions on difference. Second, a micro approach enables us to use a precise kind of radical reconsideration of the costs of war and peace – which are 'everywhere', from civilian employment to marital bedrooms to high schools – by directing 'serious attention' at individual's lives (Enloe 2010). Future research could use a feminist relational approach to hybridity in order to examine in more detail the politics of difference within particular cases or across particular issues. This may help to unpack the nuances that determine which actors are considered the good kind of 'different' and are allowed to take part in hybrid peace initiatives while other 'different' actors and initiatives are pushed to the margins, as well as helping us to understand how different narratives emerge on how to implement those initiatives which are deemed worthy of implementation.

Notes

1. And in this case it is I, the researcher, who is part of this international audience collective before which she, the activist, felt obliged to perform a certain identity.
2. Fieldwork notes, Kinshasa, 24 May 2017.
3. Interview with a staff member of an international NGO, Kinshasa, 26 May 2017.
4. At the time of writing (September 2017), the legal status of the petition to modify the electoral law and the procedures to follow are unclear.
5. Fieldwork notes, Kinshasa, 25 May 2017.
6. Interview with the leader of a women's organization, 24 May 2017; interview with the leader of a women's organization, 25 May 2017; interview with the leader of a women's organization, 26 May 2017.
7. Intervention by a female lawyer and member of the RSLF movement at a presentation of the RSLF movement, Swedish Embassy, 24 May 2017. Kinhasa, direct quoatation.
8. Interview with the leader of a national women's organization, Kinshasa, 24 May 2017.

50 THE POLITICS OF PEACEBUILDING IN A DIVERSE WORLD

9. Intervention by a high-ranking MONUSCO staff member at a presentation of the RSLF movement, Swedish Embassy, 24 May 2017. Kinhasa, rephrase of her intervention.
10. The word 'club' was used by several of the interviewees to explain the intricacies and divisions of the women's movement in the country.
11. Interview with a member of staff of an international NGO, Kinshasa, 25 May 2017.
12. Fieldwork notes, Kinshasa, 24 May 2017.
13. Interview with the leader of a national women's association based in Kinshasa, 24 May 2017.
14. Interview with the leader of a women's organization from Sud-Kivu, Kinshasa, 27 May 2017.
15. Interview with the president of the main women's organization of national dialogue framework, Kinshasa, 23 May 2017.
16. Interview with a UN Women staff member, Kinshasa, 24 May 2017.
17. This also points to another issue on the gendered dynamics of power in hybrid peace wherein 'soft' issues such as women's issues and the implementation of the Women, Peace, and Security agenda are resisted or ignored by international and national organizations due to being considered 'unimportant' matters in post-conflict contexts (for a developed argument on this issue, see Ryan and Basini 2016).
18. Interview with a staff member of an international NGO, Kinshasa, 25 May 2017.
19. Informal conversation with two members of staff from international NGOs, Kinshasa, 22 May 2017.

Disclosure statement

No potential conflict of interest was reported by the author.

Funding

This work was supported by H2020 Marie Skłodowska-Curie Actions [grant number 706888].

ORCID

Maria Martin de Almagro ⓘ http://orcid.org/0000-0002-3760-0638

References

Autesserre, Séverine. 2014. *Peaceland: Conflict Resolution and the Everyday Politics of International Intervention*. Cambridge: Cambridge University Press.
Bargués-Pedreny, Pol and Xavier Mathieu. 2018. 'Beyond Silence, Obstacle and Stigma: Revisiting the 'Problem' of Difference in Peacebuilding,' *Journal of Intervention and Statebuilding* 12 (3): 283–299.
Basham, Victoria. 2013. *War, Identity and the Liberal State: Everyday Experiences of the Geopolitical in the Armed Forces*. London: Routledge.
Butler, Judith. 1999. *Gender Trouble: Feminism and the Subversion of Identity*. Abingdon: Routledge.
Daigle, Megan 2016. 'Writing the Lives of Others: Storytelling and International Politics.' *Millennium: Journal of International Studies* 45 (1): 25–42. doi:10.1177/0305829816656415.
Dyvik, Synne L. 2016. '"Valhalla Rising": Gender, Embodiment and Experience in Military Memoirs.' *Security Dialogue* 47 (2): 133–150. doi:10.1177/0967010615615730.

Enloe, Cynthia. 2010. *Nimo's War, Emma's War: Making Feminist Sense of the Iraq War*. Berkeley: University of California Press.

Enloe, Cynthia. 2014. *Bananas, Beaches and Bases: Making Feminist Sense of International Politics*. Berkeley: University of California Press.

Eriksson Baaz, Maria, and Maria Stern. 2013. *Sexual Violence as a Weapon of War? Perceptions, Prescriptions, Problems in the Congo and Beyond*. London: Zed Books.

Foucault, Michel. 1991. *Discipline and Punish: The Birth of the Prison*. London: Penguin.

Gatens, Moira. 1996. *Imaginary Bodies: Ethics, Power and Corporeality*. Abingdon: Routledge.

Grosz, Elizabeth. 1994. *Volatile Bodies: Towards a Corporeal Feminism*. Bloomsbury: Indiana University Press.

Gouvernement de la Republique Democratique du Congo. 2009. Stabilisation and Reconstruction Plan for Eastern DRC (Programme de Stabilisation et de Reconstruction des Zones sortant des conflits armés).

Gouvernement de la Republique Democratique du Congo. 2010. The Government's Action Plan of the Democratic Republic of Congo for the purposes of Resolution 1325 of the United Nations Security Council. https://www.peacewomen.org/sites/default/files/drc_nap_english_2010.pdf.

Haraway, Donna. 1988. 'Situated Knowledges: The Science Question in Feminism and the Privilege of Partial Perspective.' *Feminist Studies* 14 (3): 575–599. doi:10.2307/3178066.

Heathershaw, John. 2013. 'Towards Better Theories of Peacebuilding: Beyond the Liberal Peace Debate.' *Peacebuilding* 1 (2): 275–282. doi:10.1080/21647259.2013.783260.

Holland, Jack, and Ty Solomon. 2014. 'Affect is What States Make of it: Articulating Everyday Experiences of 9/11.' *Critical Studies on Security* 2 (3): 262–277. doi:10.1080/21624887.2014.921454.

Holmes, Georgina. 2013. *Women and War in Rwanda: Gender, Media and the Representation of Genocide*. London: IB Tauris.

Holmes, Georgina. 2015. 'Negotiating Narratives of Human Rights Abuses: Image Management in Conflicts in the Eastern DRC.' In *Images of Africa: Creation, Negotiation and Subversion*, edited by J. Gallagher, 144-166. Manchester: Manchester University Press.

International Conference on the Great Lakes Region. 2006. Pact on Security, Stability and Development in the Great Lakes Region. https://www3.nd.edu/~ggoertz/rei/rei245/rei245.02tt1.pdf.

International conference on the Great Lakes Region. 2008. The Goma Declaration on Eradicating Sexual Violence and Ending Impunity in the Great Lakes Region. https://www.eassi.org/new/sites/default/files/GOMA%20DECLARATION.pdf.

International Conference on the Great Lakes Region. 2011. Kampala Declaration on Gender and Sexual-based violence. https://www.icglr-rtf.org/wp-content/uploads/2017/06/15-16th-December-2011-Kampala-Declaration-by-Heads-of-State-from-icglr.pdf.

Jackson, Lisa. 2007. *The greatest silence: Rape in the Congo*. New York, NY: Women Make Movies.

Joseph, Jonathan. 2018. 'Beyond Relationalism in Peacebuilding.' *Journal of Intervention and Statebuilding* 12 (3): 425–434.

Landy, Donna and MacLeon, Gerald. 1996. *The Spivak Reader*. London: Routledge.

Lefebvre, Henri. 1991. *The Production of Space*. Translated by Donald Nicholson-Smith. Malden, MA: Blackwell.

Mac Ginty, Roger. 2010. 'Hybrid Peace: The Interaction Between Top-Down and Bottom-up Peace.' *Security Dialogue* 41 (4): 391–412. doi:10.1177/0967010610374312.

Martin de Almagro, Maria. 2017. *Transitional Justice and Women, Peace and Security: A Critical Reading of the EU Framework*. London: LSE.

McLeod, Laura. 2015. 'A Feminist Approach to Hybridity: Understanding Local and International Interactions in Producing Post-Conflict Gender Security.' *Journal of Intervention and Statebuilding* 9 (1): 48–69. doi:10.1080/17502977.2014.980112.

Michel, Thierry and Braeckman, Colette. 2015. *The Man Who Mends Women*. Belgium, USA, Congo: Centre du Cinéma et de l'Audiovisuel de la Fédération Wallonie-Bruxelles.

Millar, Gearoid, Jaïr Van Der Lijn, and Willemijn. Verkoren. 2013. 'Peacebuilding Plans and Local Reconfigurations: Frictions between Imported Processes and Indigenous Practices.' *International Peacekeeping* 20 (2): 137–143. doi:10.1080/13533312.2013.791556.

Moon, Katharine. 1997. *Sex among Allies*. New York, NY: Columbia University Press.

Nordstrom, Carolyn. 1997. *A Different Kind of War Story*. Philadelphia: University of Pennsylvania Press.

Parashar, Swati. 2013. 'What Wars and "War Bodies" Know about International Relations.' *Cambridge Review of International Affairs* 26 (4): 615–630. doi:10.1080/09557571.2013.837429.

Peace, Security and Cooperation Framework for the Democratic Republic of Congo and the region. 2013. https://peacemaker.un.org/sites/peacemaker.un.org/files/DRC_130224_FrameworkAgreementDRCRegion.pdf.

Prokhomik, Raia. 1999. *Rational Woman: A Feminist Critique of Dichotomy*. Abingdon: Routledge.

Rampton, David, and Suthaharan. Nadarajah. 2017. 'A Long View of Liberal Peace and Its Crisis.' *European Journal of International Relations* 23 (2): 441–465. doi:10.1177/1354066116649029.

Randazzo, Elisa. 2016. 'The Paradoxes of the "Everyday": Scrutinising the Local Turn in Peace Building.' *Third World Quarterly* 37 (8): 1351–1370. doi:10.1080/01436597.2015.1120154.

Read, Róisín. 2018. 'Embodying Difference: Reading Gender in Women's Memoirs of Humanitarianism.' *Journal of Intervention and Statebuilding* 12 (3): 300–318. https://doi.org/10.1080/17502977.2018.1482079.

Richmond, Oliver P. 2010. 'Resistance and the Post-Liberal Peace.' *Millennium: Journal of International Studies* 38 (3): 665–692. doi:10.1177/0305829810365017.

Richmond, Oliver P. 2011. *A Post-Liberal Peace*. Abingdon: Routledge.

Roberts, Brian. 2002. *Biographical Research*. Buckingham: Open University Press.

Ryan, Caitlin, and Basini, Helen. 2016. National Action Plans as an Obstacle to Meaningful Local Ownership in UNSCR1325 in Liberia and Sierra Leone. *International Political Science Review* 37 (3): 390-403.

Sabaratnam, Meera. 2013. 'Avatars of Eurocentrism in the Critique of the Liberal Peace.' *Security Dialogue* 44 (3): 259–278. doi:10.1177/0967010613485870.

Scott, Joan W. 1992. 'Experience.' In *Feminists Theorize the Political*, edited by Judith Butler and Joan W. Scott, 22–41. Abingdon: Routledge.

Spivak, Gayatri Chakravorty. (1985) 1996. 'Subaltern Studies: Deconstructing Historiography.' In *The Spivak Reader*, edited by Donna Landry and Gerald MacLean, 203–236. London: Routledge.

Stern, Maria. 2005. *Naming Security – Constructing Identity: 'Mayan-Women' in Guatemala on the Eve of 'Peace'*. Manchester: Manchester University Press.

Sylvester, Christine. 2013. *War as Experience: Contributions From International Relations and Feminist Analysis*. Abingdon: Routledge.

Tadjbakhsh, Shahrbanou, ed. 2011. *Rethinking the Liberal Peace: External Models and Local Alternatives*. Abingdon: Taylor & Francis.

Vaughan-Williams, Nick, and Daniel Stevens. 2016. 'Vernacular Theories of Everyday (In)Security: The Disruptive Potential of Non-Elite Knowledge.' *Security Dialogue* 47 (1): 40–58. doi:10.1177/0967010615604101.

Wallis, Joanne, and Oliver P. Richmond. 2017. 'From Constructivist to Critical Engagements with Peacebuilding: Implications for Hybrid Peace.' *Third World Thematics: A TWQ Journal*, 2 (4): 422–425. doi:10.1080/23802014.2016.1309990.

Wallstrom, Margot. 2010. 'Ending Sexual Violence: From Recognition to Action.' Speech delivered at the Women and War UNSCR1325 Tenth Anniversary Conference, Washington, DC, 3 November.

Wibben, Annick T.R. 2010. *Feminist Security Studies: A Narrative Approach*. New York: Routledge.

Wilcox, Lauren B. 2015. *Bodies of Violence: Theorizing Embodied Subjects in International Relations*. Oxford: Oxford University Press.

Wolff, Jonas, and Lisbeth Zimmermann. 2016. 'Between Banyans and Battle Scenes: Liberal Norms, Contestation, and the Limits of Critique.' *Review of International Studies* 42 (3): 513–534. doi:10.1017/S0260210515000534.

Woodward, Rachel, and K. Neil Jenkings. 2012. 'Reconstructing the Colonial Present in British Soldiers' Accounts of the Afghanistan Conflict.' In *Reconstructing Conflict: Integrating War and Post-War Geographies*, edited by Scott Kirsch and Colin Flint, 115–133. Basingstoke: Ashgate.

Young, Iris Marion. 1980. 'Throwing Like a Girl: A Phenomenology of Feminine Body Comportment Motility and Spatiality.' *Human Studies* 3 (1): 137–156. http://www.jstor.org/stable/20008753.

Peace-in-Difference: A Phenomenological Approach to Peace Through Difference

Hartmut Behr

ABSTRACT

This article develops the notion of 'peace-in-difference', based on a phenomenological approach to difference from German sociology in the 1920s to the French philosophies of Emmanuel Lévinas and Jacques Derrida. Such an attempt responds to a long-standing concern in peacebuilding theory and practice and is critical of essentialist and linear-teleological approaches to peace, as with the theoretical framework of liberal peace-building. As a consequence, 'peace-in-difference' is sceptical with attempts to define peace as a status, but rather envisions peace as a perennial process of dialogue. However, 'peace-in-difference', even though having the critique of liberal peace and subsequent research questions in common with post-liberal approaches, it is also critical with their construction of 'the local' as as a binary opposition to 'the international'. Though this binary is an attempt to overcome liberal legacies in International Relations (IR) and peace studies, it nevertheless risks reintroducing essentialism. In contrast, a phenomenological approach infers a positive understanding of difference(s) which can be generative of peace, if and when perceived in non-essentialist ways and negotiated as such.

The problem and the argument

This article responds to a long-standing pressing issue and question in peace-building theory and practice, namely that of difference (see inter alia Avruch and Black 1991; Lederach 1997; Avruch 1998; Miall, Ramsbotham, and Woodhouse 1999; Bargués-Pedreny 2017; newer attempts see also the articles in this issue; in IR more generally see inter alia Gupta and Chattopadhyaya 1998; Hallam and Street 2000; Inayatullah and Blaney 2004). The multitude of attempts to engage the question of difference seems to be reasoned, just like this article, by the incontestable, empirical circumstance that differences, whether religious, social, political, economic, etc. are at the root of conflicts. The specific argument pursued here suggests perceiving of difference(s) in a non-essentialised way as this seems to be the only way to view, and to act upon, differences which is conducive to peaceful relations. This is because all essentialist or essentialising perceptions of difference establish a hierarchy of subordination and inherent violence which trigger resistance, conflict, and fighting. In its consequence, this argument thus ultimately holds that conflicts are stimulated, maybe even caused, precisely by essentialising perceptions of difference and of respective identities. This argument is based on a phenomenological reading of the problem of difference which sees the issue of difference and the question of 'otherness'[1] as irreducible, experiential foundations of all social and political relations and suggests that a non-essentialised and normative understanding of difference(s) can render difference a positive social and political force.[2]

A phenomenological approach to peace begins with the notion that whether we as individuals, citizens, political activists, politicians, or most importantly as conflict parties act in a peaceful way, or less so, depends on our relation to our fellow humans. Thus peace always articulates (as) a relation to the 'other'. Yet, the question of our relation to the 'other' includes another question, namely that of difference. Consequently, issues around peace are to be thought of as questions of difference. Whether, or not, we act in a peaceful way is therefore a question of how we approach, think, and negotiate difference(s). The first argument developed in this article is that non-essentialist ways of thinking and acting upon difference(s) are more conducive to peaceful relations than essentialised versions of difference. The second, and subsequent argument holds that in practical terms a non-essentialist way of dealing with difference surmounts in the maxim of political dialogue, a dialogue that embraces differences and steadily attempts to de-essentialise them. I call this programme 'peace-in-difference' which is presented here in its first step as a theoretical outline.[3] This approach contributes to the literature in peace and conflict studies that is critical of how difference has been so far treated in liberal peace framings and some of the post-liberal alternatives (see, for example, Nadarajah and Rampton 2015; Sabaratnam 2017), by first adding insights from phenomenology and secondly hinting at some reflections on how 'peace-in-difference' could be practiced. The main contribution is thus not to make specific practical recommendations, but its purpose is to substantiate and guide the conversation in peace studies (and in this Special Issue) towards a de-essentialised understanding of difference that can facilitate peace. Such guidance and substantiation need careful consideration and development, therefore the mainly theoretical focus of this article.

Peace as a question of difference sounds initially banal as peace articulates always as a relation to the 'other'. The discussion of this relation leads us, however, to very complex issues. The question of our relation to the 'other' that underpins the conceptualisation of peace bears another, ontologically preceding question, namely that of difference because otherness is always and already a specific articulation of the primary human experience of difference. When framing the question of peace as a question of difference, we have to deal with two main problems according to which the article is structured: (1) The first problem relates to the legacy of thinking difference in Western philosophy and political theory. This discussion occupies the main part of this article which understands itself as a theoretical outline of the basic contours of an original, namely phenomenological, approach to peace-building (following the foundation of this argument in Behr 2014). (2) The second problem relates to the liberal legacy of how to think and deal with peace in peace studies and peace-building politics. The discussions of these two problems in sections (1) and (2) include alternative thinking to respective legacies in Western philosophy[4] and political practices and thus attempts to contribute to a rethinking and reconceptualization of peace in peace studies and peace practices. In the conclusions, I will reflect on research questions for a further research agenda which emerge from the argument (and which are derived in the second section) and further contextualise them in current peace research.

Thinking difference

When looking into modes of thinking difference as they have become handed down to us by Western philosophy, we learn that until recently, i.e. until the beginning of the twentieth century, difference has been conceptualised as a hierarchical dependency between 'self' and 'other'. From Greek Antiquity to the beginning of the twentieth century we find *cum grano salis* no philosophical or political conception of difference that would not assume or directly posit the 'self'-'other'-relation as a top down that requests the sub-ordination of the 'other' to, or the transformation and assimilation of the 'other' into, (the idea) of the 'self'.[5] This has immediate consequences for how we think peace: peace is understood hierarchically, as the 'other' always has to submit to the imaginations and practices of the 'self', be that one of the conflict parties or an outside peace builder. This kind of peace can be called 'imperial peace' to emphasise its vertical, imposing, sub-ordinating, and thus always violent nature against the 'other' (for more details on this argument, see Behr 2014). A non-hierarchical approach to difference therefore seems the only way that is conducive to peace. Only then, it appears, peace thinking and peace practices do not demand the subordination of one actor to another actor's political imaginations and practices (as this is probably the reason for the outbreak of violence in the first place).The big challenge then lies in the question: *How can we conceptualise difference in a non-hierarchical and thus peaceful way?*

Exploring Western philosophy for approaches of how to think difference alternatively to orthodoxies, we strike a movement that we can summarise as phenomenology and that comprises in chronological order as its main authors Georg Simmel, Edmund Husserl, Alfred Schütz, Martin Heidegger, Emmanuel Lévinas, and Jacques Derrida. What is characteristic of this movement (and why I group these authors together; see also Lévinas 1996a; Heidegger 2006, 2007) and what helps us thinking difference in a non-hierarchical way are the following two observations: first, phenomenologists emphasise that 'self' and 'other' are both interdependent and mutually constitutive constructions that are embedded in specific historic, political, economic, and cultural circumstances. They are subject to change and are and have no fixed or constant entities.[6] Second, underpinning such constructivist outlook is a specific notion of the temporal fabric[7] of all political and social 'things'. This implies, in short, that the meanings we give to these 'things' and that these 'things' have for us are perpetually transforming, transient and can only be grasped and understood in their passing articulations as these meanings change and be actively changed through their temporalization. With regard to understanding peace as 'peace-in-difference' this means most importantly that difference(s) is/are not insurmountable obstacles based and fixed in assigned identities as 'enemy', 'opponent', 'friend' and 'foe', or in immobilised gender, race, or ethnicity roles. Rather differences are open to become transformed in their relations towards each other as actors can change their attitudes, behaviour, and perception as difference(s) become negotiated and debated. Thus, their de-essentialisation turns them into a positive force for peaceful relations.

Early phenomenologists and temporality

Motion and transformation are, for example, fundamental in Simmel when he theorises about the individual and society. The conviction that motion and transformation are fundamental criteria of society is clearly communicated by the title of one of his main writings – *Untersuchungen über die Formen der Vergesellschaftung* (1908).[8] Referring to this book, we recognise from the German '*Vergesellschaftung*' Simmel's emphasis on the processes of becoming which is expressed in the grammatical ending '-*ung*'. We see here that society is always the product of a process of motion, fluctuation, change, and transience. Society is fundamentally a historic formation ('ein historisches Gebilde') in that there were not just one presence, but rather the past and distinct cultural, political, and economic legacies become conditions of *each* presence, inherent in the process of becoming.[9] The same notion of becoming does, however, not only apply to social formations but, as Simmel argues in 'Vom Wesen des historischen Verstehens', it also applies to the human being as an individual. Here he argues decisively against the idea of the person as a fixed substance which would, and could, be characterised by something called 'identity'. Instead, the individual always traverses an unending lively development ('eine lebendige Entwicklung'). In this context we find Simmel's strongest argument against historicism, the dominant form of historiography in the nineteenth century. Especially, he argues against Leopold von Ranke's dictum that the purpose of historiography is to demonstrate how history actually 'was' and how single events would have truly been ('*wie es eigentlich gewesen sei*'). Simmel criticises this notion of history as a chimera.[10]

But Simmel goes further. He declares that the notion of becoming is the epistemic condition for the understanding of history. This is a logical consequence of his criticism of historicism, and it is remarkable that he has asserted this point some nine years before the publication of Heidegger's *Being and Time* (1929) 1962. Simmel develops his argument by accentuating not only *how* understanding has to be aware of processes of becoming, but he also argues *that* understanding itself is sustained and carried by processes and movements. Only because of these sustaining and carrying processes and movements, history and life in general would be tangible to our understanding and become tangible only by methods of understanding, i.e. by interpretation and hermeneutics.[11] Understanding is thus only possible because it is aware of historical processes of motion and transformation with regard to its 'object' and because, consequently, it is itself a process of becoming. Understanding thus grasps the historic nature of its 'object' and, as this object is permanently transforming in time, understanding has to become transformative, too, to correspond to its 'object'. A static and identitarian understanding of the world, for instance, would not understand and mismatch the world around it which is moving and transforming while it itself remains obsolete; and in the worst, but likely case turns violent as it attempts to render things fixed which are indeed in motion. At the same time this means, however, that understanding, just as the world around it, is never terminated and finished, but is itself an endless exegetic process of unveiling, unmasking, interpreting, and creating meaning.

However, this implies that understanding is never fully possible. If understanding is a process itself, and it is engaged in grasping the meaning of phenomena which are themselves in motion, the human mind can only accomplish fractional and partial understandings of those phenomena. The phenomena are always fluctuating and thereby are transforming their appearances and articulations as they present themselves to the human experience, like a flip-book: snapshots and sectionality which, however, are the constituents of our understanding. And there are two reasons for the sectionality of our understanding and cognition: society and the individual are principally historical and

THE POLITICS OF PEACEBUILDING IN A DIVERSE WORLD 57

transformative; and the nature of understanding, focusing on such transformativities, is itself conditioned, limited, and shaped by them.

We find the same argument about temporality in Schütz. He sees that the social and political world is 'not a world of being, but a world that is at every moment one of becoming and passing away – or better, an emerging world' (Schütz 1972, 36). In his *Phenomenology of the Social World* (1972), Schütz (1962) refers to Simmel to identify two main problems of the social sciences: first, what he calls the problem of 'Verstehen' (or understanding and hermeneutics) in general; and, secondly and more specifically, 'the way in which the other self is meaningfully given to us' (1972, 19). The question of difference is thus not only related to motion, but very importantly, too, to the multiplicity and to our constitution of meaning (which is, however, also embedded in motion and development).

In order to advance the question of how meaning is constituted, Schütz refers to the idea of the intentionality of action. For Schütz meaning is constituted by social and political action and interaction. He notes, '(meaning) is thus constituted as an intersubjective phenomenon' (1972, 32/33) and, on the part of each actor involved, indicates the actor's attitude toward, as well as awareness and appreciation of, his/her own duration which becomes experienced in and through action. In other words, we find temporality at the very basis of an ontology of 'a world that is being constituted, never completed, but always in the process of formation' (1972, 36). The experience of the emergence, historicity, and transience of all being – social, political, and individual – has the same epistemic condition for understanding and knowledge as in Simmel. In short: our understanding of the social and political world is bound to, and rests upon, time and change and must be aware of this. It is rooted in 'internal time-conscious-ness' (ibid.); i.e. it is, and should be, aware of the historic and thus transformative nature of all things political and social, and must proactively base our relation to the world on time and change. This means, however, that by and through consciousness and activity, our relation to the world temporalizes and is temporal. Before discussing the temporality of acting in some greater detail, another quote which highlights the transience and transformation of being helps our understanding:

> What we, in fact, experience in duration is not a being that is discrete and well-defined but a constant transition from a now-thus to a new now-thus. (1972, 45)[12]

The way in which Schütz develops the relation between temporality, action, and meaning is through the figure of *modo future exacti*. Most basically, *modo future exacti* points to an ambiguity in the term and concept of action. This ambiguity consists of the circumstance of multiple dimensions of temporality and temporal imagination inherent in the concept of action itself. This multidimensionality speaks out against imaginations of teleological and linear time. Rather action implies two very different meanings both of which must be understood as crucial for the constitution of meaning in the social and political world. This is why understanding and meaning are fundamentally bound to temporality. They are themselves modes of being-in-time. Schütz argues that, first, action can refer to an act as a 'completed unit' (1972, 39), a finished product (he describes this as 'Handlung'); and second, action refers to the course of an action during which it is constituted and comes into being. As such, action, as Schütz says, would be 'a flow, an ongoing sequence of events' (ibid.) and always something 'enacted' ('ein *Gehandelt-worden-sein*').

In this second dimension, action involves anticipation of the future. It is future-directed and planned into a future with and in every step and moment that it evolves. This directedness into the future and the very circumstance of being anticipated is, in the words of Schütz, 'transformation of this Now into a Has-Been … (The) planned act bears the temporal character of pastness' (1972, 61). Therefore, every action has the character of a draft, project, and plan, anticipating the course of action and thereby turning each present moment into anticipated pasts prior to the manifestation of the action at some future point. There is, however, another consequence of these two temporal dimensions of action which is important for thinking and speaking of difference. Namely, what are implications and consequences of these temporalities for the perspectivity, complexity, and heterogeneity of the social and political world? Schütz writes that the social world 'is given to us in a complex system of perspectives' (1972, 8). These perspectives not only emerge in every individual with regard to his/her own action, but much more in all intersubjective social actions. A multitude of projects, anticipations, and articulations of actions emerge and vanish in complex interactions.

From the early phenomenologists to Lévinas and Derrida

The nexus of temporality, perspectivity, meaning, and social and political action implies a critique of traditional Western ontology. Within the twentieth century phenomenological discourse we can trace this critique back into the 1918-article 'Vom Wesen des historischen Verstehens' by Simmel. In this article, Simmel criticises and dismisses (what he calls) the Greek style of thought. Its firm substantialism would be unified in the belief that only identical substances could recognise and identify each other. He terms this a 'naïve mechanistic dogma' as if the imagination and 'its' object were two units which could be and needed to be brought in full swing. As it becomes obvious, this is diametrical to the nexus of temporality, perspectivity, meaning, and social and political action. And Simmel, as a phenomenologist, perceives of this kind of firm substantialism as an irrational traditionalism. In his metaphorically rich language, Simmel describes this kind of traditional epistemic naivety as the illusion of things real becoming constituted in our brain and their projection by some esoteric procedure in an empty space completely reserved for this projection – comparable to moving furniture in an empty flat.

Within the movement of phenomenological social and political theory, we observe a fundamental radicalisation of the temporal thinking from early phenomenologists to the work of Lévinas and Derrida. Both break with the notion of intentionality that supposes an epistemological relation between 'subject' and 'object' that is, according to them, characteristic of Western philosophy. Both argue that the temporalized nature of 'things' leads to a situation in which we cannot grasp and hold on to things. Therefore, our claim to *understand* something would be misleading; what can at most be accomplished is limited apprehension and empathy. Opposite to more orthodox discourses on 'otherness' (such as by Munasu Duala-M'bedy (1977)), which are also critical of Western philosophical history, Lévinas is not interested in, and does not deem possible, any kind of restoration of, and re-connection to, sources of Western philosophy. Rather he focuses on the development of an original and basic philosophy of openness – or: of infinity and exteriority ('infinité' and 'extériorité'; see Lévinas 1979 [1961; also 1985]). According to Lévinas, the main problem of Western philosophy would be symbolised in the primacy of the 'self' which delivers the intellectual, emotional, spiritual, and physical framework for understanding all other individuals. Thereby the 'other' would inevitably become reduced to the 'self' and his/her experiences which symbolises the vertical and hierarchical conception of difference mentioned in the beginning of the article as the crucial problematic underpinning a reconceptualization of 'peace-in-difference'. This is a reduction which is itself the result of Western essentialist ontology which Lévinas calls 'ontological imperialism' and 'egology' (1979), i.e. an explanation, exploration, interpretation ('logos'), and acting upon the world from the vantage point of the 'self'.[13] It is on this basis that 'peace', which is based on such a vertical 'self'-'other'-relation, was termed 'imperial peace' above.

At the basis of such an ontological imperialism and egology is, as Lévinas argues, finally the idea of intentionality which pervades Western thinking and still be key to Husserl's philosophy in his *Méditations Cartésiennes* (1965 [1931]) as well as in Heidegger's *Being and Time*. Lévinas identifies intentionality as exactly the very figure of thought which is responsible for ontological imperialism and egology. Intentionality would assume the existence of a correlation between *noesis* and *noema*, i.e. between 'subject' and 'object', between recognising consciousness and the 'thing' recognised, and thus would presuppose a chronological simultaneity and synchronism between the 'self' and everything exterior. Lévinas's (1998) fundamental criticism of intentionality appears as a consequence of a temporalized ontology. It dissolves and renders impossible synchrony and simultaneity because of the genuine openness, transformativity, transience, and processurality of being. Lévinas appears as having followed the idea of temporality consequently through and as having brought the consequence of temporality to a forceful end. In an article from 1964, 'Meaning and Sense', Lévinas notes – not dissimilar to Simmel – that '(the) intelligible is not conceivable outside of the becoming' and that 'the world [is to be conceived] in its fundamental historicity' (Lévinas 1996b, 42, 43). This picture of being as permanent fluctuation, change and transformation forbids him to speak of manifestations of Being, rather he speaks of a 'temporal series of articulations and expressions of being-in-time' (Lévinas 1996b, 66).

In declining intentionality, Lévinas creates the basis for the possibility of an unprecedented thinking of openness (or of infinity). Setting the 'thing observed' free from assumptions about its Being, and delivering the categories of its cognition – precisely through breaking with the idea of intentionality and its transcendental correlation between observer and thing – Lévinas develops this liberation and the related idea of a dialogical towards the 'other' (rather than claiming knowledge of the 'other'). It is thus precisely the abolishment of intentionality which creates a relation of each 'self' of towards the 'other'; but, we have to ask, what is this towards and what is its reference object (if at all, we can even speak of an 'object' under conditions of non-intentionality)? Lévinas puts this question himself, asking: how is this relation-less relation (this 'rapport sans rapport')? At this point, we can receive important support through Derrida's notions of 'advent'.

Derrida's notion of 'advent' – albeit we encounter typical Derridean jargon here, he is very helpful to reflect upon the problematic of 'otherness', difference, and peace – provides more specific ideas with regards to what it is that is to come in the processes of becoming. His notion of 'advent' is helpful here and is most explicit in his writings about democracy and Europe (the latter especially in *The Other Heading*, 1992). In both cases, the event – i.e. democracy and/or Europe – is not yet there as he says, but something 'that remains to be thought and to come' (Derrida 1993, 19). Derrida uses the French 'à venir' and 'survenir' to describe this situation of 'yet to be'. The French 'survenir' contains a meaning which seems to be important as it links with his emphasis on the temporality and transformativity of being (which seems, however, lost in the English translation 'to come about' (as in *Psyche. Inventions of the Other*; 2007, 24)): the distinct meaning of 'survenir' is that something, an e-vent comes about *suddenly, unexpectedly,* and *unpredictably*. This terrain or space from where the event is coming is unknown, undefined, and undefinable. Otherwise, it would not come about in a sudden and unpredictably.

To keep this terrain unknown or undefined, and thus to preserve the suddenness of the coming about of the e-vent (of democracy, of Europe; and, for our matters, of the 'other') is normatively purposeful, since it will preserve its transformativity to the highest possible degree. To do otherwise, i.e. to foreclose the openness and namelessness of the terrain from where the event is coming from would mean 'to totalise, to gather, *versammeln*' (Derrida 1997, 13). It would be a form of 'monogenealogy' (Derrida 1992, 10) and depend upon and reproduce the 'contagious or contaminating powers of a reappropriating language, (…) the language of the Same that is foreign or allergic to the Other' (Derrida 2007, 155). To preserve openness, namelessness, and dialogue and thereby the (chance of) transformativity of the event (i.e. also of the 'other') is crucial, since it means to 'prevent totalitarianism, nationalism, egocentrism' (Derrida 1997, 14).

When democracy, Europe, or the 'other' are called events to come which remain to be thought, this does not mean that there would not be democratic and/or European institutions or experienced differences among individuals. Rather it suggests that preserving a critical space of openness for their free, unpredicted, and non-forestalled development and discursive articulation is a very deliberate and normative choice. This choice is convinced of the normative value of democracy/Europe/the 'other'/difference(s) to remain open towards the future. Their value is exactly (in) their openness. Their option to be and to let be is precisely their provision of, and their demand for, opened-up spaces for different modes of being and critical dialogue where those modes are not becoming pre-defined, pre-determined, and/or anticipated, but are being expected to approach, to emerge, to come about, and to transform suddenly and unexpectedly. The demands and value of democracy, the demands and value of Europe, and the demands of the 'other' consist in opening and destabilising closed structures to allow for the passage toward the multiplicity and diversity of events. This openness is enabled to come through them; i.e. with regard to the question of 'otherness' and difference, 'one does not make the other come, one lets it come by preparing for its coming' (Derrida 2007, 45), for its advent.[14]

This choice for preserving a critical and dialogical space is, according to Derrida, grounded in the 'aporetic experience of the impossible' (Derrida 1993, 15). It proposes a reading of the question of 'otherness' and difference as *Dasein*, i.e. as not an entity or essence, but rather as a being-possible and becoming-possible (according to Heidegger, 'das Möglichsein' and 'das Möglichwerden'); as a being which 'trembles in [from, and *towards*] an unstable multiplicity' (Derrida 1993, 9) and which therefore demands the *making*-possible of Being as *Dasein*.[15] The 'aporetic experience of the impossible' assumes the intrinsic disunity of, and differences within, all things (histories, identities, cultures, institutions groups, and individual psyches) as well as the proactive elaboration on, and widening of, respective disunities and their mutual tensions as critical practice. What Derrida calls deconstruction and 'différance' is important here inasmuch as they refer to deferrals, dislocations, and disruptions of all things (mainly identities in our regard) precisely due to their intrinsic disunities, contradictions, and tensions. Derrida notes:

> 'There is no culture or cultural identity without this difference *within itself*' (Derrida 1992, 9, 10); or: '(The) identity of a culture is a way of being different from itself; a culture is different from itself; language is different from itself; the person is different from itself'. (1997, 13)

In *Margins of Philosophy* (1982), Derrida describes *différance* also as an activity of 'temporization' (p. 9) and 'spacing' (ibid.).

The question asked above about what is the referent 'object' of the 'self' in its motion towards the 'other' and of difference(s) in their relation each other receives a phenomenological answer here. The aporia (impasse) of unity and essence as both an ontological and a normative demand asks and longs for the opening up of dialogical spaces that make possible to think the impossible (as the unknown, intangible, unintentional, undefinable, or unpredictable). The impossible is here understood as unknown *what* the 'other' may be and as the terra incognita *from where* the 'other' may come from and suddenly appear ('advent') as 'naked face' (Lévinas). This out of the sudden and complete masking of the 'other' is of course not always the case, but it may be a possibility (and indeed seems to be the case very often). Thus, the ontological and normative demand is neither to work within the framework of totalities, nor to work against them and to 'move out of the impasse' (Derrida 1993, 13), i.e. to either accept their rationalities or to oppose and destroy them from outside. Instead, it demands the disruption of totalities by elaborating on, widening, and negotiating their *inherent* tensions and dis-unities through dialogue. Such disruptions open up spaces for alternatives, shall prevent totalitarianisms, nationalism, and ego-centrisms, and finally articulate the condition for the relation *towards* the 'other' as condition of peace.

It is here, in a critical perception of difference(s) and 'otherness' as transformative becomings where we find both the limits of, and conditions for, the deconstruction of Western traditions of peace thinking and peacebuilding practices as well as for a positive re-articulation of a dialogical understanding of peace. Such a perception produces and opens alternative spaces for the articulation of difference(s) and the advent of the 'other'.

To summarise: Why do temporality, transformation, and non-intentionality help us thinking difference in a non-hierarchical way? Temporality liberates difference(s) from proclamations about what they *are* or would *be*; they also set them free from declarations about why they are. Both temporality and non-intentionality therefore strongly suggest anti-essentialist views and advise us to listen to the 'other' before claiming knowledge *about* them. A *dialogical structure* is inherent here that does not make statements about difference(s) and the 'other' prior to having paid attention and having learned about the 'other' through listening to difference(s). What characterised hierarchical ways of thinking and acting upon differences, namely the stigmatisation of differences(s) as 'otherness' and their subordination under imaginations and categories of the 'self', becomes anathematic to a temporal and temporalized understanding of differences that avoid their essentialization as 'otherness' and would attend them in their own right. In conclusion of those theoretical considerations, I want to suggest the following proposition which operationalises the contribution of a phenomenological approach to peace research: *The lesser the degree of essentialist attributions to difference(s) and the lesser essentialist perceptions and definitions of 'otherness', the less likely the outbreak of conflict and the more conducive this is for peace, conflict solution, and reconciliation.*

However, one has to further investigate the practical implications of an emphatic approach to difference(s) for peace research to which the article turns now, outlining the major implications.

Difference and peace studies and practices

The most important practical implication that takes us straight to (re-thinking) peace is the appreciation of differences as *positive*. If we cannot – and should not – define the 'other' and his or her identity as someone or something definite and if we can only get momentary impressions of the 'other' whose nature is hidden from us, yet, as Morgan Brigg (2018) argues in this Special Issue, differences are something undeniable in society and politics and an irreducible, existential experience of human life ('crucial feature of life itself', as he argues), we are also practically advised to develop a way to appreciate them as positive and not as an obstacle to peaceful relations.

The practical value of a temporal and temporalized notion of 'otherness' and difference for re-thinking peace becomes thus immediately visible. The vast majority of peace thinking in Western philosophy, peace studies, and International Relations, and of peace practice by international organisations such as the United Nations and the European Union have been based on the dictum of assimilating differences. Difference into unity ('E Pluribus Unum') is the famous motto here (see for more detail on this Behr 2014) which ultimately negates difference(s) for the sake of unity and under a universal script of identity and political order. To create pathways to peace, the concept of 'peace-in-difference' presented here is suggesting precisely the opposite. Not the assimilation or ultimate nullification of difference(s), but their emphatic cultivation and dialogical negotiation, based upon an anti-essentialist approach to difference(s), are the way to peace.

Thus, 'peace-in-difference' is critical of conceptualizations of 'liberal peace', its institutions and its Kantian (in theoretical terms; see [1784] 1970, 1795) and Wilsonian (in more practical terms; see 1966, 2006) legacies that become epitomised in the contemporary 'democratic peace hypothesis' and its strategies of international democratisation in the Western image (so in Russett 2001, for instance). 'Liberal peace' is indeed the representative of a universal script – by and large composed of Western notions of democracy, rule of law, human rights, and free market economies – that is imposed in global conflict settings in order to conquer and overcome differences, promoting the perception and stigmatisation of all actors, cultures, and peoples outside the 'self', as different and as the 'other'. Respective thought and practices become most visible in politics of the US administrations under George Bush and Bill Clinton, under the UK governments of Tony Blair and Gordon Brown, and in UN and EU peace building politics over the last 25 years (Björkdahl, Richmond, and Kappler 2011). This legacy has also come under severe attack from a post-liberal peace approach suggested by Oliver Richmond and others for 10 years (see *inter alia* Richmond 2008, 2010, 2011; MacGinty 2010, 2011; Autesserre

2014) with which the concept of 'peace-in-difference' shares this criticism. However, a 'peace-in-difference' perspective suggests a novel epistemology and ontology of peace thinking and peace practice that a post-liberal perspective does not include in its, yet very important, critique and suggestions to overcome 'liberal peace'. Post-liberal peace is thus concentrating mainly on new practices as an hybrid blend of Western and local peace building instruments that is conceptually based on a Foucauldian and post-colonial critique of Western, statist politics and its discursive and institutional power apparatus; without, however, an own theoretical (i.e. ontological and/or epistemological) and normative foundation that would go beyond critique. In this vein, criticism has emerged recently with regard to a new essentialism in post-liberal peace concepts, namely that of a dichotomist binary between 'the local' and 'the international' (see, for instance, Nadarajah and Rampton 2015; see also, Bargués-Pedreny and Mathieu 2018, in the introduction to this Special Issue).[16]

This 'going-beyond' is, however, hoped to be part of a 'peace-in-difference' approach according to which peace, just as 'otherness' or difference(s), cannot be fixed and cannot be defined. Rather peace is to be seen as a permanent process of, and dialogue about, the articulation and meaning(s) as well as a critical reflection upon difference(s) as they become expressed in political, social, and cultural conflicts. This process primarily consists of *neutralising essentialist thinking and action* that are based upon defining, stereo-typing, and pigeonholing political perceptions and world views. This includes the exploration of processes of identity formation, and, if necessary, their active reorientation towards anti-essentialist 'self' and 'other'-perceptions.

Such exploration and engagement would, next to the study of Western peacebuilding approaches, focus on the study of forms of local, culturally-situated knowledge, i.e. local ontologies and epistemologies of communities as they underlie visions and practices of political and social order and scrutinise them, just like Western ones, according to their essentialist and non-essentialist character respectively. Those forms of knowledge and everyday practices of local communities that are directly involved in conflict and reconciliation are deemed more legitimate than Western, universalised peacebuilding policies implanted into and imported from outside. However, these must be conducive to peace – following the argument proposed here – and of de-essentialised or de-essentialising character, too. The following kind of questions would populate a 'peace-in-difference' agenda.

- How are perceptions of difference and 'otherness' in peace-building, peace negotiation, and conflict reconciliation processes discursively framed?
- Are difference(s) and the 'other' seen as 'natural' enemies, are their characteristics essentialized (according to ethnic, national, religious, political, gender, etc. criteria), and are they stigmatised *a priori*?
- What patterns follow 'self'-'other'-relations and definitions?
- Can distinct features of the 'self'-'other'-relation be learned from successful peace formation, peace negotiation, and conflict reconciliation processes? And *vice versa*, can failed peace negotiation, peace-building, and conflict reconciliation processes be traced back to distinct perceptions and framings of the 'self'-'other' relation?
- How and through what channels can a phenomenological approach to peace practically be communicated with conflict and warring parties?

Conclusions

'Peace-in-difference' pursues, next to its critique of essentialist (i.e. mainly of universal liberal-teleological, but also of post-liberal) approaches to peacebuilding and peace formation respectively, the interrogation *and* interlocution of different ontologies and epistemologies in specific conflict contexts and involved actors. This does neither include the uncritical reception of Western or local identities, visions and practices, many of them ultimately involved in violent conflicts and faced with the demand to reconcile and re-build society and politics, nor their eventual dichotomy between them and Western modes of thinking. Thus, there is no dualism between 'Western' and 'local' politics, however, a clear choice exists and a distinction can and must be made between productive, i.e. non-essentialist/de-essentialising, and counterproductive, i.e. essentialist/essentialising, ontologies and epistemologies of difference. 'Peace-in-difference' offers guidance on how actors involved in peacebuilding and reconciliation processes may cooperate to create more sustainable pathways to peace. In this regard, I remind of the aforementioned proposition: *The lesser the degree of essentialist attributions to difference (s) and the lesser essentialist perceptions and definitions of 'otherness', the less likely the outbreak of conflict and the more conducive this is for peace, conflict solution, and reconciliation.*[17] One may also consider and explore the circumstance that conflicts and violence broke out precisely because of the essentialised perception and framing of difference(s) in the first place.

This proposition operationalises practically the phenomenological approach to 'peace-in-difference' and the research questions derived at the end of the previous section. At the same time – and here lies its epistemological advantage over other, mainly post-colonial, post-liberal, and other so-called critical approaches to peacebuilding which seem to embrace the local too undifferentiatedly – this proposition requests to scrutinise local constructions of 'self' and 'other' according to their possible essentialisations; just as this proposition and the phenomenological tradition is critical with identitiarian Western thinking. On a the macro-political scale, examples of non-Western essentialising identity discourses are Russian or Chinese discourses on civilisation and empire (see critically for example Katzenstein 2009; Shih and Yin 2013; Joergensen 2017); on a macro-political, sociological level, we find all kinds of identity politics by state and societal actors in local conflicts who propagate fixed narratives of 'us' and 'them' in teleological, gendered, securitising, territorial, geo-political, etc. hierarchies (see instead of many Basham 2016; Hagmann 2017; Rigual 2018; with regard to narratives of belonging, see the forthcoming edition of Behr/Roesch 2019). A 'peace-in-difference' approach would consequently demand and advocate the conceptual and practical de-essentialisation of Western, non-Western, local, macro- and micro-political perceptions and constructions of difference.

Notes

1. Here and throughout the article, 'otherness', the 'other', and 'self' are written in single inverted comas to indicate that they are social and political identity constructions and no ontic entities.
2. See also Lévinas, 'Peace and Proximity' (1996c [1984]) which, however, did not yet generate much discussion of a phenomenological approach to peace. A phenomenological approach should not be confused or likened with post-structuralism or post-modernism (not at least

THE POLITICS OF PEACEBUILDING IN A DIVERSE WORLD

because both Lévinas and Derrida in many interviews tirelessly and sometimes fiercely emphasised this difference and protested against any form of appropriation). The reason for this distinction lies in phenomenologists' more explicit elaboration of own assumptions and in their subsequent normative approach to politics and questions of meaning (see essentially hereto Heidegger, 'Platon: Sophistes' [1919-1944]), a dimension which post-structuralism, at least in International Relations and Peace Studies, wilfully neglects or ignores; see representative of this neglect *inter alias* Campbell 1998; Richmond 2009, 2010; as well as critically Behr/Shani, 'Critiquing critique in "critical IR": theory, ideology, knowledge claims and the problem of normativity' (forthcoming).

3. A fuller version of this approach would need to incorporate aspects of material and discursive power to further specify the experience and negotiation of difference(s) and the subsequent construction of otherness. Such an incorporation, however, would go far beyond the scope of this article. A promising direction could be found in complementing 'peace-in-difference' with a realist concept of the political in a Morgenthauian sense (see Morgenthau 2012 and the Introduction to this edition by Behr and Roesch 2012) or with post-colonial studies of asymmetric power relations between 'the' West and 'beyond the West', their histories, legacies, and threads to humanity and security (see *inter alia* Shani 2014).

4. Maybe non-Western philosophy does suggest and offer different legacies, but that is not addressed here. However, see *inter alia* Galtung 1993 (as: see also 1967); more empirical Tambiah 1992.

5. In the legacies of Western political philosophy prior to the intellectual tradition of 'phenomenology' we can identify five historic patterns of thinking difference which, however, all establish some form of essentialism of, and hierarchical relation between, differences and are therefore, more or less, less tuned to violence and conflict. For a more detailed discussion, see Behr 2014.

6. Early twentieth century phenomenologists, mainly sociologists, are thus the inventors of what has become mainstream in the discipline of International Relations only some 60 years later, namely 'constructivism' and the focus on socially constructed norms to explain actor's behaviour.

7. 'Temporal' and 'temporality' mean in the most basic sense the fluid and transformative (in contrast to an essentialised) ontological status of a thing that we become aware of through a proactive processuralization of its empirical appearances by unpacking and destabilising its dynamics, ambiguities, disunities, and perspectives (see the more detailed discussions below p. 9, esp. on the activity of 'temporisation' in Heidegger and Derrida). This understanding is critically different to how this term is used frequently in many contemporary social science debates on time that focus on and explore very importantly the historical, present, and future time dimension of politics as these discussions elaborate and actually focus on time-framing (time-making) and time-narration, however, not on 'temporality' in the technical sense (see with regard to Peace Studies, *inter alia* McMahon 2016; also representative of this misconception is Mueller 2016). These debates should therefore speak of time dimensions, time perspectives, or time horizons and thus of 'historic' and 'transient' rather than of 'temporal' dimensions. In how far both understandings interrelate would need careful consideration elsewhere.

8. This book has not yet been translated into English. The title would be something like *Inquiries into forms of sociation*; see further two (also untranslated) articles: '*Beiträge zur Philosophie der Geschichte*' (1909; would be: 'Essays on the philosophy of history') and '*Vom Wesen des historischen Verstehens*' (1918; ditto: 'On the nature of historical understanding').

9. This important, early argument may be quoted in full in its German version:

> Dies macht die Gesellschaft zu einem, seinem inneren Wesen nach, historischen Gebilde, d.h. sie ist nicht nur ein Gegenstand der Geschichte, sondern die Vergangenheit hat in ihr noch wirksame Realität ... in der Form der gesellschaftlichen Überlieferung wird das Geschehen zum Bestimmungsgrunde des Gegenwärtigen. (1909)

In English: 'This turn society into an inherently historical constellation, i.e., it is not only an "object" of history, but the past is always lively present in the presence. As social heritage the past becomes the conditioning ground for the presence' (translation by the author).

10. Very instructive here is also Vierhaus (1977).
11. Simmel notes: '*Die stetige Bewegtheit des Lebens ist der formale Träger des Verständnisses (...) von Sachgehalten, die ihrerseits das lebendig konkrete Vorkommen dieser Sachgehalte erst verständlich machen*' (Simmel 1918; also 1980, 1977). In English: „The permanent motion of our lives is the carrier for/the condition of our understanding of 'things' which itself makes possible the existence of these things in the first place' (translation by the author).
12. See hereto also Michael Shapiro who speaks of only momentary and transient 'here and nows' (1992) as there would be no structure, essence, or identity. All we have are continually transforming appearances ('transformativity' rather than 'identity' as argued in Behr 2014), exploring their emergence and developments via genealogies, and acting towards them in dialogical empathy.
13. For a discussion of his criticism of Western philosophy see also 'Is Ontology Fundamental?' (1951); here in Lévinas 1996.
14. In *The Other Heading*, Derrida writes:

> This *duty* also dictates opening Europe (...) opening it onto that which is not [and] never was (...) The *same duty* also dictates welcoming foreigners in order not only to integrate them but to recognize and accept their alterity (...) *The same duty* dictates cultivating the virtue of such *critique, of the critical idea, the critical tradition*, but also submitting it, beyond critique and questioning, to a deconstructive genealogy that thinks and exceeds it without yet compromising it. (Derrida 1992, 77)

15. A *making*-possible of being in multiplicity links back to democracy and (Derrida's vision of) Europe as spaced for this making-possible.
16. For the post-liberal framing of the local-international dichotomy, see *inter alia* Kappler 2015.
17. There may be individual and temporary exceptions of this general proposition where conflict parties have to affirm a certain identity, for example, to gather and position themselves to be listened to and thus as a condition to mobilise and voice their political ideas. This can be called 'strategic essentialism'. See originally Spivak 1988 who, however, disapproved of her term later because of its instrumental deployment in theory and practice (see Spivak 2007*)*. For this discussion see also very interesting Benhabib et al. 1995.

Acknowledgments

I would like to thank Xavier Matthieu and Pol Bargués-Pedreny for their invitation to the workshop on 'Peacebuilding and the Politics of Difference' at the Centre for Global Cooperation Research (University of Duisburg-Essen), June 26 and 27, 2017, and for careful comments on earlier drafts of this article. I also thank two reviewers of the *Journal of Intervention and Statebuilding* whose comments hugely helped to improve the article. For intense discussions on rethinking peace and peacebuilding and the possibilities of a phenomenological approach I am grateful to Giorgio Shani and Takashi Kibe from the Rotary Peace Centre, International Christian University, Tokyo.

Disclosure statement

No potential conflict of interest was reported by the author.

References

Autesserre, Severine. 2014. *Peaceland: Conflict Resolution and the Everyday Politics of International Intervention*. New York: Cambridge University Press.

Avruch, Kevin. 1998. *Culture and Conflict Resolution*. Washington: US Institute of Peace Press.

Avruch, Kevin, and Peter W. Black. 1991. "The Culture Question and Conflict Resolution." *Peace & Change* 16 (1): 22–45.

Bargués-Pedreny, Pol. 2017. "Connolly and the Never-Ending Critiques of Liberal Peace: From the Privilege of Difference to Vorarephilia." *Cambridge Review of International Affairs* 30 (2-3): 216–234.

Bargués-Pedreny, Pol, and Xavier Mathieu. 2018. "Peacebuilding and the Politics of Difference." *Journal of Intervention and Statebuilding*.

Basham, Victoria. 2016. "Raising an Army: The Geopolitics of Militarizing the Lives of Working-Class Boys in an Age of Austerity." *International Political Sociology* 10 (3): 258–274.

Behr, Hartmut. 2014. *Politics of Difference – Epistemologies of Peace*. London/New York: Routledge. ('Global Horizons' Book Series, ed. by RBJ Walker and Richard Falk; 2015 paperback).

Behr, Hartmut, and Felix Roesch. 2012. *Hans J. Morgenthau, The Concept of the Political*. Translated from the French by Maeva Vidal, edited and with an Introduction by Hartmut Behr and Felix Rösch, Foreword by Michael C. Williams. Basingstoke/New York: Palgrave.

Behr, Hartmut, and Felix Roesh, ed. 2019, forthcoming. *Narratives of Belonging: Essays in Global Comparative Political Theory*. Basingstoke: Palgrave.

Behr, Hartmut, and Giorgio Shani. 2019, forthcoming. "Critiquing Critique in 'Critical IR': Theory, Ideology, Knowledge Claims and the Problem of Normativity".

Benhabib, Sheyla, Judith Butler, Drucilla Cornell, and Nancy Fraser. 1995. *Feminist Contentions. A Philosophical Exchange*. London: Routldege.

Björkdahl, Annika, Oliver Richmond, and Stefanie Kappler. 2011. "The Emerging EU Peacebuilding Framework: Confirming or Transcending Liberal Peacebuilding?" *Cambridge Review of International Affairs* 24 (3): 449–469.

Brigg, Morgan. 2018. "Relational and Essential: Theorising Difference for Peacebuilding. Peacebuilding and the Politics of Difference." *Journal of Intervention and Statebuilding* 12 (3): 352–366.

Campbell, David. 1998. "Why Fight: Humanitarianism, Principles, and Post-Structuralism." *Millennium: Journal of International Studies* 27 (3): 497–521.

Derrida, Jacques. 1982. *Margins of Philosophy*. Chicago: The University of Chicago Press.

Derrida, Jacques. 1989. *On Spirit: Heidegger and the Question*. Chicago: University of Chicago Press.

Derrida, Jacques. 1992. *The Other Heading. Reflection on Today's Europe*. Translated by Pascale-Anne Brault and Michael B Naas, Introduction by Michael B. Naas. Bloomington: Indiana State University Press.

Derrida, Jacques. 1993. *Aporias*. Stanford: Stanford University Press.

Derrida, Jacques. 1997. *Deconstruction in a Nutshell. A Conversation with Jacques Derrida*. Edited and with a commentary by John D. Caputo. New York: Fordham University Press

Derrida, Jacques. 2007. *Psyche. Inventions of the Other*. Vol. I. Stanford: Stanford California Press.

Duala-M'bedy, Munasu. 1977. *Xenologie: Die Wissenschaft vom Fremden und die Verdrängung der Humanitaet aus der Anthropologie*. Freiburg/München: Karl Alber.

Galtung, Johan. 1967. *Theories of Peace. A Synthetic Approach to Peace Thinking*. Oslo: International Peace Research Institute. September, 1967.

Galtung, Johann. 1993. *Buddhism: A Quest for Unity and Peace*. Ratmalana, Sri Lanka: Sarvodaya Book Publ. Services.

Gupta, Ghhanda, and D. P. Chattopadhyaya, eds. 1998. *Cultural Otherness and Beyond*. Leiden/Boston: Brill.

Hagmann, Jonas. 2017. "Security in the Society of Control: The Politics and Practices of Securing Urban Spaces." *International Political Sociology* 11 (4): 418–438.

Hallam, Elizabeth, and Brian V. Street, eds. 2000. *Cultural Encounters: Representing Otherness*. London/New York: Routledge.

Heidegger, Martin. 1919-1944. 'Platon: Sophistes', *Gesamtausgabe*, II. Abteilung: Vorlesungen 1914-1944, Band 19, Frankfurt/M: Vittorio Klostermann.

Heidegger, Martin. (1929) 1962. *Being and Time*. Translated by John Macquire and Edward Robinson. New York: Harper Collins Publishers (German edition: 'Sein und Zeit', *Gesamtausgabe*, I. Abteilung: Frühe Schriften, Band 2, Frankfurt/M: Vittorio Klostermann).

Heidegger, Martin. 2006. 'Identität und Differenz', *Gesamtausgabe*, I. Abteilung: Veröffentlichte Schriften, Band 11, Frankfurt/M: Vittorio Klostermann.

Heidegger, Martin. 2007. 'Zur Sache des Denkens', *Gesamtausgabe*, I. Abteilung: Frühe Schriften, Bd. 14, Frankfurt/M: Vittorio Klostermann.

Husserl, Edmund. 1965. *Cartesian Meditations*. The Hague: N. Nijhoff.

Inayatullah, Naeem, and David L. Blaney. 2004. *International Relations and the Problem of Difference*. New York/London: Routledge.

Joergensen, Kund Erik. 2017. "'Inter Alia: On Global Orders, Practices, and Theory'. Forum Problematizing Global Challenges: Recalibrating the 'Inter' in IR-Theory." *International Studies Review* 19 (2): 283–287.

Kant, Immanuel. 1795. *Perpetual Peace. A Philosophical Essay* (Facsimile 1795). Edited by W. Hastie. Edinburgh: T&T Clark. 1891; Online Library of Liberty, 2005, http://oll.libertyfund.org/Home3/Book.php?recordID=0426.

Kant, Immanuel. (1784) 1970. *Idea for a Universal History of Mankind from a Cosmopolitan Point of View*. Kant's political writings, ed. and with an Introduction and notes by Hans Reiss, translated by H.B. Nisbet. Cambridge: Cambridge University Press (German version: 'Idee zu einer allgemeinen Geschichte in weltbürgerlicher Absicht', *Berlinische Monatsschrift*, November 1784, pp. 385–411).

Kappler, Stefanie, et al. 2015. "The 'Field' in the Age of Intervention: Power, Legitimacy, and Authority Versus the 'Local'." *Millennium: Journal of International Studies* 44 (1): 23–44.

Katzenstein, Peter, ed. 2009. *Civilizations in World Politics: Plural and Pluralist Perspectives*. London: Routledge.

Lederach, John P. 1997. *Building Peace: Sustainable Reconciliation in Divided Societies*. Washington, DC: United States Institute of Peace Press.

Lévinas, Emmanuel. (1961) 1979. *Totality and Infinity: An Essay on Exteriority*. The Hague/Boston: M. Nijhoff Publishers.

Lévinas, Emmanuel. 1985. *Ethics and Infinity*. Pittsburgh, PA: Duquesne University.

Lévinas, Emmanuel. 1996a. "Martin Heidegger and Ontology." *Diacritics* 26 (1): 11–32.

Lévinas, Emmanuel. 1996b. *Basic Philosophical Writings*. Edited by Adriaan T. Peperzak, Simon Critchley, and Robert Barnasconi. Bloomington and Indianapolis: Indiana University Press.

Lévinas, Emmanuel. (1984) 1996c. "Peace and Proximity." *Basic Philosophical Writings*, 161–169.

Lévinas, Emmanuel. 1998. *Otherwise Than Being, or Beyond Essence*. Pittsburgh, PA: Duquesne University Press.

MacGinty, Roger. 2010. "Hybrid Peace: The Interaction Between Top-Down and Bottom-Up Peace." *Security Dialogue* 41 (4): 391–412.

Mac Ginty, Roger. 2011. *International Peacebuilding and Local Resistance. Hybrid forms of peace*. Basingstoke/New York: Palgrave.

McMahon, Sean. 2016. "Temporality, Peace Initiatives and Palestinian-Israeli Politics." *Middle East Critique* 25 (1): 5–21.

Miall, Hugh, Oliver Ramsbotham, and Tom Woodhouse. 1999. *Contemporary Conflict Resolution: The Prevention, Management and Transformations of Deadly Conflicts*. Malden, MA: Polity Press.

Mueller, Justin. 2016. "Temporality, Sovereignty, and Imperialism: When is Imperialism?" *Politics* 36 (4): 428–440.

Nadarajah, Sutharajah, and David Rampton. 2015. "The Limits of Hybridity and the Crisis of Liberal Peace." *Review of International Studies* 41 (1): 49–72.

Richmond, Oliver. 2008. *Peace in International Relations*. London/New York: Routledge.

Richmond, Oliver. 2009. "A Post-Liberal Peace: Eirenism and the Everyday." *Review of International Studies* 35: 557–580.

Richmond, Oliver. 2010. "Resistance and the Post-Liberal Peace." *Millennium: Journal of International Studies* 38 (3): 665–692.

Richmond, Oliver. 2011. *A Post-liberal Peace*. London/New York: Routledge.

Rigual, Christelle. 2018. "Rethinking the Ontology of Peacebuilding. Gender, Spaces and the Limits of the Local Turn." *Peacebuilding* 6 (2): 144–169.

Russett, Bruce. 2001. *Triangulating Peace: Democracy, Interdependence, and International Organization*. New York: W.W. Norton & Company.

Sabaratnam, Meera. 2017. *Decolonizing Intervention: International Statebuilding in Mozambique*. London: Rowman & Littlefield International Ltd.

Schütz, Alfred. 1962. *Collected Papers I*, "The Problem of Social Reality", 207–259, The Hague, Martinus Nijhoff.

Schütz, Alfred. 1972. *The Phenomenology of the Social World*. Translated by George Walsh and Frederick Lehnert, with an Introduction by George Walsh. London: Heinemann.

Shani, Giorgio. 2014. *Religion, Identity, and Human Security*. London/New York: Routledge. (Routledge studies in religion and politics).

Shapiro, Michael. 1992. *Reading the Post-Modern Polity: Political Theory as Textual Practice*. Minneapolis: University of Minnesota Press.

Shih, Chih-Yu, and Jiwu Yin. 2013. "Between Core National Interest and a Harmonious World: Reconciling Self-Role Conceptions in Chinese Foreign Policy." *Chinese Journal of International Politics* 6 (1): 59–84.

Simmel, Georg. 1908. 'Exkurs über den Fremden' ('Excursus on the Stranger'), *Soziologie*: *Untersuchungen ueber die Formen der Vergesellschaftung*, 509–512, Berlin: Duncker & Humblot.

Simmel, Georg. 1909. "Beiträge zur Philosophie der Geschichte", *International Review of Scientific Synthesis*, ed. by G. Bruni, A. Dionisi, F. Enriquez, A. Giardana, E. Rignano, Vol. VI, Anno III, 1909, Number III-4, 345–351, Bologna, Paris, Leipzig, London.

Simmel, Georg. 1918. 'Vom Wesen des historischen Verstehens', *Geschichtliche Abende im Zentralinstitut für Erziehung und Unterricht*, Heft 5, Berlin.

Simmel, Georg. 1977. *The Problems of the Philosophy of History. An Epistemological Essay*, translated and edited, with an introdcution by Guy Oakes, New York: The Free Press.

Simmel, Georg. 1980. *Essays on Interpretation in Social Science*. Translated and edited with an introdcution by Guy Oakes. Manchester: Manchester University Press.

Simmel, Georg. 1992. *Soziologie: Untersuchungen über die Formen der Vergesellschaftung*. Frankfurt/Main: Suhrkamp.

Spivak, Gayatri Chakravorty. 1988. *Can the Sub-Altern Speak?* Basingstoke: Macmillan.

Spivak, Gayatri Chakravorty. 2007. *Other Asias*. Malden, MA: Wiley-Blackwell.

Tambiah, Stanley. 1992. *Buddhism Betrayed? Religion, Politics, and Violence in Sri Lanka*. Chicago: University of Chicago Press.

Vierhaus, Rudolf. 1977. "Rankes Begriff der historischen Objektivität." In *Objektivität und Parteilichkeit in der Geschichtswissenschaft*, edited by Reinhardt Koselleck, Wolfgang J. Mommsen, and Jörn Rüsen, 63–76. München: Deutscher Taschenbuch Verlag (Beiträge zur Historik, Bd. 1).

Wilson, Woodrow. 1966. *Letters on the League of Nations*. Edited by Raymond B. Fosdick. Princeton: Princeton University Press.

Wilson, Woodrow. 2006. *Essential Writings and Speeches of the Scholar-President*. New York: New York University Press. (includes those references to *First Inaugural Address*, *Second Inaugural Address*, *Fourteen Points* [also *Conditions of Peace*], *Address to the Indians*, *We must accept war* [also *Urges to Congress to Declare War*]).

Relational and Essential: Theorizing Difference for Peacebuilding

Morgan Brigg

ABSTRACT
Engagements with difference in peacebuilding are characterized by interrelated patterns of identitiarian and de-essentializing thought that tend to crystalize or minimize difference. In response, this article theorizes difference as simultaneously relational and essential, and thus as a phenomenon that continually re-forms in the world and is crucial to life itself. A relational-essential approach is sketched by drawing upon ideas from conflict resolution and feminism, and illustrated through a micro-case of peacebuilding intervention in Aboriginal Australia. This way of theorizing difference promises pathways beyond European-derived forms of thinking and into exchange with the world and diverse peoples.

Introduction

Recent peacebuilding scholarship and practice has begun to pay significant attention to social, cultural, and religious difference following criticisms of the ethnocentrism of mainstream international efforts to bring about peace. The thinking on difference in peacebuilding comes from a relatively low base, so engagement with difference can readily be seen as a positive development that resonates with growing efforts to 'decolonize' academic disciplines. However, two interrelated shortfalls – which also occur in a similar form in many other practical and scholarly endeavours – compromise the current dominant thinking on difference in peacebuilding. First, reflecting wider patterns in mainstream scholarship, thinking on difference in peacebuilding tends to be stifled by *identitarian* logics that foreground internally coherent and self-same entities. Here, cultures, religions, and ethnic groups are conceived of as 'things' – as relatively fixed and as something 'other' in relation to the figure of the international peacebuilder. Conversely, in a second pattern, difference often tends to be conceptualized through notions of fluidity and *non-essentialism*. Here, difference is framed as ephemeral and as contested and contestable. This second pattern, which sets about *de-essentializing* difference, often emerges as a semi-triumphant response to the former identitarian logics that see difference as a thing. In the de-essentializing frame, seeing a culture or an ethnic group as a thing is usually marked as an older, somewhat naïve and dated way of thinking about difference.

Identitiarian renderings of difference can threaten to lock people into fixed categories in ways that are readily seen as problematic and oppressive. Meanwhile, the de-essentializing of difference cannot readily escape criticism because it is in many respects a call – and in some cases a demand – for people to live their difference through a type of flat pluralism that would see difference accommodate itself to liberal globalism. This risks not allowing difference any substance – any purchase or claim in respect to how the world should be ordered. It depoliticizes difference. Both problems are a longstanding feature of European engagements with difference, and even though these problems appear contradictory and thus may seem to have different sources, they combine to create a singular effect. The development of both international law and domestic legal regimes in the New World, for instance, relied upon casting indigenous peoples as incontrovertible savages incapable of political order *and* as human beings who – because they were graciously deemed by Europeans as being capable of reason – could and should accommodate themselves to European rules and frameworks (e.g. Anghie 1996, 2004; Williams 1986). A similar pattern recurs – albeit in more polite tones – in contemporary peacebuilding practice: local recipients of peacebuilding programmes are likely to be recognized as different, in line with the politics of recognition which informs liberal multiculturalism. Yet if, for instance, on this basis local people prepare to practise customary law, they are likely to quickly face discomfort or resistance on the part of their international donor partners, who point to the importance of the modern rule of law and international human rights. This generates an untenable hierarchical contradiction in which peacebuilders are bathed, as Bruno Latour points out, in the light of reason and peace 'offered by science, technology, economics and democracy' while simultaneously recognizing/celebrating and minimizing/excluding difference (Latour 2002, 7, 9).

Treating difference as a 'thing', following the dominant patterns of scholarship, or as a 'non-thing', following the relatively recent critique of de-essentialization, reproduces the cosmology, predilections and preoccupations of dominant scholarship and international peacebuilders. This pattern, which bypasses the cosmologies and knowledge of those who are the recipients of peacebuilding interventions, occludes the possibility of understanding people's differences on their own terms or of entering into a meaningful relationship with them. It is necessary to do both – strive to understand difference on its own terms and enter into a relationship – in the pursuit of developing ethically defensible and effective peacebuilding practice. Making progress with the thinking on difference in peacebuilding thus requires grappling with the untenable contradictions borne out of the foregoing two patterns of identitiarian and de-essentializing approaches. One possible way forward is to explore possibilities that go beyond *both* identitarian and de-essentializing logics and their accompanying tendencies to crystalize and minimize difference. This article aims to achieve this by theorizing difference as simultaneously *relational* and *essential*, in an approach that neither narrows nor diminishes difference but instead argues that it forms (and continually re-forms) in the world and is a crucial feature of life itself. In this way, the goal of this article is to seek out ways of supporting the process of bringing mainstream peacebuilding – and the European-derived forms of thinking that inform it – into exchange with the world and other peoples.

The first section of the article moves beyond identitarianism with the help of ideas of 'relationality' that are beginning to gain traction in section evokes the possibilities of a relational–essential approach by encountering Australian dominant scholarship. Ideas of relationality are also found in many diverse knowledge, spiritual, and religious traditions around the world, and this serves as a link to the various forms of difference encountered in peacebuilding efforts. The second section moves beyond de-essentializing approaches by building upon relationality to turn anti-essentialism on its head; by drawing upon the relational theorizing of conflict-resolution pioneer Mary Parker Follett and feminist theorist Elizabeth Grosz, it is shown that difference is essential to life itself. In this frame, difference emerges relationally yet is no less crucial for arising in this way. The final section evokes the possibilities of a relational–essential approach by encountering Australian Aboriginal difference, including through a micro-case of peacebuilding intervention.

Beyond identitarianism: Relationality new and old

Identitarianism has a long tradition in European-derived scholarship, building upon Greek heritage and, particularly, the influence of Aristotle. In this tradition, 'things' are conceived as internally consistent and have the character of 'substance', which sets them apart from other things. Per Aristotle, it is impossible 'that "being a man" should mean precisely "not being a man" … denoting the substance of a thing means that the essence of the thing is nothing else' (Aristotle 1941, 740). Such an understanding of 'thingness' – and particularly the internal consistency and separateness of things – has been very powerfully put to use in Newtonian approaches to science. These same approaches – with accompanying industrial and mechanical metaphors – have been deployed in the social sciences to isolate objects and variables, sharpen understandings, and advance causal analyses, creating a heritage that has led peacebuilding scholarship to conceive of individuals, social groupings, organizations, and states predominantly as discrete 'things'.

Within the frame of identitiarian thought, the logic of cultural recognition has become, starting in the 1970s, the predominant liberal means of dealing with difference. However, in recent years the 'recognition paradigm' has been roundly challenged, including for being conducted on European-derived terms (e.g. Coulthard 2014; Oliver 2001; Povinelli 2002). This problem arises, at the most fundamental level, because understanding the world and others through identitarian recognition converges upon 'things' in the world and brings the knower into being as a 'thing'. Recognition helps to bring into being an autonomous knowing self for whom a variety of faculties, including 'perception, memory, imagination, understanding … relate themselves to a form of identity in the object' (Deleuze 1994, 133). This 'is the meaning of the Cogito as a beginning: it expresses the unity of all the faculties in the subject' (133).

The recognition of 'cultures' and ethnic groups as things is the natural companion of recognition as a procedure for generating autonomous knowing European selves and supporting European knowledge and related projects. As Roy Wagner famously noted, 'the study of culture is in fact our culture; it operates through our forms, creates in our terms, borrows our words and concepts for its meanings, and re-creates us through our efforts' (Wagner 1975, 16). One result is that in many cases cultures and ethnicities have been produced as categorical entities and identities through colonial practices (Mamdani 2012), and subsequently in security, development, and peacebuilding scholarship and practice. Establishing firm boundaries and differences between cultures is, of course, one factor in the generation of ethno-conflict (Bargués-Pedreny and Mathieu 2018, 288–289). This is not to say that differences mobilized through boundary-making are not real, but rather to point out that difference in peacebuilding tends to be conceptualized in European-derived identitarian terms. This, in turn, can have negative effects and may not accord with people's self-descriptions and cosmologies.

The broad influence of identitarian thought in dominant scholarship is not, though, synonymous with *identity theory* in the social sciences, nor does it follow that all scholarship follows the identitarian pattern. Many variants of identity theory, for instance, stem from the work of key scholars such as George Herbert Mead and Erving Goffman, who place great emphasis on the generative and crucial role of interaction for forming individual identities, for a classic in the field, see McCall and Simmons 1978.) I use the term identitarianism not to point to identity theory, but to point to the tendency – over and above interactionist analyses of social identities – to seek out and describe entities and things even where this manifestly requires forgetting the interactions that generate individual and social wholes.

Despite the influence of identitarian thought, scholarship in the social sciences and humanities is paying increasing attention to the central importance of interactions, exchanges, and relations (for a sample, see Benjamin 2015; Emirbayer 1997; Massumi 2002; Nexon 2010; Venn 2010). Even more broadly, thinkers working in diverse fields – including relational biology, complexity theory, chaos theory, complex adaptive systems, emergence and related paradigms (e.g. Miller and Page 2007; Rosen 2000; Urry 2003) – are foregrounding the importance of relations in ways that render entities rather more unstable and contingent than has hitherto been conceived. From this standpoint, organs, organisms, ecosystems, natural phenomena, and animal and human social systems cannot be understood through Newtonian and Cartesian analyses that focus on discrete entities set in relationship with each other in mechanistic terms. Instead, a wide variety of phenomena might be understood as continuous as much as discrete, with 'things' not straightforwardly coherent but instead arising from the ongoing and evolving effects of relations.

'Relationality' can be provisionally defined as giving greater conceptual importance – and in some cases priority – to relations over entities by attending to the effects of interactions and exchanges. Rather than converging and fixing upon entities, or 'things' that are taken to be internally consistent and to have the character of 'substance' which sets them apart from other things, relationality turns attention to mobile relations that bring entities and things into being. This move represents a challenge to – and in some cases a reversal of – the pattern of thinking that has become dominant in the mainstream formal western knowledge of recent centuries. Relationality disrupts conventional approaches to difference because it eschews 'identitarian' thought. It does not – indeed cannot – recognize difference as fixed because it gives priority to being in relation. Brian Massumi terms this 'the being of the middle – the being of a relation' (Massumi 2002, 70).

The relatively recent interest in relationality in contemporary disciplines has some very old counterparts. There are antecedents and analogues for relationality in many knowledge, spiritual, and religious traditions around the world, as well as in minor traditions of dominant scholarship. Some of these are well known and renowned, even fabled, such as the cases of Daoism and Buddhism, which evoke deep interconnectedness among people and the world, including through recent manifestations such as the 'order of interbeing' established by Vietnamese monk Thích Nhất Hạnh in the 1960s.

Mystical traditions within Judaism similarly emphasize infinity-oriented process–relational thinking as the source of the divine (Cooper 1997). Mystical Judaism has also been influential in the relational scholarship of the likes of Martin Buber (Buber [1937] 2004, [1947] 1961) and Emmanuel Levinas (Levinas 1986, 1991a, 1991b). Within the secular western tradition, the Greek philosopher Heraclitus – though his famous dictum 'everything flows' (or 'streams') – is a precursor for contemporary relational thought, as is the English philosopher–mathematician Alfred North Whitehead. Some of the most spectacular and provocative scholarship evoking relational principles has arisen though quantum physics (see Nadeau and Kafatos 2001), with one of the most recent attempts to translate this into social science coming from international relations theorist Alexander Wendt (see Wendt 2015).

Many indigenous peoples also foreground relationality, and this is the case among the Aboriginal Australian peoples, the world's oldest living culture (60,000 years according to conservative estimates). One pathway into indigenous relationalities, offered by Australian Aboriginal philosopher Mary Graham, is the maxim that the 'land is the law', by which she means that relations between people and land serve as a template for social and political order (Graham 1999, 106). Land participates in a reciprocal relation with human beings, serving as a poetic ordering principle for guiding relations among people. The landscape – and more particularly, the places within it – brings humans and all of existence into being. Multiple places are related with each other, and so it is with humans. Within this schema individuality is not centred on the idea of a rational, autonomous self who is positioned against others and the world, alone as a discrete entity or conscious isolate; instead, meaning is sought and sociopolitical order is produced in a relational register.

Contra the Cartesian precept 'I think therefore I am', the Aboriginal precept is 'I am located therefore I am' (personal communication with Mary Graham, 15 April 2016). Locatedness in land implies relationship and responsibilities – with kin, totems, and ancestors, and hence with (elements of) the non-human world. Within this order, existence, security, and stability – whether for oneself or one's group – is secured through extending and maintaining relations. Australian Aboriginal relationalities resonate with those of other Indigenous people. Regarding selfhood, for instance, Jarrad Reddekop suggests that the Ojibwe self is 'not closed off and outside/over-against the world but embedded and opened out into it' (Reddekop 2014, 127). The implication is not that a discrete individual is simply *open* to the world, but that she or he is *opened* to it in her or his very being – 'exfoliated', as Jose Gil puts it (Gil 1998, 126). Within this relational register, phenomena such as dreams and visions – which in an identitarian tradition are typically cast as the internal mental activity of a discrete and autonomous self – are channels to the world, including channels for communicating and knowing with the non-human world (Reddekop 2014, 127–8).

The relational turn in the remunerated and professional academy – borne of societies that split public and private, professional and personal through the specialization of knowledge work – is a predominantly intellectual exercise. However, indigenous relationalities are, notwithstanding the damaging impact of colonialism, predominantly lived and lodged in *place* as a cosmological register for everyday existence. Within this schema the difference of each being arises through its relation with the difference of other human and non-human forms and forces of the world. The formulation is less abstract than, but resonates with, the 'being of relation' suggested by Massumi (2002, 70); because places and species and landscapes vary, people who have formulated their culture and existence through imbrication with the differences of the world similarly foreground difference in relation (Graham 1999). Each person comes into existence by coinciding with itself and differences in relation – totems, kin, and ancestors, for instance. One becomes a self in relation with – and as – a totem or ancestor.

There are, then, a range of relational theoretical resources, both new and old, for moving beyond identitarian approaches to conceptualizing difference in peacebuilding. The foregoing discussion only sketches the broad outlines of a small selection of such underappreciated theoretical approaches – but by drawing upon these resources, peace-building may be able to put to one side conventional ways of thinking about difference. In particular, drawing upon cutting-edge scholarship and diverse knowledge traditions – including those of indigenous traditions in the environments where peacebuilders operate – it should be possible to avoid attempting to know difference as a 'thing'. In this way peacebuilding might avoid returning to its own forms of thought and come into engagement with the ways in which people conceptualize their difference on their own terms. This may, in turn, provide a platform for avoiding untenable hierarchical con-tradictions of contemporary approaches to difference in peacebuilding, and avoid related problems such as the facilitation of ethno-conflict through seeing difference as unduly bounded and identitarian.

My argument thus far resonates with de-essentializing approaches in which difference is seen as fluid, contested, and contestable. Indeed, a relational approach to difference does have the effect of de-essentializing understandings of difference. However, as noted in the introduction, anti-essentialist arguments tend towards a flat pluralism in which difference can have no meaningful purchase in a world that is framed and governed through Euro-pean-derived liberal globalism. Anti-essentialism responds to shortfalls in identitarian think-ing yet, in the process, the grounds upon which people may claim difference and resist dominance – including the framing and control of their lives – are undermined. Moreover, because essentialism is an effect of identitarianism, anti-essentialism responds to a symptom of identitarianism rather than its underlying cause. It is unsurprising, then, that peacebuilders who attempt to recognize difference through anti-essentialism turn to liberal globalism – including modern rule of law and international human rights – for key ethical and political referents. The interlinked problems of identitarianism and essentialism thus need to be tackled in a more fundamental way. As I have shown thus far, relationality – drawn from a variety of knowledge and cultural traditions – provides an avenue for funda-mentally moving beyond identitarianism. As the next section shows, relationality also offers a far more ambitious outlook than anti-essentialism, and this includes turning anti-essenti-alism on its head. My argument is that relationality is better paired with an argument that difference is *essential* than with anti-essentialism. To develop this argument I turn first to pioneer conflict-resolution theorist and relational thinker Mary Parker Follett, and then to contemporary feminist philosopher Elizabeth Grosz.

Essential difference

Mary Parker Follett deployed relational theorizing to rethink ways of managing conflict, yet her relational approach also led her to a strikingly novel interpretation of difference. Follett was active in the United States (US) in the late nineteenth and early twentieth centuries, but it is only in recent decades that she is increasingly and belatedly becoming recognized as an important figure in the development of conflict resolution and the American pragmatist philosophical tradition. Follett is most well known in conflict resolution for her advocacy of 'integrative' and creative approaches to conflict which, in the archetypal interaction between two parties, generates a 'solution … in which both [of their] desires have found a place' (Follett 1941, 32). Because integration promotes open communication and collaboration to broaden the zone of possible agreement for all parties, it is very different from the classical compromise or bargain between entities that predominates in the idiom of rational choice and bargaining. Follett's frustration with commonplace efforts is thinly veiled, alongside her advocacy of integration: compromise 'does not create, it deals with what already exists; integration creates something new' (35).

Of difference, Follett states that '[t]he essence of society is difference, related difference' (Follett [1918] 1998, 33). Difference and integration are not incompatible, moreover, because – in a relational frame in which phenomena can be continuous as well as discrete – 'we can at the same moment be the self and the other … we can be forever apart and forever united' (33). Among her other striking claims about difference are the following: 'We may wish to abolish conflict, but we cannot get rid of diversity. We must face life as it is and understand that diversity is its most essential feature … Fear of difference is dread of life itself' (Follett 1941, 31). Follett does not appear to elaborate substantially on these points, so there is a need to further develop her thinking, including by drawing upon other theoretical resources. Developing these threads of thinking also requires bold innovation because to speak of 'life' and 'life itself' is to make large and bold claims typically beyond those made by today's theorists of difference, focused as they tend to be on the social and the cultural.

One resource for building upon Follett can be found in Elizabeth Grosz's bold and innovative form of feminism of difference. Grosz (2004, 2005, 2008) provides a startling and provocative set of feminist insights by re-reading Charles Darwin (alongside others, including Nietzsche and Bergson in *The Nick of Time*). She shows that difference – both sexed and cultural – is essential because it arises as central to life in response to the 'problems that nature poses to the living' (Grosz 2005, 51). In this frame, Darwin's natural selection is 'a theory of the becoming of life, and of the human, from earlier forms of life, a becoming made possible only by reproduction, and primarily by sexual reproduction' (Grosz 2013, 4). This encompassing view places the human as continuous with life, neither trading in the nature–culture split nor engaging in the reductionism that is usually associated with engaging with the material and biological world. In this frame the forces of nature 'have enabled rather than inhibited cultural and political production' (Grosz 2008, 2). The problem of essentializing and narrowing discussions of difference, diagnosed by contemporary cultural and political theorists, thus lies not with Darwin but, rather ironically, with the sociobiological essentialism that proudly flies the flag of Darwin's legacy.

Against reductionist understandings, Grosz argues that Darwin is 'the first and most significant theorist of difference as the engine of becoming' because he 'devised a theory of species as vast series of differences within forms of resemblance' (Grosz 2013, 4). This is a profoundly relational approach because it inverts the traditional dominance of identities over relations by foregrounding the play of differences: 'Difference is the "principle of identity" for all identities to the extent that no entity is self-producing or self-identical, with each entity and relation a product of the encounter of differences of different things and different orders' (4).

Grosz hereby overturns, via Darwin, the conventional positioning of identitarian and relational thought. All living entities derive from relations of difference, so it is this difference which is essential. Crucially, making such difference essential does not involve 'essentializing' because what is hereby seen as essential is not any given entity but instead the principles and processes of differentiation, which is both fundamental to life itself and in continual flux.

Grosz shows that Darwin does not account for social and cultural difference by reducing them to biology in the manner of sociobiology or other means; for Darwin there is no simple nature–culture split, so 'the biological structure of man in no way pre-empts the forms of social organization within which he will live', meaning that culture is not a derivative or culmination of nature but rather the 'ramifying product and effect of a nature that is ever prodigious in its techniques of production and selection' (Grosz 2004, 89). Grosz points out that Darwin consistently converts differences of *kind* into differences of *degree* (61). In this schema, man, for instance, has no intrinsically particular or unique standing. Darwin suggests that 'some of the rudiments or preconditions for language, and all the other contenders for distinctively human attributes [such as learning, reason, and problem-solving] are there in animals, simply awaiting adequate stimulus and development' (59). Differences in kind, between species, take shape through natural selection, but difference itself – in terms of sexed difference, genetic variation, and its ramifying effects on culture – is the engine.

It is indeed, then, difference that is life's most essential feature, as Follett ([1918] 1998, 33) says. 'According to Darwinian precepts, culture is not different in kind from nature' (Grosz 2004, 59). Here it is important to note that Darwin does not think of nature (or culture) in the ways that are usually attributed to him and taken up by many in the natural sciences. Natural selection is not a limited and knowable battleground that allows us to interpret human behaviour in reductionist ways; rather, evolution has no particular trajectory or direction – it produces variety and change incessantly without any particular ends, although in ways that are spectacularly creative and essential to the survival of life itself. The effect of evolution is life as we know it, but this life is highly contingent on the difference essential to its realization. In this schema, culture is not the overcoming of nature or its logical end point; rather, change and the future arise from the relational interplay of cultural–biological–environmental factors such that 'each culture [is] a surprise to and a development of nature itself' (59). Difference of all types, including social and cultural diversity, is the non-teleological engine of life on Earth.

Darwin's natural selection, then, is at bottom a relational (interactive) process in line with Follett's relational thought. Follett's statement that we can be 'forever apart and forever united' (1918 [1998], 33) also takes on greater sense and meaning in Grosz's reading of Darwin. We are apart and united *through* difference. At the risk of simplicity, relational difference is what we share, for it is the sacred and sublime force which makes us who we are. Difference is the essential shared phenomenon, and engaging with it opens to the world rather than returning to the knower. It is not, as occurs in identitarian thought, the name for the demarcating of a bounded and identitarian phenomenon that asserts the autonomy of the knower and risks division in the world. Grosz thus shows that difference is essential without taking differences of a kind as fixed or as essences. Each living being comes into existence by coinciding with itself in relation to other differences that are, in turn, also set in relation. Adopting this stance involves, following Brian Massumi, aligning 'with a logic of relation', or the 'being of a relation' (Massumi 2002, 70). Because each entity is an effect of related difference and is invariably dynamic, it cannot be conceptualized in identitarian or essentialist terms.

No doubt it may be hard for some theorists of difference to shake off discomfort about parleying with nature, but there are good reasons for doing so. Discomfort in relation to engaging with nature can in part be attributed simply to the strength of the nature–culture split in dominant European-derived scholarship. While numerous forms of domination – racism and patriarchy in particular – are mobilized and perpetuated through discourses of 'nature', this is no reason for theorists of difference to repeat the problem in inverse form by continuing to reproduce – in the face of considerable critique and alternatives such as those on offer through Darwin – the nature–culture distinction. Second, as Grosz points out, 'there is a certain absurdity in objecting to the notion of nature or biology itself if this is (even in part) what we are and always will be' (2005, 13). Part of the challenge, instead, is to understand how biological and cultural life interact. Finally, and as discussed in the first section, many peoples in world history have developed complex forms of knowledge and ways of being that do not entertain the nature–culture split but instead actively weave 'nature' and 'culture' together. Reluctance to consider nature and culture together may be a rather perverse and recent affliction that is somewhat unique to progressive scholarship about difference.

Relational difference offers a far richer and more appropriate foundation for theorizing difference in peacebuilding than approaches that merely de-essentialize difference. While de-essentialization responds to the problems of essentialism that arise from identitarian thought, it does so by reacting to symptoms and, in turn, diminishing difference by suggesting that it has no essence. In contrast, Follett and Grosz help us to understand how relational difference is essential to life itself in all its forms. In this frame, difference is fluid and contingent but essential to life in ways which suggest that it deserves to be taken far more seriously than is implied by de-essentializing approaches. Because difference is central to life and part of our response to nature and our environment, it simultaneously binds us together and holds us apart from each other. In this way difference may be of a people and of a place in ways that de-essentializing approaches do not countenance. Difference thus deserves to be thought of not as a matter of identity or lifestyle but as a sacred and sublime phenomenon that makes us (respectively) who we are, and engaging with this phenomenon in a serious manner is essential to the development of peaceful responses to instances of human differences. To concretize this proposition, the next section stages an encounter with Australian Aboriginal difference.

Knowing indigenous difference for peacebuilding?

Indigenous difference is difference par excellence for peacebuilding because it is indigenous dispossession which founds the New World and the modern international system, and which nurtures some of the loudest voices for the pursuit of progressive peace (see Byrd 2011). The hierarchical contradictions embedded within identitarian and de-essentializing approaches to difference in contemporary peacebuilding have their very foundation in colonial regimes that cast indigenous peoples, on an ongoing basis, as simultaneously autochthonous (of the land/place) and subject to imported political orders. European-derived engagements with difference and efforts to build peace proceed by simultaneously sustaining and denying the colonial violence of Indigenous dispossession. What would it mean, then, to attempt to reverse dominant patterns of knowing difference in peacebuilding in the colonial heartland of settler–colonial states through the relational–essential frame developed thus far? And what might this suggest for engaging difference more broadly in peacebuilding? This section considers, in an abbreviated overview enumerated in four steps, how a relational–essential approach might be deployed to support engagement with Australian Aboriginal people. Writing about another people's being is obviously sensitive, and for this reason I aim only to evoke for illustrative purposes (rather than to specify). I also offer a further overall caveat by putting a question mark over this section.

First, responding to difference through a relational–essential frame requires foregrounding not the theoretical *frame* per se but the act of relating in combination with according difference the respect that comes with viewing it as essential. A relational–essential approach therefore cannot assume an overarching a-priori standing vis-à-vis the world and others, as occurs through the identitarian and de-essentializing approaches which permeate most dominant approaches to peacebuilding and which assume that the international peacebuilder – and the knowledge tradition to which she or he belongs – holds the necessary authority and capacity to know the world over and above the recipients or 'others' of peacebuilding. Instead of knowing through and recreating European-derived forms and meanings, the first move in a relational–essential approach thus acknowledges other registers and forms of knowing, which involves demoting the usually ascendant figure of the one who knows by placing him or her into relationships with others.

Taking this step challenges dominant scholarship by placing knowing in the world of interaction rather than over and above the world and the peoples who inhabit it. Doing so is no doubt unsettling for some as it renders knowing, including the very viability of the relational–essential approach that is being brought to bear, contingent upon interaction with the knowledge schemas and ways of being of the peoples encountered through peacebuilding practice. Peacebuilders are not accustomed to having their frames of reference brought into question to this extent; however, they are often familiar with dealing with high levels of uncertainty and contingency in the field, and are capable of negotiating these circumstances in order to undertake programmes and projects that support the conditions for peace. Bringing these capacities to bear suffices to develop shared commitments and processes between international peacebuilders and local peoples.

This first move may take the form of an in-principle commitment that guides interaction with people in the field and, in many cases, an acknowledgement of pre-existing knowledge traditions, including forms of political ordering, managing conflict, and securing and maintaining peace. In the case of Aboriginal Australia, this requires acknowledging the primacy of Aboriginal thought on the Australian continent (Muecke 2009, 209), including – as discussed in the first section – remarkably long-standing ways of knowing (greater than 60,000 years) that link peoples with places and the elaboration of sophisticated forms of political order, governance, and conflict management. In this system, reciprocal relations between places and people provide the foundation for sociopolitical ordering.

The understanding and acknowledgements developed in this first step must be continually applied in encountering the difference at hand in any given case.

Second, adopting a relational–essential approach avoids attempting to understand peoples' difference – that which sets people apart from others – as a fixed phenomenon and instead experiments with relational rather than identitarian understandings of difference. To be sure, some amount of purely descriptive analysis of who people understand themselves to be is valuable and necessary, but this should be paired with attention to the mobile relations – historical, contemporary, and ongoing – that bring people into being. In the case of Aboriginal Australia, the relations that bring people into being are profoundly divided into two parts by the experience of British colonization. The available evidence suggests that until colonization impacted heavily upon individual Australian Aboriginal peoples (several hundred at the time of contact), people came into being, primarily, through the ontogenetic relationships established with places in their respective landscapes, as described above. It seems that contact and relationships with neighbouring groups (for trade, ceremony, resource-sharing, and intermarriage) were also significant, although these were also mediated through the system of relations established through place and landscape. On some parts of the continent, relations with others (e.g. people from present-day Indonesia) may have also played a role in people's self-understanding.

British colonization profoundly disrupts (but does not eliminate) precolonial self-understandings, and in time it generates a secondary set of equally complicated self-understandings, this time in terms of 'Aboriginality' in relation to the incoming settler regime. Successive policy approaches apply a shifting mix of policy instruments that, as in other encounters between indigenous peoples and colonial states, variously and paradoxically set about destroying, creating, and incorporating indigenous peoples (Sider 1987). Aboriginal people, in turn, attempt to secure some rights in the context of a grossly asymmetrical relationship with the colonizer by variously drawing upon both their own and colonizers' understandings of justice and political order. These dynamics are inextricably bound with settlers or newcomers to Aboriginal lands, thus reiterating the centrality of relationship with would-be peacebuilders of today.

Third, within a relational–essential approach, interpreting Aboriginal difference in relational terms is not a de-essentializing device for pointing to the contingency and fluidity of Aboriginality. Rather, it is a means of seeking to understand how Aboriginal difference is essential – that is, it does not assert that Aboriginality is unreal for having formed through relations, but asks what, in indigenous terms, might be essential about Aboriginality. The relational is not relativist, in other words. Absolutes exist within relationally established orders, even though they do not necessarily arise through science or take the form which modernity imagines that they should. At the broadest level, Aboriginal absolutes are likely to take the form of a particular type of ancient connection lodged in the land and a form of sociopolitical ordering (described above) which is mobilized today against the onslaught of colonial violence (Muecke 2009). This type of stance is simultaneously a statement of difference and a negotiating position which the colonizer–peacebuilder may, from his or her position in a very different set of political and power relations, enter into relation and exchange with.

Fourth, the foregoing macroscopic application of a relational–essential approach to difference can be brought to bear upon peacebuilding practice in concrete and particular terms. In 2007, the Aboriginal community of Mornington Island was chosen by the

Australian attorney-general's department as the location for the establishment of a restorative justice programme (for a project report, see Venables 2012). As the project rolled out, and in response to Aboriginal scepticism, the project manager and steering group successfully advocated – with the government agency delivering the project and against initial plans – for a consultation approach that responded to Aboriginal difference articulated in Aboriginal terms. In particular, consultations proceeded according to the local kinship system. During the consultations, the Aboriginal people partially appropriated the project as a customary initiative, with the result that their kinship system informed the development and operation of a hybridized mediation model (see Brigg et al. 2017). This process represents a successful negotiation between two social–legal orders, and it led to a highly effective peacebuilding intervention (see Colmar Brunton 2014). The Aboriginal difference articulated by the project was relationally formed through the kinship system, through (largely negative) interactions with the colonial society, and through contemporary relations with government. The project manager engaged with Aboriginal difference thus-formed as essential (though not as an essence). Difference was taken to be both relational and essential; thus, the project and its design, implementation, and success were underpinned by a relational–essential approach to difference.

Conclusion

Peacebuilding has begun to engage with difference, but thus far its ways of doing so have tended to be characterized by relatively conventional scholarly approaches. The two dominant tendencies are to approach difference in 'identitarian' terms: as a 'thing', or – in order to counter the essentializing tendencies of identitarian thought – to de-essentialize difference. Although apparently contradictory, these two approaches are fused in a long and problematic history of European engagements with difference through a tendency to simultaneously identify difference and minimize it. The contemporary liberal politics of recognition and multiculturalism are the most recent incarnation of this approach. While recognition-multiculturalism ostensibly represents a platform for respectful engagement with difference, it tends to mark out difference as a thing and to minimize its capacity to exert purchase over the ordering of political life, including the management of conflict. This pattern repeats in contemporary peacebuilding practice in the form of untenable contradictions arising from a discourse about respect for difference yet reticence to draw seriously upon non-western and non-liberal approaches to political ordering and conflict management or resolution.

In response to dominant tendencies to think of difference in identitiarian or de-essentializing terms, this article has theorized difference as *relational* and *essential*. Relational thought, found in diverse cultural and knowledge traditions as well as in cutting-edge contemporary scholarship, gives greater conceptual importance – and in some cases priority – to relations rather than things, and therefore foregrounds interactions and exchanges. Drawing upon relationality avoids attempting to know difference as a 'thing' and potentially connects with diverse cultures and knowledge traditions that are routinely encountered in peacebuilding practice. This provides a potential platform that peacebuilders can use to avoid returning to dominant forms of thought and to come into engagement with the ways in which people conceptualize difference on their own terms. This in turn may help to avoid the untenable hierarchical contradictions of contemporary approaches to difference in peacebuilding, while also sidestepping the facilitation of ethno-conflict through seeing difference as unduly bounded and identitarian. Relationality also offers a powerful counter to anti-essentialism. Indeed, I have demonstrated that relationality inverts anti-essentialism by showing – following Follett in combination with Grosz's reading of Darwin – that difference is essential to life itself.

While de-essentializing difference responds to the symptoms of essentialism that arise from identitarian thought, a relational approach offers a more fundamental and effective remedy. Relationality shows that difference is fluid and contingent, but it helps us to understand that difference is no less essential for arising in this way. Indeed, as Grosz shows in her reading of Darwin, continuously mobile difference is necessary for life itself, including through an ongoing engagement with nature, environment, and biology. Difference is thus a sacred and sublime phenomenon that makes us who we are, simultaneously binding us together and holding us apart from each other. Applying a relational–essential approach to peacebuilding requires acknowledging that difference arises relationally yet is no less essential for this. Several steps are suggested to operationalize such an approach, beginning, naturally enough, with the need to put the relational–essential frame into exchange as dictated by relational encounters with peoples' difference. Beyond this, relationality helps to move past both identitarian and de-essentializing renderings of difference in ways that enable difference to stand on its own terms in the context of peacebuilding interventions, as demonstrated through the micro-case of a restorative justice project in Aboriginal Australia.

Acknowledgements

My thanks to the editors of this special issue and to the anonymous reviewers.

Disclosure statement

No potential conflict of interest was reported by the author.

References

Anghie, Antony. 1996. 'Francisco De Vitoria and the Colonial Origins of International Law.' *Social & Legal Studies* 5 (3): 321–336. doi:10.1177/096466399600500303

Anghie, Antony. 2004. *Imperialism, Sovereignty, and the Making of International Law*. Cambridge: Cambridge University Press.

Aristotle. 1941. *Basic Works*. Edited by Richard McKeon. New York: Random House.

Bargués-Pedreny, P., and X. Mathieu. 2018. 'Beyond Silence, Obstacle and Stigma: Revisiting the "Problem" of Difference in Peacebuilding.' *Journal of Intervention and Statebuilding* 12 (3): 283–299.

Benjamin, Andrew. 2015. *Towards a Relational Ontology: Philosophy's Other Possibility*. New York: State University of New York Press.

Brigg, Morgan, Paul Memmott, Philip Venables, and Berry Zondag. 2017. 'Gununa Peacemaking: Informalism, Cultural Difference and Contemporary Indigenous Conflict Management.' *Social and Legal Studies* 27 (3): 345–366. doi:10.1177/0964663917719955.

Buber, Martin. (1937) 2004. *I and Thou*. London: Continuum.

Buber, Martin. (1947) 1961. *Between Man and Man*. Translated by Ronald Gregor-Smith. London: Collins.

Byrd, Jodi A. 2011. *The Transit of Empire: Indigenous Critiques of Colonialism*. Minneapolis: University of Minnesota Press.

Colmar, Brunton. 2014. *Mornington Island Restorative Justice Project Evaluation: Final Report*. Canberra: Commonwealth of Australia.

Cooper, David A. 1997. *God Is a Verb: Kabbalah and the Practice of Mystical Judaism*. New York: Riverhead Books.

Coulthard, Glen S. 2014. *Red Skin, White Masks: Rejecting the Colonial Politics of Recognition*. Minneapolis: University of Minnesota Press.

Deleuze, Gilles. 1994. *Difference and Repetition*. London: Athlone Press.

Emirbayer, Mustafa. 1997. 'Manifesto for a Relational Sociology.' *American Journal of Sociology* 103 (2): 281–317. doi.org/10.1086/231209.

Follett, Mary Parker. (1918) 1998. *The New State: Group Organization, the Solution of Popular Government*. University Park: Pennsylvania State University Press.

Follett, Mary Parker. 1941. *Dynamic Administration: The Collected Papers of Mary Parker Follett*. Edited by Herny C. Metcalf and L. Urwick. London: Pitman.

Gil, Jose. 1998. *Metamorphoses of the Body*. Minneapolis: University of Minnesota Press.

Graham, Mary. 1999. 'Some Thoughts about the Philosophical Underpinnings of Aboriginal Worldviews.' *Worldviews: Global Religions, Culture, and Ecology* 3 (2): 105–118. doi:10.1163/156853599X00090.

Grosz, Elizabeth. 2004. *The Nick of Time: Politics, Evolution and the Untimely*. Crows Nest: Allen & Unwin.

Grosz, Elizabeth. 2005. *Time Travels: Feminism, Nature, Power*. Crows Nest: Allen & Unwin.

Grosz, Elizabeth. 2008. *Chaos, Territory, Art: Deleuze and the Framing of the Earth*. New York: Columbia University Press.

Grosz, Elizabeth. 2013. 'Significant Differences: An Interview with Elizabeth Grosz.' *Interstitial Journal*. https://interstitialjournal.files.wordpress.com/2013/03/grosz-interview1.pdf.

Latour, Bruno. 2002. *War of the Worlds: What about Peace?* Translated by Charlotte Bigg. Chicago: Prickly Paradigm Press.

Levinas, Emmanuel. 1986. 'The Trace of the Other.' Translated by Alphonso Lingis. In *Deconstruction in Context*, edited by Mark C. Taylor, 346–359. Chicago: Chicago University Press.

Levinas, Emmanuel. 1991a. *Otherwise Than Being or Beyond Essence*. Translated by Alphonso Lingis. Dordrecht: Kluwer Academic.

Levinas, Emmanuel. 1991b. *Totality and Infinity*. Translated by Alphnso Lingis. Dordrecht: Kluwer Academic.

Mamdani, Mahmood. 2012. *Define and Rule: Native as Political Identity*. Cambridge, MA: Harvard University Press.

Massumi, Brian. 2002. *Parables for the Virtual: Movement, Affect, Sensation*. Durham, NC: Duke University Press.

McCall, George J., and J. L. Simmons. 1978. *Identities and Interactions: An Examination of Human Associations in Everyday Life*. New York: Macmillan.

Miller, John H., and Scott E. Page. 2007. *Complex Adaptive Systems: An Introduction to Computational Models of Social Life*. Princeton: Princeton University Press.

Muecke, Stephen. 2009. 'Cultural Science? The Ecological Critique of Modernity and the Conceptual Habitat of the Humanities.' *Cultural Studies* 23 (3): 404–416. doi:10.1080/09502380902858000.

Nadeau, Robert, and Menas Kafatos. 2001. *The Non-Local Universe: The New Physics and Matters of the Mind*. Oxford: Oxford University Press.

Nexon, Daniel H. 2010. 'Relationalism and New Systems Theory.' In *New Systems Theories of World Politics*, edited by Mathias Albert, Lars-Erik Cederman, and Alexander Wendt, 99–126. New York: Palgrave.

Oliver, Kelly. 2001. *Witnessing: Beyond Recognition*. Minneapolis: University of Minnesota Press.

Povinelli, E. 2002. *The Cunning of Recognition: Indigenous Alterities and the Making of Australian Multiculturalism*. Durham, NC: Duke University Press.

Reddekop, Jarrad. 2014. 'Thinking across Worlds: Indigenous Thought, Relational Ontology, and the Politics of Nature; or, If Only Nietzsche Could Meet A Yachaj.' PhD diss., University of Western Ontario.

Rosen, Robert 2000. *Essays on Life Itself*. New York: Columbia University Press.

Sider, Gerald. 1987. 'When Parrots Learn to Talk, and Why They Can't: Domination, Deception, and Self-Deception in Indian–White Relations.' *Comparative Studies in Society and History* 29 (1): 3–23. doi:10.1017/S0010417500014328.

Urry, John. 2003. *Global Complexity*. Cambridge, MA: Polity.

Venables, Phil. 2012. *Mornington Island Restorative Justice (MIRJ) Project: Report on Its Development, Implementation and Transition to Community Management 2012*. Brisbane: Queensland Government.

Venn, Couze. 2010. 'Individuation, Relationality, Affect: Rethinking the Human in Relation to the Living.' *Body & Society* 16 (1): 129–161. doi:10.1177/1357034X09354770.

Wagner, Roy. 1975. *The Invention of Culture*. Englewood Cliffs, NJ: Prentice-Hall.

Wendt, Alexander. 2015. *Quantum Mind and Social Science: Unifying Physical and Social Ontology*. Cambridge: Cambridge University Press.

Williams, Robert A., Jr. 1986. 'The Algebra of Federal Indian Law: The Hard Trail of Decolonizing and Americanizing the White Man's Indian Jurisprudence.' *Wisconsin Law Review* 219: 219–299.

The Politics of Difference in Transitional Justice: Genocide and the Construction of Victimhood at the Khmer Rouge Tribunal

Julie Bernath

ABSTRACT

Although aiming to disrupt the othering that enables political violence and mass victimization, transitional justice processes – which are integral to international peacebuilding – may also (re)produce difference in intricate and possibly problematic ways. This article argues that as this dilemma is inherent to the politics of difference, it is crucial to consider how difference is constructed in transitional justice processes, and with what consequences, as this can feed into problematic processes of othering. This article focuses on the genocide charges at the Khmer Rouge tribunal in Cambodia, using transcripts of the legal proceedings and qualitative fieldwork conducted between 2013 and 2018.

Introduction

The United Nations (UN) defines transitional justice as the 'full range of processes and mechanisms associated with a society's attempts to come to terms with a legacy of large-scale past abuses, in order to ensure accountability, serve justice and achieve reconciliation' (UNSC 2004, 4). Although transitional justice has emerged as a distinct field of policy, research, and practice in relation to the transitions from authoritarian regimes during the third wave of democratizations in Latin America and Eastern Europe, transitional justice processes have increasingly been deployed in so-called 'post-conflict' contexts, thus becoming an integral part of international peacebuilding interventions (Sriram 2007).

The question of difference is at the core of peacebuilding debates, and has permeated critical scholarship on transitional justice too. Although the notion of difference is not explicitly mobilized, questions related to how to deal with distinct interpretations of justice and peace have been raised in the context of the field's epistemological turn to the 'local' (e.g. Shaw and Waldorf 2010). Whilst being cautious not to romanticize local understandings, researchers have increasingly questioned the ways in which local responses to mass atrocities differ from the practices that are circulated, reproduced, and promoted in international interventions. Taking an actor-oriented perspective 'from below' (McEvoy and McGregor 2008) indeed raises unsettling questions in relation to the instruments, practices, and proclaimed aims of transitional justice interventions. This scholarship highlights how the notions of justice, accountability, and reconciliation may mean very different things in different contexts, as well as encapsulate multiple meanings within a single context.

These discussions echo the academic debates of the local turn in research on peacebuilding, even though the scholarships on peacebuilding and transitional justice seem to run on parallel tracks rather than constituting an integrated academic field (Sharp 2013). Scholars have indeed started to locate transitional justice as an integral part of liberal peace, illustrating how peacebuilding and transitional justice both represent 'discourses and practices of intervention aimed at (post)violent societies' (Baker and Obradović-Wochnik 2016, 281). As such, critical scholarship analyses transitional justice as a political project and questions the types of knowledge, needs, and practices that are made to count in the field. Some scholars have for instance identified how transitional justice sidelines certain justice claims, such as socio-economic justice (Lai 2016) and gender justice (Buckley-Zistel and Stanley 2011), while others have explored how transitional justice is linked to the invisibility of certain categories of harm, such as the violation of economic, social, and cultural rights (Schmid 2015), structural inequalities (Miller 2008), and gender-based violence. In analysing transitional justice as a political project, scholars have also criticized the dominance of legalistic approaches that construct law as an apolitical tool for intervention (McEvoy 2007).

This scholarship thus questions the ways in which transitional justice interventions, and in particular interventions shaped by legalistic approaches, deny difference when it comes to defining the goals of transitional justice and deciding how to get there. In other words, critical scholarship has engaged with what Bargués-Pedreny and Mathieu (2018) in the introduction to this special issue identify as the first error in peacebuilding when dealing with difference: the silencing of difference.

More recent works have questioned the ways in which different approaches to transitional justice easily become constructed as deviant. In these cases, therefore, resistance to transitional justice is cast as problematic and in need of transformation, belying the political nature of transitional justice interventions (Arnould 2016; Jones and Bernath 2017). The reflections on how resistance to transitional justice is constructed as disruptive can be said to be critiquing what Bargués-Pedreny and Mathieu (2018) call the second error in peacebuilding approaches: the problematization of difference as an obstacle to be assimilated.

But transitional justice scholarship also engages with difference in relation to what may be described as the dilemma inherent to the politics of difference of transitional justice; while transitional justice processes aim at disrupting the processes of othering that initially enable political violence and mass victimization, they may (re)produce difference in intricate ways, or even contribute to essentializing identities. Although the acknowledgment of victims and the ways in which they suffer due to processes of othering and ascribed identities lies at the core of transitional justice endeavours, at least rhetorically, mobilizing these categories of difference may indeed reproduce problematic stereotypes and exclude more fluid identifications in post-conflict contexts (Arthur 2011). This dilemma highlights the ways in which the construction of difference is always relational, as it is linked to the unstated comparison with what is considered to constitute normalcy (Behr 2018). As Minow (1990) argues, rather than being intrinsic to law, difference is 'made to matter' by law in specific ways and in relation to unstated points of reference. The dilemma of the politics of difference in transitional justice therefore illustrates how defining who is different, and in relation to what, constitutes an exercise of power.

These reflections are central to reflections on reconciliation, as well as to more recent works that look at how transitional justice affects identity (Arthur 2011; Wilke 2011). A prominent example refers to the discussions of the International Criminal Tribunal for former Yugoslavia, and the ways in which its findings play into – rather than transform – narratives that strengthen interethnic boundaries (Baker and Obradović-Wochnik 2016). Research on victim participation also examines these questions when analysing how transitional justice has the potential to create problematic victim hierarchies within already divided societies (e.g. Killean 2018).

Drawing from these discussions, this article proposes to analyse how difference is constructed in transitional justice processes, and more specifically in international legal practices, by focusing on the Extraordinary Chambers in the Courts of Cambodia (ECCC). Established in 2004 by the UN and the Cambodian government, and based in the capital city, the ECCC constitutes a so-called 'hybrid' or mixed tribunal, i.e. a court of 'mixed composition and jurisdiction, encompassing both national and international aspects' (OHCHR 2008, 1). Both national and international criminal offences can be prosecuted at the ECCC, and all offices are staffed with national and international personnel. The ECCC's mandate is to bring to justice the senior leaders and those most responsible for the crimes committed during Democratic Kampuchea (DK), also known as the Khmer Rouge regime, between 17 April 1975 and 6 January 1979. The ECCC deals with a relatively small number of suspects. In Case 001, the accused – Kaing Guek Eav, alias Duch, former deputy and chairman of the DK security centre S-21 – was sentenced to life imprisonment in February 2012. Case 002 consists of charges against senior DK leaders and is therefore considered the most important case. Two of the accused however died before the completion of the case. The remaining defendants are Nuon Chea, former deputy secretary of the Communist Party of Kampuchea (CPK), and Khieu Samphan, former head of state. The first portion of the trial, Case 002/01, focused on charges of crimes against humanity in the form of the forced transfer of the population and the execution of soldiers of the Khmer Republic, and was finalized in June 2017. Case 002/02 examines charges of genocide against Vietnamese and Cham minorities, forced marriages and rape, internal purges, the persecution of Buddhists, forced labour in work camps, and cooperatives and crimes committed at security centres. The Trial Chamber judgement in Case 002/02 is still pending at the time of writing. Cases 003, 004, 004/01, and 004/02 concern four suspects indicted under the category of 'most responsible' for crimes committed under DK. It still remains uncertain as to whether, and how, these cases will move to trial.

This article investigates how the ECCC orders and classifies difference when dealing with the crimes committed during the Khmer Rouge regime. How is difference performed during the legal proceedings, and what are the implications for the construction of victimhood in contemporary Cambodia? Whilst the focus lies on the legal institution and practices, this article is primarily interested in the implications and effects of the ways in which the ECCC deals with difference for the victims involved in the transitional justice process.

This article is divided into two parts. The first part provides a brief overview of the processes that were used to manufacture difference under the Khmer Rouge regime, then discusses how these processes were subsequently ordered and classified at the ECCC according to existing legal categories before exploring how the use of different categories has introduced difference between victim groups. The second part analyses the dilemma inherent to the politics of difference at the ECCC. It argues that whilst recognizing the construction of difference in contexts of mass atrocity has a transformative potential, this process can also essentialize identities in ways that disrupt strategies for the assimilation of groups who continue to be subject to discrimination, as well as singling out certain victim groups from collective experiences of suffering.

This article is based upon an analysis of the publicly available transcripts of the legal proceedings related to the genocide charges in Case 002/02, in particular an analysis of all the related testimonies of experts, as well as the Cham and Vietnamese civil parties. It further draws from qualitative, semi-structured interviews conducted between 2013 and 2018 with ECCC staff members, civil society actors, and civil parties on the transitional justice process in Cambodia. However, this article remains exploratory in nature, as the trial proceedings in Case 002/02 are still ongoing. More importantly, additional empirical research on affected victims is necessary in order to analyse in a more systematic manner how the politics of difference play out empirically, how and whether they match the subjective experiences of affected victims, and how they shape the micropolitics of victimhood construction. Indeed, in this regard, this article is based on a limited set of qualitative interviews that were conducted with only four Cham civil parties on their perspectives and experiences of the ECCC genocide charges.

The ECCC and the manufacturing of difference under the Khmer Rouge regime

The manufacturing of difference under the Khmer Rouge regime

Contexts of mass atrocity tend to produce rigid identities and exclude alternative identity constructions, which become either unavailable or unliveable (Wilke 2011, 121). In his analysis of genocidal regimes, anthropologist Alexander Hinton refers to this as the process of 'manufacturing difference':

> Difference is manufactured as genocidal regimes construct, essentialize, and propagate socio-political categories of difference, crystallizing what are normally more fluid forms of identity … stigmatize victim groups in accordance with the differences that are being crystallized … initiate a series of institutional, legal, social, and political changes that transform the conditions under which the targeted victim group live … and inscribe difference on the bodies of the victims … . (Hinton 2005, 33)

Perspectives in the social sciences thus focus on the processes of othering in defining what constitutes genocide. What emerges from this analysis is that the construction of difference is always influenced by the perspectives of the perpetrators and does not rely on supposedly objective criteria that can be proven scientifically. Rather than being static, group categories such as ethnicity, race, and gender constitute 'metaphors of otherness' (Feierstein 2014, 20) that are mobilized in contexts of mass atrocity.

Such processes of manufacturing difference were central to the DK regime. Identities that were previously more fluid became sharpened and essentialized whilst narrowly defined groups became targeted for extermination. In this context, an estimated 1.5 to 2.2 million died, i.e. at least 1 in 5 of the 1975 population.

In spite of its communist rhetoric of building a classless society, the Central Committee of the CPK established a strict social hierarchy. Those who before 17 April 1975 had lived in rural areas controlled by the CPK were classified as 'old' or 'base' people; of this group, those whose relatives had not worked for the former regime were categorized as 'full rights candidates' and could access leading positions within cooperatives (Becker 1989), whereas the rest were subject to particular scrutiny and classed as 'trial candidates' (Dy 2007, 30–31). Those who in April 1975 were forcibly evicted from cities were called the 'new' or '17 April' people; relegated to the bottom of the hierarchy (Dy 2007, 31), they had little access to proper food rations or to the Khmer Rouge cadre's 'benefit of the doubt', in what often amounted to life and death situations (Ponchaud 2001, 74, 132).

The CPK ideology further relied on constant class warfare and revolution, thus requiring a permanent provision of enemies. In February 1975, the CPK leadership decided to exterminate the former cadres of the previous regime, the Khmer Republic (Chandler 1991, 247), and the vague category of 'intellectuals' was also targeted during the forced transfers of the population. In January 1976, the party leadership moved to the 'second stage of revolution', which comprised the elimination of the 'remaining bourgeois elements' (Becker 1989, 246–47). This led to a second wave of executions, with the Buddhist clergy and the ethnic Vietnamese and Muslim minorities particularly targeted.

When the agrarian 'miracle' that had been aspired to did not materialize, the search for enemies was extended to elements that had allegedly infiltrated the CPK's ranks (Becker 1989, 259). As of April 1976, inner party purges increasingly targeted CPK cadres (Chandler 1991, 273). Moreover, in a process of cumulative radicalization, the likelihood of certain groups being perceived as having the ability to 'reform their consciousness' or 'be re-educated' gradually diminished, whilst certain groups were stigmatized to the point of being explicitly targeted for extermination. This applied in particular to the ethnic Vietnamese minority; in the early months of the DK regime, around 150,000 to 170,000 ethnic Vietnamese were forced to leave the country. Almost all of the ethnic Vietnamese who remained in Cambodia were killed.[1] With the growing paranoia of the CPK, the Khmer Krom community that has historically inhabited the Mekong River delta, which became part of southern Vietnam during the twentieth century, also became targeted, designated as 'Vietnamese enemies' (Ciorciari 2008, 2).

The ordering of difference in the legal categories of the ECCC

Almost thirty years later, the ECCC was established in order to examine the individual responsibilities for the crimes committed under the DK regime. The targeting of specific groups on the basis of difference was dealt with under the legal categories of crimes of genocide and crimes against humanity. Both of these crimes are inherently linked to difference, as their legal constitutive elements require the targeting of specific groups on discriminatory grounds (Aptel 2011, 152).

The definition of genocide adopted at the ECCC is based on the UN Convention on the Prevention and Punishment of the Crime of Genocide.[2] It therefore entails a traditional and narrow definition of genocide, as it restricts acts of genocide to crimes targeting a specific set of groups. The ECCC law (article 4) indeed defines genocide as 'any acts committed with the intent to destroy, in whole or in part, a national, ethnical, racial or religious group'.[3] These acts may include:

killing members of the group; causing serious bodily or mental harm to members of the group; deliberately inflicting on the group conditions of life calculated to bring about its physical destruction in whole or in part; imposing measures intended to prevent births within the group; forcibly transferring children from one group to another group.[4]

As a result, the ECCC only examines the crime of genocide against groups that are qualified as national, ethnic, racial, or religious, which includes the Cham group, described as 'an ethnic and religious group', and the Vietnamese minority in Cambodia, presented as 'an ethnic and national group, who may also have been considered as a racial group by the CPK' (ECCC [OCIJ] 2010, §§1336, 1343). After a long invisibility of Khmer Krom victims in the ECCC proceedings (Ciorciari 2008; Mohan 2008), the charge of genocide against this group was included in Case 004.

During the protracted negotiations between the UN and the Royal Government of Cambodia for the establishment of the ECCC, the definition of genocide did not seem to be a matter of contention (Jarvis and Fawthrop 2004, 221),[5] in comparison to more controversial issues such as the court's structure, jurisdiction, and decision-making processes. This is surprising, as it stands in contrast to suggestions at the international policy level to broaden the list of protected groups in the definition of genocide, for instance in the 1985 report of Benjamin Whitaker, then UN Special Rapporteur on the Prevention of Discrimination and the Protection of Minorities (Whitaker 1985). Over the past decades, jurists and judicial and legislative bodies across the world have also adopted broader definitions of genocide. Countries such as Bangladesh, Ivory Coast, Peru, France, and Switzerland have also enlarged their definitions of genocide to include other groups in their penal codes, such as political groups, sexual groups, health groups, and even any type of group (Feierstein 2014, 219, n. 12). These developments acknowledge that the 1948 Genocide Convention is the result of an inherently political drafting process. The initial resolution adopted by the UN General Assembly in November 1946 defined the crime of genocide in a much broader manner as 'a crime under international law which the civilised world condemns … whether the crime is committed on religious, racial, political or any other grounds' (quoted in van Schaack 1996–7, 2263). However, since the Soviet bloc and Latin American countries did not support a draft including political groups, the definition was subsequently restricted to national, religious, ethnic, and racial groups, argued to constitute 'homogenous and stable' categories (2268).

Whether or not the ECCC would also examine cases of genocide against national groups was however open to debate.[6] In this regard, the reasoning was that the targeting of members of subgroups of the Khmer national group – who constituted the majority of the victims of the DK regime – could be seen as genocide in relation to an intent on the part of the CPK to purify the national group and eradicate imperialism, feudalism, and reactionary capitalism. The Group of Experts, appointed by the UN in 1998 to evaluate existing evidence and assess the feasibility of a tribunal, did not necessarily rule out such an option. Whilst their report mainly identified the need for investigation into the commission of genocide against the Cham, the Vietnamese, and the Buddhist monkhood as ethnic, religious, and possibly 'racial' groups, they took note of the debates on whether or not the CPK regime committed genocide with regard to the Khmer national group (United Nations Group of Experts 1999, §63). The experts stated that although they did not take a position on this matter, any tribunal would 'have to address this question should Khmer Rouge officials be charged with genocide against the Khmer national group' (§65).

Although this was the position of some international and national civil party lawyers[7] in Case 002 who wanted to bring more attention to the fate of the 'new people' under the DK regime (see Vianney-Liaud 2014), the co-prosecutors and co-investigating judges did not examine the crime of genocide against a national group. This contrasts with recent innovative interpretations of the crime of genocide within the restricted list of protected groups.[8] In this regard, a senior government adviser and former ECCC official regretted the lack of innovation from the Cambodian judges:

> it would have been a very interesting discussion, and could have moved the international jurisprudence forward ... to a certain extent they [the national judicial officials] allow themselves to be ... led by the internationals. They considered, understandably that they had less legal judicial education and experience ... often on legal points, they have allowed the international viewpoint to prevail, without challenging it when perhaps they could have.[9]

As a result of the ECCC's approach to genocide, many groups are excluded as victims of the crime of genocide. The targeting of these groups was however dealt with under the separate legal category of crimes against humanity. The ECCC law (article 5) defines these crimes as 'any acts committed as part of a widespread or systematic attack directed against any civilian population, on national, political, ethnical, racial or religious grounds'.[10] These acts may include 'murder, extermination, enslavement, deportation, imprisonment, torture, rape, persecutions on political, racial, and religious grounds, other inhumane acts'.[11]

In Case 001, the accused was found guilty of the crime of persecution on political grounds of the S-21 detainees. The accused in Case 002/01 were found guilty for the crime of persecution on political grounds with regard to the targeting of former officials of the Khmer Republic and so-called 'new people' during the forced population transfers. In Case 002/02, the co-investigating judges also indicted the defendants for crimes against humanity, regarding the persecution of the Vietnamese minority on racial grounds, and of the Cham and Buddhist groups on political and religious grounds. The indictment for crimes against humanity also relates to the targeting of several groups for political reasons, including former officials and officers of the Khmer Republic (ECCC [OCIJ] 2010, §§1363–9).

An advantage of using the legal category of crimes against humanity to account for the targeting of specific groups on discriminatory grounds is that it also applies to political groups at the ECCC. Moreover, it is arguably less difficult to establish the occurrence of crimes against humanity, since unlike the charge of genocide it does not require proving an intent to destroy a targeted group. This ordering of the processes of manufacturing difference under the DK regime however has significant implications for the construction of victimhood in contemporary Cambodia.

Creating difference between victims of genocide and other victims?

The restricted legal definition of genocide at the ECCC differs from the widespread sociopolitical use of the term in Cambodia. The Khmer term for genocide (ប្រល័យពូជសាសន៍[12]) has indeed become a 'shorthand description of what happened' under the DK regime.[13] It is used interchangeably as a synonym for the DK regime. This use in common parlance is closely linked to the political self-legitimation strategies of the People's Republic of Kampuchea (PRK), the government established after the fall of the DK regime. The PRK quickly classified the DK crimes as genocide in its quest for legitimacy in a context of political isolation during the Cold War (Chandler 2008). Until today, this term remains central to the self-legitimation rhetoric of the ruling Cambodian People's Party, which portrays itself as the liberator of the population from the 'genocidal' DK regime.

After the general elections organized by the UN peacekeeping mission in 1993, and even after the establishment of the ECCC, political officials continued to use the term 'genocide' to refer to the DK regime. As a result, civil parties – including those accepted in relation to the charge of genocide – have difficulty understanding the legal terminology used at the ECCC.[14] A national civil party lawyer who represents Cham civil parties at the ECCC, observed:

> In general, the Cambodian population, when they talk about the Khmer Rouge, say that the Khmer Rouge regime is a *genocidal* regime. After the ECCC was established … even up to this date, the general public is still confused by the terms 'genocide' and 'crimes against humanity'.[15]

Beyond a lack of comprehension of the intricacies of the legal definition adopted at the ECCC, there is also evidence that some victims feel offended and angry that the court does not recognize that genocide occurred beyond the Cham and Vietnamese groups.[16] This is something that the co-investigating judges, especially the national judge, feared might happen due to only pursuing genocide charges for two minority groups (Giry 2014). This reaction is not only linked to the broad use of the notion of genocide in common parlance and the ways in which it has been shaped by the political discourse since the end of the DK regime – it also relates to how calls at the international level for interventions to stop the crimes committed by the Khmer Rouge, and later on for their acknowledgment, also centred on the notion of 'genocide'.[17] The use of the term of 'genocide' to describe the crimes committed under the DK regime thus quickly became part of the 'human rights nomenclature' (Schabas 2001, 39; see also van Schaack 1996–7). Interestingly, it remains part of the language of some civil-society transitional justice projects today, despite the restricted interpretation at the ECCC. Most importantly, genocide is often presented as being the worst of all crimes (Schabas 2001, 37). Whilst such a hierarchy of crimes is actively refuted by civil-party lawyers working at the ECCC,[18] civil parties may still feel that such a hierarchy is implied. A senior government adviser and former ECCC official observes:

> Crimes against humanity are supposedly on a similar level to genocide. But on the other hand, people talk about the 'crimes of crimes' and as … most people in Cambodia have always thought that they were survivors of genocide, and now, if you say, no, what happened to your people is not genocide … I don't think it's very conducive to national harmony … it's likely to … backfire.[19]

The use of the different legal categories of genocide and crimes against humanity to qualify the targeting of specific groups on discriminatory grounds may thus create difference between victim groups, thereby possibly introducing problematic hierarchies of victims.

This analysis furthermore highlights the multiplicity of meanings of the notion of genocide that exist in the context of a hybrid transitional justice process such as the ECCC. Whilst the term 'hybrid tribunal' is part of the common vocabulary used in transitional justice and international criminal justice scholarship to classify different types of tribunals (domestic, hybrid, international; see e.g. OHCHR 2008), the mixed composition of a tribunal's staff and jurisdiction is often framed as a technical aspect. Only a few scholars have proposed analysing the hybrid nature of mixed tribunals such as the ECCC from a socio-cultural perspective (Kent 2013). A salient example is the anthropological work of Kelsall (2009, 17) on the Special Court for Sierra Leone, which shows the inadequacy of legal doctrines and Western procedures when they are employed in a context with different understandings of 'social space and time, causation, agency, responsibility, evidence, truth and truth-telling'.

The present article analysis speaks to this scholarship, as it shows that hybridity also implies that the legal concepts used within a legal process entail multiple meanings for diverse actors. As discussed above, the notion of genocide has specific implications in the Cambodian context, given its embeddedness in the post-DK political discourse. It also has to be seen in terms of the complex political and historical relations between Vietnam and Cambodia. A national civil-party lawyer for instance explained that, personally, he felt that the ECCC's limited genocide charges were not 'fair' and would affect the image of Cambodia at the international level:

> They [the Khmer Rouge] killed everyone, not just specific groups … actually 95% of the victims are Khmer … with some of my [national] colleagues, we are concerned that [because of this limited approach], history will show that Cambodia committed genocide against Vietnam. We are concerned that those who know international law [will think] that Cambodia is a very bad nation, although Cambodians suffered.[20]

Struggles with regard to the meaning of genocide also take place in a divide between on the one hand social scientists, legal experts, and civil-society actors with a more open view to the interpretation of genocide, and on the other hand legal actors who take a legalistic or 'purist' approach.[21] This divide long precedes the establishment of the ECCC (Stanton 2001; Schabas 2001) and also relates to historiographical discussions on the DK regime (Bruneteau 2004). This issue emerged in the Case 002/02 proceedings during the testimony of the anthropologist Hinton, who was invited by the prosecution to testify as an expert on genocide studies but was then asked to refrain from discussing the definition of genocide and using the term in ways which would exceed the court's legal definition.[22]

The struggles around the meanings of the notion of genocide thus take place at different levels and inform the hybrid nature of the transitional justice process in Cambodia. However, whilst the debate on hybridity and hybrid peace tends to reify the categories of the international vs local (Jones and Péclard 2014), this analysis shows that the differences in understandings of genocide cannot simply be separated along such a binary.

The dilemma of the politics of difference at the ECCC

Having discussed the ECCC's use of different legal categories to analyse the specific targeting of groups on discriminatory grounds under the Khmer Rouge regime, this section turns specifically to the people recognized as victims of genocide, and analyses the dilemma inherent to the politics of difference at the ECCC. It is argued that whilst recognizing the construction of difference in contexts of mass atrocity is important and can promote tolerance, this process can also essentialize identities in problematic ways and single out certain victim groups from shared experiences of suffering.

Potential for transformation

The genocide charges at the ECCC facilitate the recognition of how individuals were targeted on the basis of their ascribed identity and the acknowledgement of the specificity of victimization against these groups. The significance of this acknowledgment can be illustrated with the belated inclusion of genocide charges regarding the Khmer Krom minority. Before these charges were included in Case 004, a civil-party applicant argued that not recognizing them as victims of genocide would constitute an affront to his family precisely because it would deny the specific discrimination they were subjected to: 'The [ECCC's] lawyers can say whatever they want, but if they don't make it clear that we were screened and killed because of who we are, because we were called Vietnamese traitors, then they insult my loved ones!' (Mohan 2008, 49). It is here that the discussions of genocide charges at the ECCC have a transformative potential; they can help to erode the negative connotation of difference that made the crimes possible in the first place, and address the patterns of discrimination that still persist today. A lawyer for Khmer Krom civil parties observes that this was in fact precisely the aim of his clients:

> [The] Khmer Kampuchea Krom ... were separated [as the enemy] ... [but] they didn't do anything wrong! They say that they're humans also ... people still think that the Khmer Kampuchea Krom who come to Cambodia are Vietnamese ... [and they face problems in Vietnam too] ... this is what they want to prove; [they want] this court to tell the world that the Khmer Kampuchea Krom always face threats every time, throughout all of the regimes.[23]

Nguyen and Sperfeldt (2014, 114) argue that the inclusion of genocide charges may help the ethnic Vietnamese minority to reconstruct their identity as 'a distinct group in Cambodia whose rights need to be respected', in a context where 'some mainstream Cambodians still consider it implausible that these Vietnamese hold a status as "victims"'. The lawyers of the ethnic Vietnamese civil parties have also made creative use of the reparations provisions at the ECCC; they have requested assistance services for their clients to facilitate the application process for Cambodian citizenship, which could arguably 'help put an end to the transgenerational harms caused by continuing statelessness' (Killean, Moffett, and Chilshom 2016, 36).

In the Case 002/02 trial proceedings, the discrimination against the ethnic Vietnamese minority was also raised through the discussion of the term 'Yuon (យួន)'. During his testimony, Hinton explained that whilst this term 'may be used in colloquial speech in a way where people aren't knowing about the use of it', when mobilized 'in context of broader incitement, of anger, of ethnic stereotyping', it clearly constitutes 'a rhetoric of ... racist hatred'.[24] As such, it enables the spread of stereotypes of the Vietnamese as 'thieving, covetous of Khmer territory, people who use trickery, people who are bad'.[25] Hinton further described how Cambodian governments throughout history have portrayed the Vietnamese as the 'other'. These discussions during ECCC hearings are significant in the context of continued xenophobia – indeed, 'Yuon-ness' constitutes a 'universal key to explain failures of social, economic and national development in Cambodia', a trope that

THE POLITICS OF PEACEBUILDING IN A DIVERSE WORLD   95

is used across ideological divides and political regimes (Edwards 1996, 64). More recently, this rhetoric has been dangerously mobilized in the context of the contested 2013 national elections, leading to an escalation of violence against the ethnic Vietnamese minority.

With regards to the Cham minority, the inclusion of genocide charges against this group has allowed the discussion of their history, everyday practices, and common mis-conceptions in the context of Islamophobia.[26] These important discussions however take place in the limited space of the court proceedings, highlighting the importance of civil-society projects that engage with, and can affect, the broader population.

Risks of essentializing difference

Whilst acknowledging that the construction of difference in contexts of mass atrocity can be transformative, it can however also contribute to essentializing difference. Legal definitions of genocide do not imply that the difference on the basis of which victims are targeted corresponds to their subjective identities, as they focus on the identities externally ascribed by the perpetrators (Aptel 2011). Prosecutorial strategies may therefore lead to a problematic essentialization of identities in the attempt to prove that victims were specifically targeted for their difference, and for being part of a group protected under the Genocide Convention. This challenge can be illustrated with the following excerpt of the testimony of a civil party whose ethnic Vietnamese wife was killed under the DK regime. He answers the questions of the international civil-party lawyer:

> *Could you describe your wife, what did she look like?*
> She's healthy and has a light complexion. Her height was about 1.55 m and her age was similar to my age.
> …
> *What languages did she speak?*
> She – we studied in the same class up to the Grade 8 in the old education system. So she could speak Khmer fluently.
> *Did she have Cambodian nationality or an ID card?*
> We had our marriage certificate, and of course, she held a Khmer nationality.
> *Did she speak the Vietnamese language?*
> Yes, she knew Vietnamese, but she did not use it. She only spoke Khmer and French.
> *Did she look Vietnamese or did she look Cambodian?*
> Her facial figure was that of Khmer but she had a lighter complexion.
> *Were her parents both ethnically Vietnamese?*
> The mother was ethnically Vietnamese, but the father was half-blood Chinese.
> …
> *Did her parents look or dress Vietnamese?*
> The way they dressed was truly Vietnamese. And when they spoke Khmer, they spoke with a severe accent.
> …
> *Did her family follow Vietnamese traditions?*
> Yes. For example, during the Chinese New Year celebration they celebrated according to their culture. But they did not practise such a ceremony according to the Buddhist religion.[27]

This excerpt shows how the lawyer is searching for 'detectable differences' to provide evi-dence that her client's wife was targeted on this basis. Civil-party lawyers thus make use of strategic essentialism methods, i.e. of the instrumental use of essentialized identity cat-egories for emancipatory purposes, during a struggle for equal rights (Martin de

Almagro 2018). As Caswell (2012) has shown, strategic essentialism can even be traced back to the work of the archivists of the Documentation Center of Cambodia, which provides the main evidentiary documentation for the ECCC, since the classification system they introduced rendered visible the specific targeting of ethnic groups under the DK regime.

However, as is widely discussed in feminist and postcolonial scholarship, strategic essentialism can also possibly constitute a self-defeating political tactic for minority groups (Spivak 1985). There is indeed a fine line between on the one hand identifying and naming difference, and on the other hand portraying these characteristics of difference as static or natural, thereby running the risk of essentializing identities. The strategic essentialism of civil-party lawyers may conceal the ways in which identities were primarily defined by the perpetrators of the crimes committed under the DK regime. Also, this can reproduce the 'reverse principles of absolute inclusion and exclusion' which are inherent to these crimes, i.e. the practice whereby one either necessarily belongs to, or is excluded from, one specific group (Aptel 2011, 154). These practices can therefore contribute to the reduction of the multilayered identities of the victims to a single, static belonging to a homogenous group. This is Wilke's (2011) conclusion in her analysis of the Auschwitz trials in Frankfurt between 1963 and 1965, in which she shows that the legal process problematically reproduced 'German' and 'Jewish' identities as mutually exclusive categories, rather than formulating these as fluid and overlapping identity groups.

With regard to the ECCC, a Cambodian researcher and member of a civil society organization working closely with the Cham community observed:

> the Court wants to look at only the specific and related information, not allowing space for people to express multiple identities … sometimes I don't wear a scarf, but then it doesn't mean that I am not Cham. But when you look at those who testified [at the ECCC], usually they have all these signifiers … you can tell immediately … for men they wear the *kufi* and women would wear headscarves … the other thing is about [their] accent … but the Court should also allow … multiple identities or plurality.[28]

Besides the risk of essentializing difference, the singling out of specific victim groups may also lead to the exacerbation of difference in problematic ways, in contexts of continued experiences of discrimination. When the civil-party lawyers first introduced their reparation requests in Case 002/02, the national defence lawyers for instance strongly questioned the legal status of the Vietnamese victims of the DK regime in a way which seemed to reproduce prejudices against the ethnic Vietnamese.[29] Singling out certain groups of victims, even by transitional justice actors who mean well, can thus expose them to potentially harmful situations in which the legitimacy of their victimhood claims is questioned, as well as their place in society today.

Exclusion from narratives of shared suffering

In addition to the risk of essentializing difference, the categorization of the Cham and ethnic Vietnamese civil parties as the only recognized victims of genocide at the ECCC may not always relate to their subjective experiences of victimization, or at least to the public narratives thereof. During their testimonies in the Case 002/02 public hearings, Cham and even Vietnamese civil parties indeed surprisingly emphasized that they had suffered as the rest of the population had, that they were not treated differently from the majority population. This also emerged during the interviews conducted for this research with four Cham civil parties in January 2016. Most of them for instance high-lighted that they were treated harshly because they were categorized as 'new people' or '17 April people'. Moreover, whilst acknowledging that they were subject to differential treatment, for instance being forced to eat pork, they repeatedly emphasized a sense of shared suffering with other victims: 'I don't know about what crimes, only about my suffer-ings … I don't know what the other civil parties who are not Cham have recounted, but in terms of suffering, it is the same'.[30]

This can also be illustrated with an interview conducted with a Cham civil-party repre-sentative. When I asked him why the Cham civil parties in his village were grouped sep-arately and represented by lawyers different from those of the non-Cham civil parties, he did not explain that this was because they were victims of genocide and the others were not. Rather, he argued that this was because their lawyers particularly 'liked' the Cham minority and therefore only represented Cham clients:

> [The national lawyer] only takes civil parties who are Cham, because the French lawyer told him so. I don't understand why … because he likes us. He likes the Cham people … It's like an affection, when you like someone, you go with him. Everybody likes [the national civil party lawyer].[31]

It is important to know here that as a civil-party representative, this respondent had a sig-nificantly better understanding of the legal proceedings at the ECCC than other civil parties in his village. However, rather than explaining the separate grouping of Cham civil parties on the basis of how they were treated under DK or how the court recognized them as victims of genocide, he viewed this through the prism of local power relations, through what can be analysed as an affection-based patron–client relationship with his civil-party lawyer.

Narratives of differential treatment produced through the genocide charges at the ECCC thus possibly diverge from subjective experiences of victimization for victims from the Cham community. However, additional empirical research with civil parties that are recognized as victims of genocide at the ECCC is required before being able to reach any conclusion. Also, the fact that the different civil parties do not emphasize differential treatment under the DK regime has to be considered with caution in the context of ongoing discrimination, in particular with regard to the ethnic Vietnamese civil parties. Such a position may indeed be linked to strategies of assimilation, or attempts to deflect exposure and divert attention away from being different from the majority popu-lation. It has indeed been reported that some ethnic Vietnamese civil parties hold a 'real fear of repercussions for speaking out about their experience of crimes', especially given the 'actual and structural violence' that continues to be exercised against this minority in contemporary Cambodia (Nguyen and Sperfeldt 2014, 117).[32]

Conclusion

Focusing on the context of Cambodia, this article has analysed the dilemma inherent to the politics of difference in transitional justice. In order to acknowledge how victims were specifically targeted on the basis of processes of othering and externally ascribed identities, transitional justice processes have to mobilize these same categories of differ-ence. As a result, they can contribute to reinforcing stereotypes and essentializing identities. At the ECCC, this tension emerges in relation to the notion of genocide; because it refers to the specific targeting of specific groups, examining the notion of genocide used at the ECCC allows for specific experiences of victimization to be acknowledged. This can have a transformative potential, especially since groups identified as victims of genocide, such as the ethnic Vietnamese minority, continue to be subject to discrimination in Cambodia. However, the discussion of the genocide charges can also limit the emergence of more fluid identities or disrupt the strategies of assimilation of these groups. Here, civil-party lawyers fighting for the acknowledgment of their clients as victims of genocide face the challenges inherent to strategic essentialism.

Whilst focusing on the case study of the ECCC, this article thus shows that engaging with difference in transitional justice raises epistemological questions as to how difference is categorized within a society in the aftermath of mass atrocity, who is involved in this ordering process, and how this affects social reconstruction. It highlights the heuristic implications of a broader understanding of the hybrid nature of transitional justice processes, including legal processes such as the ECCC. Indeed, it shows how different actors at different levels are involved in the construction of difference, adding to the field's critiques of how legalistic approaches construct law as neutral and thereby 'silence difference'.

But this contribution also shows that reflecting upon difference raises questions of a more instrumental or strategic nature about how to best protect those groups and individuals who have suffered extreme harm, and how to avoid creating new harm in singling out these groups who can become exposed again to discrimination. Research on this matter can thus contribute to recent considerations in the field of transitional justice in relation to conflict sensitivity.

Notes

1. ECCC Democratic Expert Report, 30.09.2009, Doc. No. D140/1/1. Available at: https://www.eccc.gov.kh/sites/default/files/documents/courtdoc/D140_1_1_Public_Redacted_EN.PDF [last accessed 01.10.2017].
2. See Vianney-Liaud (2014) for a comparative analysis of the definitions of genocide in the 1948 Genocide Convention and the ECCC Law. The International Criminal Court (ICC) has also adopted this definition (Article 6, Rome Statute).
3. Article 4, *Law on the Establishment of the ECCC, with inclusion of amendments as promulgated on 27.10.2004 (NS/RKM/1004/006)*, available at: https://www.eccc.gov.kh/sites/default/files/legal-documents/KR_Law_as_amended_27_Oct_2004_Eng.pdf [last accessed 20.09.2017].
4. Ibid.
5. From a legal perspective, it is also argued that the adoption of the 1948 Genocide Convention definition upholds the basic principle of justice of *nullum crimen sine lege* (Ciorciari 2008, 5; Vianney-Liaud 2014, 8).
6. See e.g. the diametrically opposed positions of Schabas (2001) and Stanton (2001).
7. Co-Lawyers for Civil Parties (04.02.2010) *Sixth Investigative Request of Co-Lawyers for Civil Parties Concerning the Charge of Genocide against the Khmer Nationals*, Case 002, ECCC Document No. D349, available at: www.eccc.gov.kh/sites/default/files/documents/courtdoc/D349_EN.PDF [last accessed 20.09.2017].
8. In his indictment against members of the Argentine military junta for genocide, Judge Garzón for instance argued that the perpetrators attempted to substantially change the social relations in Argentine and thereby partially annihilated the national group (Feierstein 2014, 18–21).
9. Interview with a senior adviser to the Royal Cambodian government and former ECCC official, 26 January 2016, Phnom Penh.

THE POLITICS OF PEACEBUILDING IN A DIVERSE WORLD   99

10. Article 5, *Law on the Establishment of the ECCC, with inclusion of amendments as promulgated on 27.10.2004 (NS/RKM/1004/006)*, available at: https://www.eccc.gov.kh/sites/default/files/legal-documents/KR_Law_as_amended_27_Oct_2004_Eng.pdf [last accessed 20.09.2017].
11. Ibid.
12. This term was already used in Cambodia before the DK regime. According to Edwards (1996), it has to be analysed in relation to the specific cultural context which shapes the meaning of genocide as the destruction of the Khmer race.
13. Interview with a senior adviser to the Royal Cambodian government and former ECCC official, 26 January 2016, Phnom Penh.
14. Interview with a civil party (female, age 46), 31 January 2016, Kampot province; interview with a civil-party representative (male, age 64), 31 January 2016, Kampot province.
15. Interview with a national civil-party lawyer at the ECCC, 7 February 2014, Phnom Penh.
16. Interview with an international civil-party lawyer, 29 January 2016, Phnom Penh; interview with a national civil-party lawyer, 30 January 2014, Phnom Penh. See also Giry (2014).
17. E.g. the 1994 Cambodian Genocide Justice Act of the US Congress, or the 1978 request from the Canadian government to the UN Human Rights Council Sub-Commission Report pursuant to the 31st Session of the Human Rights Council Sub-Commission on the Prevention of Discrimination and Protection of Minorities.
18. Interview with an international civil-party lawyer, 29 January 2016, Phnom Penh.
19. Interview with a senior adviser to the Royal Cambodian government, 26 January 2016, Phnom Penh.
20. Interview with a national civil-party lawyer, 7 February 2018, Phnom Penh.
21. Interview with an international defence lawyer, 14 February 2014, Phnom Penh.
22. ECCC Public Transcript of Trial Chamber Proceedings, 14 March 2016, Case 002/02, ECCC Doc. No. E1/401.1, 41–3.
23. Interview with a national civil-party lawyer, 30 January 2014, Phnom Penh.
24. ECCC Public Transcript of Trial Chamber Proceedings, 17 March 2016, Case 002/02, ECCC Doc. No. E1/404.1, 35.
25. ECCC Public Transcript of Trial Chamber Proceedings, 15.03.2016, Case 002/02, ECCC Doc. No. E1/402.1, p.8.
26. See ECCC Public Transcript of Trial Chamber Proceedings, 9.02.2016, Case 002/02, ECCC Doc. No. E1/388.1, p.38.
27. ECCC Public Transcript of Trial Chamber Proceedings, 02.02.2015, Case 002/02, ECCC Doc. No. E1/361.1, p. 44-46.
28. Interview with a researcher and civil society actor, 2 February 2018, Phnom Penh.
29. Informal discussion with an international ECCC staff member, 26 January 2016, Phnom Penh. See also ECCC Public Transcript of Hearing on Specification of Civil Party Reparations Awards and Accused Ieng Thirith's Fitness to Stand Trial, 19.10.2011, Trial Chamber, Case 002, ECCC Doc. No. E1/11.1, p. 62-63. Many civil parties from the Cambodian majority population also did not understand, or felt uncomfortable with, this reparation request; see interview with a national civil-party lawyer, 7 February 2018, Phnom Penh; interview with a national civil-party lawyer, 13 February 2018, Phnom Penh.
30. Interview with a civil party (female, age 54), 31 January 2016, Kampot province.
31. Interview with a civil-party representative (male, age 64), 31 January 2016, Kampot province. Translation is my own.
32. Interview with a national civil-society actor working with minority groups, 8 February 2018, Phnom Penh.

Acknowledgements

My sincere thanks go to the two anonymous reviewers and the editors of the *JISB* for their helpful comments. I also warmly thank Pol Bargués-Pedreny and Xavier Mathieu, the co-editors of this special issue, and Elisabeth Baumgartner, who provided feedback on earlier drafts of this article. I am also grateful to the respondents quoted in this article, who shared their thoughts and experiences during my research.

Disclosure statement

No potential conflict of interest was reported by the author.

Funding

This work was supported by the Swiss National Science Foundation [grant number 100017_140289]; and the Fund for Early Career Researchers of the University of Basel [grant number DGK2612].

References

Aptel, Cécile. 2011. "International and Hybrid Criminal Tribunals: Reconciling or Stigmatizing?" In *Identities in Transition: Challenges for Transitional Justice in Divided Societies*, edited by Paige Arthur, 149–186. Cambridge: Cambridge University Press.

Arnould, Valérie. 2016. "Transitional Justice in Peacebuilding: Dynamics of Contestation in the DRC." *Journal of Intervention and Statebuilding* 10 (3): 321–338.

Arthur, Paige. 2011. *Identities in Transition: Challenges for Transitional Justice in Divided Societies*. Cambridge: Cambridge University Press.

Baker, Catherine, and Jelena Obradović-Wochnik. 2016. "Mapping the Nexus of Transitional Justice and Peacebuilding." *Journal of Intervention and Statebuilding* 10 (3): 281–301.

Bargués-Pedreny, Pol, and Xavier Mathieu. 2018. "Beyond Silence, Obstacle and Stigma: Revisiting the 'Problem' of Difference in Peacebuilding." *Journal of Intervention and Statebuilding* 12 (3): 283–299.

Becker, Elisabeth. 1989. *Les larmes du Cambodge*. Paris: France Loisirs.

Behr, H. 2018. "Peace-in-Difference: Peace through Dialogue about and across Difference(s)." *Journal of Intervention and Statebuilding* 12 (3): 335–351.

Bruneteau, Bernard. 2004. *Le siècle des génocides. Violences, massacres et processus génocidaires de l'Arménie au Rwanda*. Paris: Armand Colin.

Buckley-Zistel, Susanne, and Ruth Stanley, eds. 2011. *Gender in Transitional Justice*. Basingstoke: Palgrave Macmillan.

Caswell, Michelle. 2012. "Using Classification to Convict the Khmer Rouge." *Journal of Documentation* 68 (2): 162–184.

Chandler, David. 1991. *The Tragedy of Cambodian History: Politics, War and Revolution since 1945*. New Haven/London: Yale University Press.

Chandler, David. 2008. "Cambodia Deals with Its Past: Collective Memory, Demonisation and Induced Amnesia." *Totalitarian Movements and Political Religions* 9 (2–3): 355–369.

Ciorciari, John D. 2008. "The Khmer Krom and the Khmer Rouge Trials." The Documentation Center of Cambodia. http://www.d.dccam.org/Tribunal/Analysis/pdf/Summer_Assn_John_KRT_Khmer_Krom.pdf.

Dy, Khamboly. 2007. *A History of Democratic Kampuchea (1975–1979)*. Phnom Penh: Documentation Center of Cambodia.

ECCC Co-Investigating Judges. 2010. "Closing Order in Case 002 (Case File No. 002/19-09-2007-ECCC-OCIJ., September 15." ECCC. https://www.eccc.gov.kh/sites/default/files/documents/courtdoc/D427Eng.pdf.

Edwards, Penny. 1996. "Imagining the Other in Cambodian Nationalist Discourse before and during the UNTAC Period." In *Propaganda, Politics, and Violence in Cambodia: Democratic Transition under United Nations Peace-keeping*, edited by Steve Heder and Judy Ledgerwood, 50–72. Armonk, NY: M.E. Sharpe.

Feierstein, Daniel. 2014. *Genocide as Social Practice: Reorganizing Society under the Nazis and Argentina's Military Juntas*. New Brunswick, NJ: Rutgers University Press.

Giry, Stéphanie. 2014. "The Genocide That Wasn't." *New York Review of Books*, August 25. www.nybooks.com/daily/2014/08/25/khmer-rouge-genocide-wasnt/.

Hinton, Alexander. 2005. *Why Did They Kill? Cambodia in the Shadow of Genocide*. Berkeley: University of California Press.

Jarvis, Helen, and Tom Fawthrop. 2004. *Getting Away with Genocide? Elusive Justice and the Khmer Rouge Tribunal*. London: Pluto Press.

Jones, Briony, and Julie Bernath. 2017. *Resistance and Transitional Justice*. Abingdon: Routledge.

Jones, Briony, and Didier Péclard. 2014. "Critical Notes on Categories of Peacebuilding and Peace Research." In *Challenges of Peace Research*, edited by Laurent Goetschel and Sandra Pfluger, 35–42. swisspeace Working Paper 7/2014. Bern: *swisspeace*.

Kelsall, Tim. 2009. *Culture under Cross-Examination: International Justice and the Special Court for Sierra Leone*. Cambridge: Cambridge University Press.

Kent, Alexandra. 2013. "Friction and Security at the Khmer Rouge Tribunal." *SOJOURN: Journal of Social Issues in Southeast Asia* 28 (2): 299–328.

Killean, Rachel. 2018. "Constructing Victimhood at the Khmer Rouge Tribunal: Visibility, Selectivity and Participation." *International Review of Victimology*.

Killean, Rachel, Luke Moffett, Andrew Chilshom, Rachel Hanna, Egle Vasiliauskaite, and Katarina Schwarz. 2016. *Working Paper on Acknowledging and Repairing the Moral and Collective Harm of Ethnic Vietnamese Victims of the Khmer Rouge Genocide*. Belfast: QUB Human Rights Centre.

Lai, Daniela. 2016. "Transitional Justice and Its Discontents: Socioeconomic Justice in Bosnia and Herzegovina and the Limits of International Intervention." *Journal of Intervention and Statebuilding* 10 (3): 361–381.

Martin de Almagro, M. 2018. "Hybrid Clubs: A Feminist Approach to Peacebuilding in the Democratic Republic of Congo." *Journal of Intervention and Statebuilding* 12 (3): 319–334.

McEvoy, Kieran. 2007. "Beyond Legalism: Towards a Thicker Understanding of Transitional Justice." *Journal of Law and Society* 34 (4): 411–440.

McEvoy, Kieran, and Laura McGregor, eds. 2008. *Transitional Justice from Below: Grassroots Activism and the Struggle for Change*. Oxford: Hart.

Miller, Zinaida. 2008. "Effects of Invisibility: In Search of the 'Economic' in Transitional Justice." *The International Journal of Transitional Justice* 2 (3): 266–291.

Minow, Martha. 1990. *Making all the Difference: Inclusion, Exclusion and America Law*. Ithaca, NY: Cornell University Press.

Mohan, Mahdev. 2008. "Reconstituting the 'Un-Person': The Khmer Krom and the Khmer Rouge Tribunal." *Singapore Year Book of International Law and Contributors* 12: 43–55.

Nguyen, Lima, and Christoph Sperfeldt. 2014. "Victim Participation and Minorities in Internationalised Criminal Trial: Ethnic Vietnamese Civil Parties at the Extraordinary Chambers in the Courts of Cambodia." *Macquarie Law Journal* 14: 97–126.

OHCHR (Office of the United Nations High Commissioner for Human Rights). 2008. *Rule-of-Law Tools for Post-Conflict States: Maximizing the Legacy of Hybrid Courts*. New York: United Nations.

Ponchaud, François. 2001. *Cambodge année zéro*. Paris: Kailash.

Schabas, William. 2001. "Should Khmer Rouge Leaders be Prosecuted for Genocide or Crimes against Humanity?" *Magazine of Documentation Center of Cambodia*, October, 37–39. http://www.d.dccam.org/Projects/Magazines/Previous%20Englis/Issue22.pdf.

Schmid, Evelyne. 2015. *Taking Economic, Social and Cultural Rights Seriously in International Criminal Law*. Cambridge: Cambridge University Press.

Sharp, Dustin. 2013. "Beyond the Post-Conflict Checklist: Linking Peacebuilding and Transitional Justice Through the Lens of Critique." *Chicago Journal of International Law* 14 (1): 165–196.

Shaw, Rosalind, and Lars Waldorf, eds. 2010. *Localizing Transitional Justice: Interventions and Priorities after Mass Violence*. Stanford: Stanford University Press.

Spivak, Gayatri C. 1985. "Subaltern Studies: Deconstructing Historiography." In *Subaltern Studies IV: Writings on South Asian History and Society*, edited by Ranajit Guha, 330–363. New Delhi: Oxford University Press.

Sriram, Chandra L. 2007. "Justice as Peace? Liberal Peacebuilding and Strategies of Transitional Justice." *Global Society* 21 (4): 579–591.

Stanton, Gregory. 2001. "The Khmer Rouge Did Commit Genocide." *Magazine of Documentation Center of Cambodia*, November, 32–33. http://www.d.dccam.org/Projects/Magazines/Previous%20Englis/Issue23.pdf.

United Nations Group of Experts. 1999. *Report of the Group of Experts for Cambodia Established Pursuant to General Assembly Resolution 52/135*. New York: United Nations.

UNSC (United Nations Security Council). 2004. *The Rule of Law and Transitional Justice in Conflict and Post-Conflict Societies: Report of the Secretary General. No. S/2004/616*. New York: United Nations.

van Schaack, Beth. 1996–1997. "The Crime of Political Genocide: Repairing the Genocide Convention's Blind Spot." *The Yale Law Journal* 106: 2259–2291.

Vianney-Liaud, Mélanie. 2014. "Controversy on the Characterization of the Cambodian Genocide at the Extraordinary Chambers in the Courts of Cambodia." International Crimes Database. http://www.internationalcrimesdatabase.org/upload/documents/20141022T141836-ICD%20Brief%20-%20Vianney-Liaud_FINAL%20VERSION.pdf.

Wilke, Christiane. 2011. "Staging Violence, Staging Identities: Identity Politics in Domestic Prosecution." In *Identities in Transition: Challenges for Transitional Justice in Divided Societies*, edited by Paige Arthur, 118–148. Cambridge: Cambridge University Press.

Whitaker, Benjamin (1985) Revised and Updated Report on the Question of the Prevention and Punishment of the Crime of Genocide Prepared by Mr. Benjamin Whitaker for the United Nations Sub-Commission on Prevention of Discrimination and Protection of Minorities, UN Document E/CN.4/Sub .2/1985/6 (2 July 1985).

Governing Conflict: The Politics of Scaling Difference

Andreas Hirblinger ⓘ and Dana M. Landau ⓘ

ABSTRACT

The dynamics of peace and conflict are fundamentally shaped by a *politics of scaling difference*. Based on the insight that difference is widely associated with both the *causes of* and *cures for* violent conflict, this article explores how practices of scaling mediate this duality. Drawing on South Sudan and Kosovo, it is argued that the governance of conflict is characterized by efforts to skilfully accommodate diversity, straddling the line between recognizing, reinforcing, and reconfiguring difference and investing it with political power at the 'right' scale. This is read as a conflictual process involving the unravelling, rescaling, and counter-scaling of difference.

Introduction

Difference plays a central yet ambiguous role in the praxis of conflict and in its theorization and study. Spanning from Schmitt's (1996) existential philosophy of the friend–enemy distinction and Doty's (1996) concern with the discursive construction of difference in North–South relations to Hobsbawm's (2012) historical study of the emergence of nationalism and Anderson's (2006) work on imagined communities, scholars widely agree that difference matters greatly for politics and conflict. Difference also continues to yield an emancipatory appeal, particularly in critical, feminist, and postcolonial thought. This heterogeneous body of work does not purport to deliver a single theory enunciating the merits of difference; however, many contributions arguably share a dissatisfaction with liberal thought for homogenizing and covering up differences that indeed shape the lives of individuals and communities. This is strongly expressed in arguments emphasizing that politics rest on relational identities that are constituted through an affirmation of difference (Mouffe 2005, 2). Moreover, feminist and postcolonial thought has pointed to the need for 'strategic essentialism' as an emancipatory strategy (Spivak 1988), not least against imperial and colonial rule and its legacies, operating through the deliberate construction of identities in order to govern societies and territories (Barkey and Gavrilis 2016; Erk 2015).

Difference thus informs political – and often violent – conflict, both as a means of invoking and waging conflict and as a means of managing it. As Bargués-Pedreny and Mathieu (2018) note in the introduction to this special issue, peacebuilders have often viewed difference as a problem to be solved, or conferred to it a positive (even though stigmatized) role. In this article, we show that difference has played a central, yet somewhat contradictory, role in the governance of conflict: difference is widely viewed as both the cause of *and* the cure for conflict. This was true in both colonial and imperial strategies of rule, and continues to be the case in contemporary peacebuilding and statebuilding practice, where difference is viewed as simultaneously holding a destructive potential for conflict and being key to peacefully resolving it. Building on earlier works on the 'politics of scale' in peacebuilding, we particularly demonstrate that it is the *scaling* of difference through administrative and political practices – making difference politically salient at one level of a given political order rather than another – which mediates the duality between cause and cure. The article sheds light on how the dynamics of peace and conflict are characterized by a politics of scaling difference – a continued process of negotiation through which difference is conflictingly (re)constructed and made politically viable at different scales.

We illustrate our argument with the cases studies of South Sudan and Kosovo, where recent peacebuilding and statebuilding endeavours have been strongly concerned with scaling difference, largely in the context of decentralization processes. This empirical exploration points to a phenomenon of global reach, which is found in contexts that vary in regard to geography and history, while sharing certain legacies of external intervention that can be understood as precursors of contemporary practices of scaling difference.[1] Despite their different locations and recent history, the two countries share a couple of commonalities. First, both have been under the influence of Ottoman rule, which like other imperial regimes operated through the skilful management of difference between ethno-religious groups. In both cases, ethnic identity continued to shape the territories' postcolonial and post-imperial histories, and gained increased salience towards the end of the Cold War as geopolitical changes redefined political and military power structures and overarching political ideologies vanished vis-à-vis ethnic and nationalist forms of identification. The countries' more recent political histories also share a number of common features; as in many other cases, peacebuilding in Kosovo and South Sudan manifested itself as a vast and complex undertaking involving a range of actors that were attempting to rebuild and remake these states and societies. In both cases this involved *inter alia* attempts to create systems of governance that could accommodate diversity. We show that, in both cases, the interventions involved political and administrative practices that were preoccupied with making difference politically salient at the 'right' level of government and for the 'right' kind of groups. Specifically, in both South Sudan and Kosovo, peacebuilding interventions were preoccupied with defining the number and nature of groups to recognize, as well as the appropriate administrative level at which to endow them with political power.

The analysis herein illustrates that in both cases the scaling of difference took place through discursive and non-discursive practices, such as knowing and defining difference through naming and mapping exercises, managing difference through the demarcation of boundaries, and producing difference through political activism. Through the analysis of the politics of scaling difference in the two cases we identify three shared patterns: firstly, a preference for the term 'community' over other more explicitly scalar terms – such as 'minority' – in an *effort to unravel* scalar configurations; secondly, the targeted use of scaling practices in order to change power dynamics between groups in an *effort*

THE POLITICS OF PEACEBUILDING IN A DIVERSE WORLD

to rescale difference; and thirdly, in response to such practices, intense contestation by political entrepreneurs in an *effort to counter-scale* difference.

By studying the two cases, we find that the various scales are not stable, but rather are continuously contested through tactics that construct and deconstruct difference epistemologically, while materially investing it with political power. We suggest that scaling difference should therefore be understood as a continuous, conflictual process involving a variety of practices that construct difference and make it politically salient at specific scales. In both cases, these conflicting practices have tangibly affected the dynamics of peace and conflict. The article starts with a short theoretical reflection on the relationship between peace, conflict, and difference before we advance our approach to studying the scaling of difference in the South Sudanese and Kosovan peacebuilding processes. Thereafter we present our case studies, followed by concluding remarks that highlight common patterns and directions for further research.

Governing conflict and governing difference

Dealing with difference is not only a key concern for contemporary peacebuilding and statebuilding – it has also been at the core of colonial and imperial rule, characterized by discourses on conflict that portrayed difference as a potential source of violence, and as a threat to stability and peace. Most of these discourses frame difference in ethnic terms, subsuming a variety of socially constructed distinctions, including regarding culture, religion, economic status, and language. Our analysis focuses in particular on attempts to govern difference associated with *ethnic* identity. However, this focus is not intended to reify ethnicity or assert its primacy over other forms of identity; rather, our analysis traces the construction of difference along these categories in order to demonstrate that both interpretations of conflict and practices of peacebuilding in contemporary South Sudan and Kosovo are located in a historical trajectory of practices in which ethnic difference takes centre stage.[2]

Academic approaches have in recent decades undergone a shift from primordial understandings of ethnicity as a fixed attribute to formulations that stress its socially constructed and instrumental properties. It is now commonly understood that tribes and 'tribal' customs and traditions, or the category of the 'native', were wilfully created or invented by colonial administrations (Spear 2003). Moreover, many authors stress that ethnic identity is flexible, fluid, multilayered, and context-dependent (Brubaker 2004). Consequently, terms such as 'tribe' and 'tribalism' have become unfashionable, not only because they are associated with the antiquated language of colonial bureaucracy and anthropology, but also because they rest on biological concepts of race and thus wrongly convey a notion of fixity. However, this is not to suggest that as a socially constructed reality ethnicity has no tangible effects; indeed, it appears to be much more of a political than a biological category. Lentz (1995, 304) suggests understanding '"ethnicity" like the joker in a card game: it can be introduced into various play sequences, taking on the characteristics – in this case, connotations and conceptual vagueness – of the card it replaces'. Although – or maybe because – the concept and adjacent terms are so difficult to grasp, they can be used effectively to further specific political agendas. As we illustrate below, ethnic difference has historically been seen as both a cause of and cure for conflict; it has traditionally been associated with the presence of intercommunal conflict and instability, yet at the same time the management and (re)production of ethnic difference has also been employed to ensure stability and peace.

Anglo-Egyptian rule in the Sudan (1899–1956) is a case in point. At the turn of the twentieth century, for instance, British officers viewed the Sudan as 'far from being under any kind of control' and as 'a wild and turbulent land where warfare and violence, springing from the way of tribal life of the peoples, were deep-rooted and traditional' (Collins and Herzog 1961, 120). However, Anglo-Egyptian rule over the Sudan soon also faced resistance from emerging nationalist movements. These were quelled through a variety of mechanisms of indirect rule and native administration in the British colonies which installed a system of decentralized despotism that was operated through 'traditional authorities' (Mamdani 2012). Similar structures were created in German and French colonies, and were adopted by postcolonial regimes which continued to utilize ethnic identity with the aim of creating stable polities (Lange 2015). Postcolonial Sudan was similarly occupied with this management of difference, particularly in the context of efforts to quell the southern Sudanese resistance movements that formed after Sudan's declaration of independence and challenged Khartoum's authority during two long and bitterly fought civil wars (1955–72, 1983–2005). This process also entailed efforts to understand or define the population's various groups in terms of their most salient categories and boundaries, and this has been at the heart of attempts to govern and pacify what is now South Sudan since colonial times. In South Sudan, the different terms denoting ethnic identity such as 'tribe' and 'community' thus often have a comparably vague meaning. Whenever administrators and experts – both colonial and postcolonial – undertook efforts to precisely define and describe the composition of the Sudan's peripheries, they faced great difficulties in coming up with generally valid, palpable categories and classifications. Terms such as 'tribe', 'community', and the more recently used 'ethnicity' usually remained vague and ill-defined. However, there was a shared assumption that the peacebuilding process, which followed the Comprehensive Peace Agreement (CPA) of 2005, was challenged by *some* kind of ethnic difference, and that this difference needed to be dealt with in order to manage the conflict. Instead of taking difference at face value in an attempt to understand and analyse it, this article is interested in the practices through which difference has been remade, managed, and sorted, and how these practices have related to the struggle over power, and ultimately to the dynamics of peace and conflict.[3]

Turning to Kosovo, the Ottoman Empire – which extended into both the Balkans and the Sudan – was comparably occupied with managing difference. The so-called millet system offered religious communities substantial autonomy in areas such as education, family law, religious affairs, and even taxation, enabling communal leaders to exert considerable control over their communities (Barkey and Gavrilis 2016; Erk 2015; Hisket 1994, 90). The granting of such autonomy to religious communities was employed in the interest of sustaining imperial governing power and served to manage ethno-religious difference for imperial stability (Barkey and Gavrilis 2016). With the end of empire in the Balkans, and the rise of the nation state in the nineteenth and twentieth centuries, various groups proceeded to base their claims for self-determination on assertions of religious, linguistic, and ethnic distinctiveness, often finding international support (Lynch 2002). Post-Ottoman Kosovo in particular saw its territory engulfed in competing claims of the Albanian and Serbian nationalist movements. Consequently, Kosovo's historical and contemporary demographic make-up has been highly politicized, including through allegations of politically engineered migration and conflict-related displacement (Malcolm 1998). Even in a socialist, multinational federation such as Yugoslavia following the Second World War, difference played a critical role in the institutional design and discursive framing of the state, where it was made salient in terms of *nations* whose right to self-determination was embodied in the republics (Lampe 2000). Under the banner of 'Brotherhood and Unity', Tito's Yugoslavia devised a complex system of quotas and rotation among republics as well as autonomous provinces in order to engineer balance within the state (Ramet 2002). Following the violent dissolution of Yugoslavia in the early 1990s, difference hardened along ethnic lines, most prominently expressed through the thesis of 'ancient ethnic hatreds', which traced the perceived interethnic conflicts in the former Yugoslavia back to presumed centuries-old and irreconcilable antagonisms between the various groups (R.D. Kaplan 1993). The peacebuilding efforts thereafter were similarly prone to the 'dominance of an ethnicity-centred discourse, which reduce[d] both the causes of conflict and the post-conflict reality to ethnic identity' (Bieber 2004a, 9). Ethnic groups were assumed to be entirely fixed entities with little internal diversity, and intergroup relations appeared to be of a zero-sum nature. The governance of diversity came to be a key element of international peacebuilding and statebuilding efforts in the region (Caplan 2014). In Kosovo, this resulted in a pronounced focus on institutional and legal measures for managing ethnic diversity during the international peacebuilding period following 1999, including through extensive provisions for groups' self-government, special representation, and minority rights (Landau 2017).

The remainder of this article discusses how scaling difference has had an impact on the dynamics of peace and conflict in South Sudan and Kosovo. We acknowledge that the study of difference, including any attempt to account for its complexity, itself inevitably entails some fixation of difference. Aiming to avoid this pitfall, we focus our analysis not on difference per se in the peacebuilding cases we study, but rather on the practices through which difference is enacted, and particularly how the understanding, management, and (re)production of difference affects peace processes. Contributing to the emerging literature on the politics of scale in peacebuilding and statebuilding contexts, we ask how practices of difference-making and scale-making – in other words, scaling difference – relates to dynamics of peace and conflict.

The politics of scaling difference

Scale and difference are deeply intertwined, as seminal works on the subject such as Horowitz's (2000) *Ethnic Groups in Conflict* suggest. By definition, ethnicity – like all group identification – is characterized by what Horowitz refers to as a 'minimal scale requirement', i.e. the fact that 'ethnic membership transcends the range of face-to-face interactions' (53). The practices through which ethnic identity is subjectively constructed – Horowitz builds on Weber's conception of a subjective belief in a common descent – thus reach beyond a single relationship between two subjects. Following this understanding, scale is fundamental to difference. Ethnic identification can operate at different scales, including in 'large-scale society' (45). While this thinking still stands in the trajectory of colonial science which portrayed ethnic 'groups' in contrast to larger, universal forms of social and political organizations, it also disavows the neat differentiation between commonly portrayed 'parochial' ethnic identifications and more 'enlightened' and universal identifications. Difference is always scalar. This insight also underpins much of the post-structuralist literature in political geography, since Massey's (1999) claim that 'identities/entities, the relations "between" them, and the spatiality which is part of them are all co-constitutive' (3). More recently, Herb and Kaplan for instance have demonstrated how identity can manifest itself – and be significant – across different scales, thus forming nested scalar hierarchies, which they associate with regional, national, and supra-national levels (Herb and Kaplan 2018; D.H. Kaplan 2018).

Importantly, Horowitz's (2000) early work also hints at the importance of scale in mediating between conflict, identity, and difference; for example, the fact that difference can become manifest at different scales – including in differently sized territories or at different levels of political authority – has been shown to directly affect the likelihood of violent conflict. Of course, difference only matters to conflict if it is politicized *and* implicated in incompatible claims to power. This requires that identity-bearing actors are implicated in a 'shared social relation' in which at least one party exercises some form of power or coercion (Tilly 2002, 61; see also D.H. Kaplan 2018, 32). During armed conflict and war, political identities form the shared beliefs around which claims to political power over a given territory are made and violence is mobilized. Vice versa, peace processes can indeed be understood as efforts to construct a political order in which a monopoly of violence is established; following Weber, such a monopoly of violence is usually associated with the state. However, the state itself is a heterogeneous, relational entanglement that is ultimately enacted by human beings engaging in relational practices (Lottholz and Lemay-Hébert 2016, 1474; see also Migdal and Schlichte 2005). While the ideal typical understanding of a nation state suggests that these practices may be conjoined under the same national identity, states have always struggled to accommodate different and often competing manifestations of identity. Practices of dealing with conflict are thus methodologically nationalist for pragmatic reasons, although it would be analytically imprudent to limit an analysis of the politics of difference to the national scale.

The importance of scale has more recently also caught the attention of peacebuilding scholars who are preoccupied with making sense of the 'local', in particular following the surge of debates about the merits of 'hybridity' and the differentiation between the 'local' and the 'international' (Mac Ginty and Richmond 2013; Paffenholz 2015). Contributing to an effort to overcome the aforementioned local–international binary that has constrained peacebuilding research, there is now a burgeoning literature which incorporates the notion of a 'politics of scale' into the study of peacebuilding and international intervention. For instance, Hirblinger and Simons (2015, 426) contend that fact and value claims about the local have informed the dynamics of peacebuilding, arguing that scholars' and experts' views about the local form part of a 'politics of scale' that empowers some actor groups over others and shapes political agendas. Similarly, Hameiri and Jones (2017, 54) posit that in peacebuilding 'different social forces promote and resist alternative scales and modes of governance, depending on their interests and agendas', and that contestation between these forces explains the outcomes of international intervention. More recently, Hameiri, Hughes, and Scarpello (2017, 72–5) have introduced a systematic theoretical perspective on the politics of scale in international intervention, drawing on Gramscian state theory. They suggest focusing on how flexible coalitions of social forces contest scales in a struggle over power and resources, and they apply this approach in the context of international programmes in the field of public administration reform.

Speaking to this emerging research interest, we investigate the practices of scaling difference in two case studies. We understand practices as 'socially meaningful patterns of action which … simultaneously embody, act out, and possibly reify background knowledge and discourse in and on the material world' (Adler and Pouliot 2011, 4). Practices are thus the 'dynamic material and ideational processes that enable structures to be stable or to evolve, and agents to reproduce or to transform structures' (4). We are particularly interested in understanding two matters: how practices dynamically co-produce scale and difference, and how this influences peacebuilding outcomes. We do not apply a preconfigured scale but instead advance an interpretative approach which focuses on how difference is made politically salient through practices of scaling. Commensurate with the emerging literature on peacebuilding and intervention, we define scale as a hierarchy of territorial spaces, constructed through conflicting practices and characterized by distinctly material dimensions (Hameiri, Hughes, and Scarpello 2017, 150; Hameiri and Scarpello 2018, 166–72; Marston, Jones, and Woodward 2005). Importantly, scales create not neat, discrete, separable entities but overlapping, relationally defined, fuzzy territories that contain mutually exclusive social relations and oftentimes remain contested. As Brenner (2001, 606) puts it, they should be understood as constituting a 'mosaic of unevenly superimposed and densely interlayered scalar geometries'.

Our article takes a particular interest in the politics of scaling difference: we ask how various identity traits are expressed, performed, or inscribed into different scales, thus creating difference in the very act of scaling. Our case studies show that peacebuilding interventions are preoccupied with identifying the appropriate level and loci at which to make difference politically salient, such as the number or nature of groups to recognize and the appropriate level of government at which to institutionalize difference. Clearly, attempts to scale difference to the level perceived to be most conducive to peace risk glossing over the multidimensionality of difference and identity highlighted by other contributions to this issue (Bargués-Pedreny and Mathieu 2018). This perspective sheds light on how difference remains perpetually dynamic and unstable. While we assume that difference comes into being and is made salient through practices of scaling, we are particularly interested in the tensions and frictions produced by such practices. We describe this as a conflictual process, through which difference is continuously contested and (re)negotiated.

Scaling difference in South Sudan and Kosovo

The following section presents the two case studies of Kosovo (1999–2013) and South Sudan (2003–13), elucidating how, in both cases, politics of scaling difference mediated the duality of difference as both a cause of and cure for conflict. This examination of these two cases, which are rarely if ever studied jointly, demonstrates a number of common patterns in the ways in which the scaling of difference can affect the dynamics of war and peace. These include recurring and competing efforts to unravel, rescale, and counter-scale difference in an attempt to foster peace through practices of knowing, naming, and managing difference. In the two cases, these dynamics straddled the line between recognizing, reinforcing, and reconfiguring divisions, and involved scholars, experts, administrators, and political leaders alike. We argue that efforts to analyse and understand the ethnic set-up of societies have been closely related to the remaking, managing, and sorting of difference. Furthermore, we find that the most salient feature in the two cases is the attempt to scale difference in order to make it salient at the 'right' level of government and for the 'right' kind of groups. We moreover find that the various scales have not been stable, but contested. We suggest that scaling difference can be understood as a conflictual process involving a variety of practices that advance different scales through which difference becomes politically salient at different levels of administration, for different people, and in different loci. We find that these scaling practices are often discursive – for instance, related to knowledge production or the public narration or legislation of difference. Moreover, they can also be non-discursive, involving enactments of difference that are primarily bodily or material – in the most extreme cases through the use of force.

South Sudan: Unity in diversity?

South Sudan declared independence from Sudan in July 2011, following the stalled implementation of the CPA signed in 2005 between the Sudan People's Liberation Movement/Army (SPLM/A) and the government in Khartoum. The peacebuilding and state-building process that followed was however characterized by continuity, particularly in regard to the role attributed to difference. Fears about 'tribalism' and 'tribal conflict' have a long history in South Sudan, dating back at least to the advent of Anglo-Egyptian colonialism – but so has the notion that the recognition of South Sudan's ethnic diversity could guarantee the country's unity. The Second Sudanese Civil War (1983–2005) was at its core an armed conflict between the regime in Khartoum and a variety of southern rebel groups, with the SPLM/A at the forefront. However, the SPLM/A's liberation struggle, as well as the period after the CPA, have also been characterized by widespread worries about armed clashes between different groups. While some of these conflicts were local and small in scale, such as different 'clans' or 'sections' fighting over land and natural resources, there existed larger concerns about 'regionalism' and 'divisionism', and thus conflicts which would pitch agglomerates of ethnic groups against each other.

The SPLM, as well as the government of South Sudan under the presidency of Salva Kiir Mayardit, have particularly been held captive by the claim of 'Dinka domination' of government institutions and the armed forces (Johnson 2011). These allegations have a long history. Following the Addis Ababa Agreement of 1972 that ended the First Sudanese Civil War, southern Sudan obtained regional autonomy. This was followed by years of quarrels about the political administration of the southern region, and growing accusations that it had become dominated by the Dinka (Arou 1982, 324). Supported by a broad political opposition, as well as the government in Khartoum, these claims gave rise to what came to be known as the 'Kokora' – the administrative redivision of southern Sudan, a process that weakened the south politically, intensified the animosity between the different regions, and provided a cause for the SPLM/A's insurgency (Willems and Deng 2015).

On the eve of the CPA, concerns about regionally defined, ethnic fault lines were present, just as they had been before the war, and they influenced the SPLM's considerations about institutional reform. The rebel movement had governed its liberated territories through a rudimentary system of civil administration, the so-called Civil Administration of the New Sudan (CANS). From 2003, when a settlement of the conflict became more likely, a commission composed of SPLM experts, supported by international organizations, initiated a process aimed at the 'recovery' and 'reform' of local governments. Since 2006, this process has been guided by the newly established Local Government Board (LGB), tasked with, among other things, drafting a new legal framework and the capacity development of local administrations. The experts emphasized that the policy framework for local government should 'provide principles and policies for managing the culturally diverse communities and offer tools for managing ethnic conflict' (Skills 2004, 3). Decentralization should 'strengthen national unity and solidarity by recognizing diversity in ways that promote the sense of all citizens that they belong to [South Sudan] and participate in its government' (Skills 2004, 5). Local government could 'diffuse regional feelings' – the strengthening of county administrations would foster a sense of belonging at a much smaller scale and thus serve as a strategy for preventing the disintegration of the south along larger, regionally defined categories (SPLM Governance Cluster 2004). Consequently, the reform process led to the establishment of local administrations at three administrative tiers: county, *payam*, and *boma*.

Interestingly, this thinking resembles earlier efforts to undermine the possibility of 'trans-ethnic' mobilization (Mamdani 1996, 152–8), particularly the British policy of establishing native administrations to contain the spread of nationalist movements through the creation of 'self-contained racial or tribal units' based 'upon indigenous customs, traditional usage and beliefs' (Bakheit 1965, 208). The SPLM leadership's considerations were similar in that they aimed to prevent the rise of regionally defined movements that could pose a challenge to central government. Both historically and in independent South Sudan, the task was to scale ethnic difference correctly: to make ethnic belonging salient at the right level of government. Importantly, the SPLM's policy also sat well with the considerations of international organizations, which assumed that devolution of power would be central to building peace in the ethnically diverse South Sudan (Sarzin and Mehta 2011, 53). As is discussed in the following, these scaling attempts are characterized by conflicting practices, including: portraying difference in political and technical discourse; knowing difference, for instance through assessments and mapping exercises; managing difference, such as through the demarcation of territories; and efforts to produce difference through political activism.

Over the course of the reform process, references to 'tribes' and 'tribalism' completely vanished from policymakers' discourse, arguably because they were aware of the terms' negative connotations. As an antidote, the far less politically laden term 'community' emerged, for example in key legislative documents, which portrayed local government as 'community government' (Government of Southern Sudan 2009, sect. 107). The equalization of local government with community government was pursued through the formal integration of traditional authorities into the administrative structure. A leading expert assumed that traditional authorities would 'relate organically to historical, cultural and ethnic groups' (Skills 2004, 2012). The new legal framework therefore established clear links between an ethnically framed understanding of community, traditional authority, and the territorially defined administrative entities of local government. Strikingly, the term 'community' no longer carried any clear scalar connotation, in the same way that 'tribe' did for instance in relation to 'clans' or 'sections' at respective lower scales.

This approach however stood in conflict with the knowledge practices of local administrations, which maintained an interest in the scalar configurations of difference. Training manuals for local government officials, for example, recounted the history of southern Sudan as one of 'peoples and tribes' (LGB and GTZ, n.d.), and government officials began to produce lists of southern Sudanese 'indigenous communities' (LGB, n.d.). A 'county form', circulated in 2009 as part of the beginning of a formal process through which counties would be legally established, asked specifically about the names of the ethnic groups, clans, and sub-clans of the county. Moreover, a 'county mapping tool' was used to ask about the different 'ethnic' and 'section' groups of the county and whether or not the 'ethnic balance in the Administration' would 'reflect that of the county' (Government of Southern Sudan and LGB 2010).

While some involved in the reform process thus sought to clearly delineate the ethnic composition of administrative units, the final legal framework eschewed any reference to an 'organic' or homogenous composition of administrative units, and only made vague provisions. Nonetheless it identified the lowest level of local government, the *boma*, as the 'main domain of traditional authority' and thus as the main level at which ethnic difference would retain its meaning (Government of Southern Sudan 2009, sect. 19). Political authority would mainly be exercised through the commissioner at the county level, where county councils should be created on the basis of 'a common interest of the communities'. Given that these would be multi-ethnic entities populated by a diverse range of groups under different traditional authorities, guidance was given for councils to be created under 'consideration of minority or majority ethnic group cases as may be decided by the Southern Sudan Legislative Assembly; and administrative convenience' (Government of Southern Sudan 2009, appendix I). Through reference to the ethnic minorities or majorities that would be created depending on the size and composition of a given local government unit, the new legal framework exhibited the continued concern for scale among the legislators: which levels of government would be invested with power and where the administrative boundaries would be drawn remained closely linked with the construction of ethnic difference to establish majorities and minorities.

The prospect of a system of government that would cater to community interests led to increased concerns about the demarcation of administrative boundaries. In consequence, an increasing number of political initiatives arose that were aimed at carving out ethnically homogenous units for specific communities. In 2008, a leading technical expert acknowledged that the many 'disputes perceived as arising from the demarcation of [the] administrative boundaries of the States and Counties' were 'caused by the grand designs to curb [sic] *bomas* and *payams* out of existing counties to meet group and personal interests' (Guok 2008, 1). The demarcations on which the SPLM based its system of civil administration during the war were inherited from Sudan and constituted relatively large entities that provided little opportunity for pursuing the goal of establishing ethnically homogeneous local government units. While the number of counties had already proliferated in an uncontrolled manner during the war, self-proclaimed 'communities' aimed to renegotiate existing county boundaries even more forcefully in the course of the reform process, often justified through concerns about ethnic conflict (Skills 2004, 8).

For example, in a letter addressed to President Kiir in October 2006, representatives of the Pari community requested the establishment of an 'independent Lafon County for the Pari people alone' due to a 'conflict over the county' between different communities

THE POLITICS OF PEACEBUILDING IN A DIVERSE WORLD

caused by a lack of 'common interest', offering justification for the creation of a separate local administration: 'a Pari based Lafon County without the Lopit will be one of the most prosperous and peaceful County [sic] in Eastern Equatoria State' (Pari Community Delegates 2006). A response from the chairman of the LGB was generally affirmative of their demands:

> [it] is the stand [sic] of the GOSS [Government of Southern Sudan] of which [the] LGB is part, that since the CPA brought about the peace … we cherish the peaceful living together of our people of different communities in harmony, far away from inter-tribal conflicts … If it is true that the Pari Community find [sic] it impossible to live in peace together with some other communities in their area … this could be one of the strong reasons to enable the Pari Community [to] deserve an Administrative unit of their own … [in other words] a separate County. (LGB 2007)

In many other cases conflicts over county demarcations have turned violent since the CPA, and have motivated community leaders to seek the establishment of ethnically homogeneous government units. Some experts have therefore expressed concerns that the introduction of democratic principles into ethnically diverse local government units ensured that competition over local government positions would unfold along ethnic lines. Local democracy could strengthen ethnic sentiments and be abused by political entrepreneurs invoking ethnic belonging (Hirblinger and Simons 2015, 428–9). Thus, the SPLM leadership delayed the implication of its own 'Unity in Diversity' policy on the grounds that the new arrangements could produce renewed trouble, unfolding along ethnic lines. Given the emphasis on communal belonging and the numerous conflicts over demarcations in consequence, the attempt to reconcile democratization with ethnic belonging led the local government reform process into a deadlock. The politics of scaling difference in the case of South Sudan thus justified a protracted and ineffective devolution of power and an increase in the centralization of governance, and finally brought about the causes that for many justified a return to armed conflict in December 2013.

Decentralization and the scaling of difference in Kosovo

In Kosovo, too, peacebuilding interventions entailed discursive and administrative practices of scaling difference, in particular through repeated negotiations of local government arrangements that would recognize certain groups and endow them with political power at the right scale. Following the Yugoslav wars of dissolution and a protracted period of state repression in Kosovo during the 1990s, violent conflict broke out between the Kosovo Liberation Army and the Yugoslav security forces in 1998. The North Atlantic Treaty Organization (NATO) intervened in 1999 with a bombing campaign against Yugoslavia that was justified under the doctrine of humanitarian intervention (Judah 2002). Thereafter, the United Nations Interim Administration Mission in Kosovo (UNMIK) was tasked with administering Kosovo pending the determination of its final status. The 'status question', i.e. whether Kosovo would become an independent state or remain part of Serbia, was left unresolved. Nevertheless, Serbia effectively retreated from Kosovo and UNMIK took over all state functions (Caplan 2005), except in the predominantly Serb-inhabited north, where Serbian sovereignty continued de facto. Kosovo entered a prolonged period of international administration, during which attempts were made to negotiate a settlement between Belgrade and Pristina on its political future. The status of the Serbian minority in Kosovo, which overwhelmingly opposed independence, was a key consideration. Following unsuccessful UN-mediated negotiations, Kosovo unilaterally – although with significant international backing – declared its independence in 2008 on the basis of the Ahtisaari Plan, which was not signed by both parties.[4] Group-differentiated rights and a decentralization process which aimed to empower the Serb minority in Kosovo formed a key part of the plan, whose implementation was monitored and supported by international actors.

Ethnic difference was considered central to both conflict and peace in Kosovo by key actors involved in its expansive peacebuilding and statebuilding endeavours, during which the recognition and skilful management of Kosovo's diversity thus took central stage (Landau 2017). Concerns for the appropriate scaling of difference are already evident in the terminology used: in UN-administered Kosovo, provisions for group-differentiated rights were granted to so-called 'communities', rather than to minorities. This terminology served to deflect from scalar framings of ethnic difference and to defuse the politicization implied in the term 'minority', as an attempt was made to avoid prejudging Kosovo's future status by defining which group would be in the minority: Albanians within an undivided Serbia, or Serbs within an independent Kosovo (Bieber 2004b, 117). The term 'community rights' has also been referred to as 'a euphemism for minority rights' (Perritt 2010, 155). While the Kosovo Serbs have always been the politically most vocal and well-represented minority in Kosovo, others also benefit from the group-differentiated rights, including the Roma, Ashkali, Egyptian, Turkish, Bosnian, and Gorani communities, as well as the Albanian communitywhich makes up the overwhelming majority of Kosovo's population – in cases where it represents a local minority. From the late 1990s onwards, the various proposed settlements became progressively more favourable to Kosovo's smaller minorities. This was in all likelihood a way to lower the stakes in the conflict between Kosovo's Serbs and Albanians – and it also contained a historical dimension, since the initial recognition of some of Kosovo's smaller minorities came as part of an 'often-deliberate fragmentation of minorities' (Bieber 2015, 883). Importantly, the Ahtisaari Plan's provisions for community rights included asymmetrical elements favouring the Kosovo Serbs, most notably in the decentralization of enhanced competencies to certain Serb-majority municipalities only (*Comprehensive Proposal for the Kosovo Status Settlement* 2007, Annex 3).

Decentralization was used as a tool to institutionally recognize and manage ethnic difference in Kosovo, and it played a prominent role in the negotiations about Kosovo's status. The scaling of difference was negotiated in numerous proposals for decentralization, which varied in the territorial units of local governance (municipalities, sub-municipal units, or groups of municipalities) and in the degree of political authority vested in them. By creating new minorities at the local level, the practice of redrawing administrative boundaries also constituted a rescaling and reconfiguring of difference.

Decentralization in Kosovo must be understood in light of two factors: firstly, the ethnically homogenizing displacement and return patterns that characterized the war and immediate postwar periods, which had led to a pattern of territorial segregation between communities and given rise to a 'consolidation of the "enclavisation" of minority life in Kosovo' (OSCE and UNHCR 2002, 47); and secondly, the imperative to extend the reach of Kosovo's institutions to the Kosovan Serb enclaves who rejected these institutions' authority by replacing the so-called parallel structures financed by the Serbian state. At the heart of the decentralization debate in Kosovo was thus the hope that decentralized government, particularly for the Kosovo Serbs, would facilitate their inclusion in the emerging state structures, and it was therefore understood that 'the recognition of group difference [was the] starting point for the design of constituent units' (McCulloch 2014, 17). This understanding, however, created a tension with the peacebuilding project's discursive framing of Kosovo as first and foremost 'multi-ethnic', whereby the integration – rather than separation – of groups was often implicitly understood as a core feature of the desired peaceful order. In this context, administrative recognition of de facto ethnic segregation, and the creation of largely mono-ethnic governance units, sat uneasily with a commitment to multi-ethnicity, with difference again straddling the line of being perceived as both cause and cure of conflict. In this context, the scaling of difference was negotiated in successive attempts to engineer new local government arrangements.

The first time that decentralization was raised simultaneously as a peacebuilding tool and a strategy for the inclusion of Kosovo Serbs in the emerging political structures was in 2002 (Steiner 2002). A proposed plan for the divided city of Mitrovica was tabled to encourage its large Kosovo Serb population, concentrated in the city's north, to participate in the Kosovo-wide local elections, thus far largely boycotted by this population. Decentralization was proposed in order to bring Mitrovica's north and south under common UNMIK administration. Efforts to rescale difference, changing the scale at which it would become politically salient, took the form of a limited institutionalization of ethnically based self-government in Kosovo, as well as the idea of redrawing administrative boundaries to reflect demographic trends. Rather than devolving power to the municipal level, it foresaw separate sub-municipal units (SMUs) for the Albanian and Serb parts of the municipality, which were each to have a local council, administrative organs, and a budget, and would have authority to decide on issues of local importance while forming part of an integrated, multi-ethnic municipality of Mitrovica. The offer of establishing SMUs for 'sizeable non-majority communities' was thereafter extended to all of Kosovo in exchange for participation in local elections, which, however, did not initially materialize. Notably, the scaling of difference took the form of recognizing it at one level by creating relatively ethnically homogeneous units, while embedding these in larger, mixed-governance structures. This scaling of difference indicates a desire to avoid accusations of endorsing purely mono-ethnic governance units, and it is also evident in reactions to further developments, whereby Kosovo Serbs embraced the idea of decentralization, albeit scaling it to a different level. Continuing to reject participation with the authorities in Pristina, the Kosovo Serbs instead formed an 'Assembly of Serbian Municipalities' to which the United Nations (UN) reacted by stating that 'institutions based on mono-ethnicity' have 'no legal relevance for Kosovo' (UNMIK 2003, 1). The discursive framing of this reaction in a principled rejection of mono-ethnicity, even though the proposed SMUs had contained a level of recognition of ethnic separation as well, is indicative of conflicting visions for the scaling of difference.

As the debate on decentralization continued, the appropriate level at which to recognize difference was eventually raised to the municipality level. The Ahtisaari Plan in 2007 settled on the creation of a number of new, Serb-majority municipalities to reflect demographic realities as part of an asymmetric decentralization process that gave Serb municipalities in particular enhanced self-government rights. This policy was presented as the appropriate scaling of difference, framed in the name of multi-ethnicity and the integration of Kosovo Serbs into state structures. The recognition and institutionalization of difference in the form of mono-ethnic governance units was thus considered, while not desirable, at least acceptable as a peacebuilding measure only at the level of the municipality. At the higher level of the state, however, difference was recognized and framed in more integrative terms, as evidenced by a refusal to give anything but a 'multi-ethnic' character to the newly independent Kosovo.

Although the Ahtisaari Plan was meant to settle both Kosovo's status question and its management of ethnic difference, conflicting discursive and administrative practices of decentralization in the post-independence period – pertaining to both the 'lower' and 'higher' levels of scaling – continued to affect the country's politics. The reluctance to create further local government units for smaller minorities, along with the continued deadlock around the creation of a larger unit in the form of the proposed 'Association of Serbian Municipalities', reveals an ongoing negotiation of the scaling of difference in Kosovo.

For example, the Ahtisaari Plan provided for the establishment of new municipalities in settlements of at least 5000 inhabitants that are made up of 75% or more non-majority community members, in which case the state is encouraged to 'engage in consultations [with that community], with a view to establishing other new municipalities' (*Comprehensive Proposal for the Kosovo Status Settlement* 2007). Since independence, the Bosniak community has advocated for the creation of its own municipality in Kosovo's south, thus effectively attempting to change the scalar configurations of ethnic difference.[5] However, these attempts have remained low on the agenda and have found few backers, since the decentralization process was chiefly designed with the Kosovo Serbs in mind.[6]

On the other hand, since 2011, the dialogue between Belgrade and Pristina – mediated by the European Union (EU) – has discussed the creation of a Kosovo Serb unit at a level above the municipality, thus reopening the debate on the appropriate scaling of difference. In April 2013, an agreement was signed between the two parties agreeing on the creation of a vaguely termed 'Association/Community of Serb-Majority Municipalities' (*First Agreement of Principles Governing the Normalization of Relations* 2013). Interpretations of the nature of the association/community vary widely, ranging from a separate level of government for Serbs in Kosovo to essentially a non-governmental organization (NGO) made up of various municipalities. The possibility of full territorial autonomy for Kosovo Serbs embodied in the agreement led to a series of political crises that have subsequently paralysed key institutions in Kosovo, and it remains largely unimplemented. The scaling of difference thus continues to be contested.

Overall, the focus on ethnic difference as both cause of and cure for conflict – combined with its scaling along the parameters of ethnic decentralization at the sub-municipal, municipal, and regional levels – has had tangible effects on the peace and conflict dynamics in Kosovo, as well as on governance more broadly. Firstly, the continued renegotiation of the scaling of difference in both discursive and administrative practices has constituted an ongoing source of tension, both in Kosovo domestically and in its relationship with Serbia. Secondly, administrative practices of scaling have entailed the increasing ethnicization of all public life, in particular the provision of public services in Kosovo. Given that Kosovo is characterized by poor governance and a private sector so weak that public employment is often the only source of livelihood, the focus on self-government rights in the form of establishing new, ethnically defined municipalities – with the implied creation of public sector employment – has had the effect of further entrenching an ethnically based patronage system for majority and minority communities alike (Capussela 2015). Peace and stability in Kosovo have become understood predominantly in ethnic terms, with a minimal focus on other societal cleavages and sources of grievance.

Conclusion

Difference relates to conflict in an ambiguous manner. It is intricately related to both the causes of and cures for conflict. While difference widely retains an emancipatory appeal for political movements that seek greater political freedom, it has also taken a central place in the efforts of colonial and postcolonial regimes to create stable and peaceful political entities. This article argues that this duality of cause and cure is mediated by a politics of scaling difference. As our case studies suggest, this involves various, often conflicting discursive and non-discursive practices through which difference is recognized, reinforced, and reconfigured, as well as invested with political power at different scales of the respective political order. Scaling difference ultimately entails both shaping the identities of the governed subjects and defining the social, political, and territorial spaces and hierarchies in which these subjects are able to assert political control.

The cases of Kosovo and South Sudan demonstrate that the politics of scaling difference can be informed by a variety of influences, including historical legacies and trajectories of scale-making reaching back to colonial and imperial rule, broader political paradigms and programmes – for instance associated with liberal good governance which advances decentralization – and conflict-related grievances and narratives that reinforce identity categories and provide justifications for scale-making. We found that the politics of scaling difference in the two case studies are characterized by three common patterns. Discursively, political actors promoted the term 'community' over other terms which are negatively associated with conflict – such as 'minority' and 'tribe' – in order to eschew from public debate the scalar connotations that these terms entail. This can be understood as *efforts to unravel scalar configurations*. Furthermore, attempts were made to use scaling as a tool to fracture the dominance of certain groups, and to recognize and empower others, wherein it was hoped that this would contribute to peace and stability. These *efforts to rescale* were aimed at balancing political power and inevitably required both knowing and mapping difference; they discuss the viability of specific scalar configurations – including spatial demarcations. However, these administrative practices were met with *efforts to counter-scale* by political entrepreneurs that aimed to (re)negotiate the appropriate level at which to make difference politically salient, in order to advance their specific agendas.

The continued contestation over the scaling of difference has led to varying outcomes. In South Sudan, large-scale violence recurred in 2013 due to an increase in the centralization of power, which was partly the result of a failed decentralization process that was curtailed by fears of increasing ethnic tensions. Roughly ten years after the first local government reform efforts, the national government was accused of 'dictatorial tendencies' by a nascent opposition – and the civil war that followed has since been characterized by a re-emergence of regionally defined ethnic cleavages. In Kosovo, renegotiations of decentralization in the post-independence period have significantly contributed to political deadlock and paralysis of state institutions, in particular since the 2013 agreement between Kosovo and Serbia. This suggests that scaling difference evidently influences the dynamics of peace and conflict.

Our case studies point to the fact that the politics of scaling difference are closely related to the power struggles through which political power and nested hierarchies of difference are co-produced. Nonetheless, the practice–theoretical lens applied in this article could benefit from further efforts to flesh out the material character of these relations (Joseph 2018), for example by exploring how efforts of scaling difference are linked to the redistribution of economic resources, and how resource and capital flows interact with scalar configurations (Swyngedouw 2004). While the politics of scaling difference are first and foremost relational, they do have material effects. Our case studies point to the reproduction of material inequality and patronage linked to scalar configurations of difference, and the outbreak of renewed war in South Sudan speaks to the fact that the politics of scale even impact on the questions of life and death of the populations embedded in nested hierarchies of difference. Scaled identities are not only relational in an ideational, discursive, and practical sense but also in their material dimensions once they legitimize and pave the way for the distribution of economic resources, which can be an important underlying cause of armed violence. As such, the politics of scaling difference, which mediate the dual role of both cause of and cure for conflict, practically affect the lives of those made to differ.

Notes

1. The territory of what is now South Sudan had prior to the country's independence formed part of Anglo-Egyptian Sudan (1899–1956) and independent Sudan (1956–2011), since the Comprehensive Peace Agreement (CPA) of 2005 as the autonomous region of Southern Sudan. From 1945, Kosovo was part of the Socialist Federal Republic of Yugoslavia (SFRY) as an autonomous province of Serbia until its violent dissolution in the 1990s. It unilaterally declared independence from Serbia in 2008 after being governed under a transitional administration (1999–2001) led by the United Nations (UN) and a provisional self-government under UN executive powers (2001–8).
2. We recognize that a focus on ethnicity can blind scholars to other forms of enacted difference, as well as to the question of intersectionality. Rather than discarding these, this article proposes a frame of study that can be applied broadly, and we look forward to future studies of the scaling of difference in relation to class, gender, and other forms of difference.
3. This is a task with which scholars often struggle. In a recent contribution on the Murle for example, the author notes that she recognizes the 'multiplicity of clans and sub-ethnic groups that are often coalesced together under the banner of a wider ethnic group', but notes that 'in some cases, such detail was not forthcoming in the author's investigations' (Laudati 2011, 27).
4. The Comprehensive Proposal for the Kosovo Status Settlement plan is commonly referred to as the Ahtisaari Plan, after Martti Ahtisaari, the Finnish diplomat who led the negotiations in his role as Special Envoy for Kosovo appointed by the UN Secretary-General from 2006–7.
5. Interview conducted via Skype with a project manager of the European Centre for Minority Issues (ECMI) Kosovo, 13 May 2009. See also Krasniqi (2015, 209).
6. Interview conducted via Skype with a former senior International Civilian Office (ICO) official, 18 September 2014.

Disclosure statement

No potential conflict of interest was reported by the authors.

ORCID

Andreas Hirblinger ⓘ http://orcid.org/0000-0003-1193-1903
Dana M. Landau ⓘ http://orcid.org/0000-0003-2900-4163

References

Adler, Emanuel, and Vincent Pouliot. 2011. "International Practices." *International Theory* 3 (01): 1–36. https://doi.org/10.1017/S175297191000031X.

Anderson, Benedict. 2006. *Imagined Communities: Reflections on the Origin and Spread of Nationalism*. Rev. ed. London: Verso.

Arou, Mom Kou Nhial. 1982. *Regional Devolution in Southern Sudan, 1972–81*. Edinburgh: University of Edinburgh.

Bakheit, Gaafar Mohed Ali. 1965. *British Administration and Sudanese Nationalism, 1919–1939*. Cambridge.

Bargués-Pedreny, Pol, and Xavier Mathieu. 2018. "Beyond Silence, Obstacle and Stigma: Revisiting the 'Problem' of Difference in Peacebuilding." *Journal of Intervention and Statebuilding* 12 (3): 283–299.

Barkey, Karen, and George Gavrilis. 2016. "The Ottoman Millet System: Non-Territorial Autonomy and Its Contemporary Legacy." *Ethnopolitics* 15 (1): 24–42. https://doi.org/10.1080/17449057.2015.1101845.

Bieber, Florian. 2004a. "Institutionalizing Ethnicity in the Western Balkans: Managing Change in Deeply Divided Societies." *ECMI Working Paper*, no. 19: 1–28.

Bieber, Florian. 2004b. "The Legal Framework for Post-War Kosovo and the Myth of Multiethnicity." In *Managing Hatred and Distrust: The Prognosis for Post-Conflict Settlement in Multiethnic Communities in the Former Yugoslavia*, edited by Dimitrijeviç Nenad, and Kovacs Petra, 118–135. Budapest: Open Society Institute.

Bieber, Florian. 2015. "The Construction of National Identity and Its Challenges in Post-Yugoslav Censuses." *Social Science Quarterly* 96 (3): 873–903. https://doi.org/10.1111/ssqu.12195.

Brenner, Neil. 2001. "The Limits to Scale? Methodological Reflections on Scalar Structuration." *Progress in Human Geography* 25 (4): 591–614. https://doi.org/10.1191/03091320 1682688959.

Brubaker, Rogers. 2004. *Ethnicity without Groups*. Cambridge, MA: Harvard University Press.

Caplan, Richard. 2005. *International Governance of War-Torn Territories: Rule and Reconstruction*. Oxford: Oxford University Press.

Caplan, Richard. 2014. "European Organizations and the Governance of Ethnocultural Diversity after the Cold War: The Yugoslav 'Laboratory'." *Nationalism and Ethnic Politics* 20 (3): 269–286. https://doi.org/10.1080/13537113.2014.937623.

Capussela, Andrea Lorenzo. 2015. *State-Building in Kosovo: Democracy, Corruption, and the EU in the Balkans*. London: I.B.Tauris.

Collins, Robert, and Richard Herzog. 1961. "Early British Administration in the Southern Sudan." *The Journal of African History* 2 (1): 119–135. https://doi.org/10.2307/179587.

Comprehensive Proposal for the Kosovo Status Settlement. 2007. https://www.kuvendikosoves.org/common/docs/Comprehensive%20Proposal%20.pdf.

Doty, Roxanne Lynn. 1996. *Imperial Encounters: The Politics of Representation in North–South Relations*. Minneapolis: University of Minnesota Press.

Erk, Jan. 2015. "Non-Territorial Millets in Ottoman History." In *Minority Accommodation Through Territorial and Non-Territorial Autonomy*, edited by Tove H. Malloy and Francesco Palermo, 119–131. Oxford: Oxford University Press.

First Agreement of Principles Governing the Normalization of Relations. 2013.

Government of Southern Sudan. 2009. *Laws of Southern Sudan. The Local Government Act*.

Government of Southern Sudan and LGB. 2010. "County Development Plan and Budget. Mayendit County, Unity State.".

Guok, David Koak. 2008. "Local Government Presentation to the Sixth Governors Forum on Demarcation of State and County Administrative Boundaries in Southern Sudan.".

Hameiri, Shahar, Caroline Hughes, and Fabio Scarpello. 2017. *International Intervention and Local Politics*. Cambridge: Cambridge University Press.

Hameiri, Shahar, and Lee Jones. 2017. "Beyond Hybridity to the Politics of Scale: International Intervention and 'Local' Politics." *Development and Change* 48 (1): 54–77. https://doi.org/10.1111/dech.12287.

Hameiri, Shahar, and Fabio Scarpello. 2018. "International Development Aid and the Politics of Scale." *Review of International Political Economy* 25 (2): 145–168. https://doi.org/10.1080/09692290.2018.1431560.

Herb, Guntram H., and David H. Kaplan. 2018. "Introduction: Scaling the Nation." In *Scaling Identities: Nationalism and Territoriality*, edited by Guntram H. Herb and David H. Kaplan, 1–3. Lanham, MD: Rowman & Littlefield.

Hirblinger, Andreas T., and Claudia Simons. 2015. "The Good, the Bad, and the Powerful: Representations of the 'Local' in Peacebuilding." *Security Dialogue* 46 (5): 422–439. https://doi.org/10.1177/0967010615580055.

Hisket, Mervyn. 1994. *The Course of Islam in Africa*. Edinburgh: Edinburgh University Press.

Hobsbawm, Eric John. 2012. *Nations and Nationalism since 1780: Programme, Myth, Reality*. 2nd ed. Cambridge: Cambridge University Press.

Horowitz, Donald L. 1985. (2000) *Ethnic Groups in Conflict*. Berkeley and London: University of California Press.

Johnson, Douglas H. 2011. *The Root Causes of Sudan's Civil Wars: Peace or Truce*. Rev. ed. Woodbridge: James Currey and Fountain.

Joseph, J. 2018. "Beyond Relationalism in Peacebuilding." *Journal of Intervention and Peacebuilding* 12 (3): 425–434.

Judah, Tim. 2002. *Kosovo: War and Revenge*. 2nd ed. New Haven, CT: Yale University Press.

Kaplan, Robert D. 1993. *Balkan Ghosts: A Journey through History*. New York: St Martin's Press.

Kaplan, David H. 2018. "National Identity and Scalar Processes." In *Scaling Identities: Nationalism and Territoriality*, edited by Guntram H. Herb and David H. Kaplan, 31–48. Lanham, Maryland: Rowman & Littlefield.

Krasniqi, Gëzim. 2015. "Equal Citizens, Uneven Communities: Differentiated and Hierarchical Citizenship in Kosovo." *Ethnopolitics* 14 (2): 197–217. https://doi.org/10.1080/17449057.2014.991152.

Lampe, John R. 2000. *Yugoslavia as History: Twice There Was a Country*. 2nd ed. Cambridge: Cambridge University Press.

Landau, Dana M. 2017. "The Quest for Legitimacy in Independent Kosovo: The Unfulfilled Promise of Diversity and Minority Rights." *Nationalities Papers* 45 (3): 442–463. https://doi.org/10.1080/00905992.2016.1267137.

Lange, Matthew. 2015. "State Formation and Transformation in Africa and Asia." In *The Oxford Handbook of Transformations of the State*, edited by Stephan Leibfried, Evelyne Huber, Matthew Lange, Jonah D. Levy, Frank Nullmeier, and John D. Stephens, 216–230. 1st ed. Oxford: Oxford University Press.

Laudati, Ann. 2011. "Victims of Discourse: Mobilizing Narratives of Fear and Insecurity in Post-Conflict South Sudan – The Case of Jonglei State." *African Geographical Review* 30 (1): 15–32. https://doi.org/10.1080/19376812.2011.10539133.

Lentz, Carola. 1995. "'Tribalism' and Ethnicity in Africa: A Review of Four Decades of Anglophone Research." *Cahiers Des Sciences Humaines* 31 (2): 303–328.

LGB (Local Government Board). 2007. "Letter Addressed to Mark Akio Ukuibul, Secretary for Social and Public Relations, Pari Community, Juba." Local Government Board Library.

LGB (Local Government Board). n.d. "The Southern Sudan Indigenous Communities (Tentative)." Local Government Board Library.

LGB (Local Government Board), and Gesellschaft für Technische Zusammenarbeit (GTZ). n.d. "Training Course for Local Government Administrative Officers." Local Government Board Library.

Lottholz, Philipp, and Nicolas Lemay-Hébert. 2016. "Re-Reading Weber, Re-Conceptualizing State-Building: From Neo-Weberian to Post-Weberian Approaches to State, Legitimacy and State-Building." *Cambridge Review of International Affairs* 29 (4): 1467–1485. https://doi.org/10.1080/09557571.2016.1230588.

Lynch, Allen. 2002. "Woodrow Wilson and the Principle of 'National Self-Determination': A Reconsideration." *Review of International Studies* 28 (2): 419–436. https://doi.org/10.1017/S0260210502004199.

Mac Ginty, Roger, and Oliver P. Richmond. 2013. "The Local Turn in Peace Building: A Critical Agenda for Peace." *Third World Quarterly* 34 (5): 763–783. https://doi.org/10.1080/01436597.2013.800750.

Malcolm, Noel. 1998. *Kosovo: A Short History*. London: Macmillan.

Mamdani, Mahmood. 1996. *Citizen and Subject: Contemporary Africa and the Legacy of Late Colonialism*. Princeton: Princeton University Press.

Mamdani, Mahmood. 2012. *Define and Rule: Native as Political Identity*. 1st ed. Cambridge, MA: Harvard University Press.

Marston, Sallie A., John Paul Jones, and Keith Woodward. 2005. "Human Geography without Scale." *Transactions of the Institute of British Geographers* 30 (4): 416–432. https://doi.org/10.1111/j.1475-5661.2005.00180.x.

Massey, Doreen B. 1999. "Philosophy and the Politics of Spatiality: Some Considerations." *Geographische Zeitschrift* 87 (1): 1–12. https://www.jstor.org/stable/27818829.

McCulloch, Allison. 2014. *Power-Sharing and Political Stability in Deeply Divided Societies*. London: Routledge.

Migdal, Joel S., and Klaus Schlichte. 2005. "Rethinking the State." In *The Dynamics of States: The Formation and Crises of State Domination*, edited by Schlichte Klaus, 1–40. Aldershot: Ashgate.

Mouffe, Chantal. 2005. *The Return of the Political*. London: Verso.

OSCE (Organization for Security and Co-operation in Europe), and UNHCR (United Nations High Commissioner for Refugees). 2002. *OSCE/UNHCR Ninth Assessment of the Situation of Ethnic Minorities in Kosovo (Covering Period September 2001–April 2002)*. Pristina: OSCE/UNHCR.

Paffenholz, Thania. 2015. "Unpacking the Local Turn in Peacebuilding: A Critical Assessment Towards an Agenda for Future Research." *Third World Quarterly* 36 (5): 857–874. https://doi.org/10.1080/01436597.2015.1029908.

Pari Community Delegates. 2006. "Demand for an Independent Lafon County for Pari People Alone. Letter Addressed to the 1st Vice President of the Republic of Sudan and President of the Government of Southern Sudan (GOSS), Juba." Local Government Board Library.

Perritt, Henry H., Jr. 2010. *The Road to Independence for Kosovo: A Chronicle of the Ahtisaari Plan*. Cambridge: Cambridge University Press.

Ramet, Sabrina R. 2002. *Balkan Babel: The Disintegration of Yugoslavia from the Death of Tito to the Fall of Milosevic*. Boulder, CO: Westview Press.

Sarzin, Zara, and Bajor Mehta. 2011. "Republic of South Sudan: Issues in Urban Development. Phase 1 – Overview of the Urban Landscape. Final Draft, August 2011." Local Government Board Library.

Schmitt, Carl. 1996. *The Concept of the Political*. Edited by Leo Strauss, George Schwab, J. Harvey Lomax, and Tracy B. Strong. Chicago: University of Chicago Press.

Skills. 2004. "2nd Draft Report of the Local Government and Civil Administration Consultative Workshop Held between 26th to 29th January 2004 Rumbek, and Follow-up Meeting of the

Technical Team Held on 12th and 13th February at New Site, South Sudan." Local Government Board Library.

Skills. 2012. Prah, Kwesi Kwa, Moving Forward with COTALs. Address to the "Council of Traditional Authority Leaders Forum III (3rd COTAL Conference)", Juba, Southern Sudan, 25/26 May 2011, p. 12.

Spear, Thomas. 2003. "Neo-Traditionalism and the Limits of Invention in British Colonial Africa." *The Journal of African History* 44 (1): 3–27. https://doi.org/10.1017/S0021853702008320.

Spivak, Gayatri Chakravorty. 1988. "Can the Subaltern Speak?" In *The Post-Colonial Studies Reader*, edited by Bill Ashcroft, Gareth Griffiths, and Helen Tiffin, 24–28. London: Routledge.

SPLM (Sudan People's Liberation Movement) Governance Cluster. 2004. "The Governance Cluster. Local Government Sub-Committee, Rumbek." Local Government Board Library.

Steiner, Michael. 2002. "A Choice for Mitrovica – the Seven Point Plan.".

Swyngedouw, Erik. 2004. "Scaled Geographies: Nature, Place, and the Politics of Scale." In *Scale and Geographic Inquiry*, edited by Eric Sheppard and Robert B. McMaster, 129–153. Malden, MA: Blackwell.

Tilly, Charles. 2002. *Stories, Identities, and Political Change*. Lanham, MD: Rowman & Littlefield.

UNMIK (United Nations Interim Administration Mission in Kosovo). 2003. *UNMIK Press Release: '1244 Does Not Foresee Mono-Ethnic Institutions.' UNMIK/PR/906*.

Willems, Rens, and David K. Deng. 2015. "The Legacy of Kokora in South Sudan. Intersections of Truth, Justice and Reconciliation in South Sudan." South Sudan Law Society.

Old Slogans Ringing Hollow? The Legacy of Social Engineering, Statebuilding and the 'Dilemma of Difference' in (Post-) Soviet Kyrgyzstan

Philipp Lottholz ⓘ

ABSTRACT
This article illustrates the 'dilemma of difference' of post-conflict peacebuilding in the Kyrgyz Republic in Central Asia. Following inter-communal clashes in 2010, the country has received significant support in the form of peacebuilding and conflict prevention programmes and aid. Still, national policy makers retained their sovereignty and carried out peacebuilding in line with the country's historical legacy and cultural specificities. I illustrate the 'dilemma of difference' precluding sustainable peacebuilding and conflict transformation in this context because, as Minow argues, difference and the disadvantage and stigma associated with it is either silenced and ignored or over-emphasised, leading to marginalisation through victimisation. I trace the establishment of a territorialised and essentialised understanding of ethnicity through the social transformations of Kyrgyzstan in the early Soviet and the post-Soviet period. I then show how, since the '2010 events', authorities attempted to do peacebuilding and conflict prevention with appeals to multicultural peace and diversity through the Soviet-era idea of 'people's friendship'. Such efforts and corresponding peacebuilding initiatives in southern Kyrgyzstani communities face, as I show, inherent contradictions given exclusionary national-level language and cultural policies and a focus on donor satisfaction which serve to brush over reported tensions, exclusion and conflict.

Introduction

Ethnic and national identity have been core issues in peacebuilding scholarship since the end of the Cold War and the subsequent rise of sub-national and ethnic conflicts. The mixed record of scholarly and practical attempts to tackle these issues in the past two decades inspired new thinking about the role of identity in post-conflict peacebuilding. Scholars have acknowledged the necessity to address issues of identity but also find a way of forging peaceful social relations in a way that does not depend on invoking identity in the first place (e.g. Behr 2014; Bargués-Pedreny 2016). Bargues-Pedreny and Mathieu (2018) propose Minow's (1990) 'dilemma of difference' as a concept to capture the difficulty of dealing with situations of identity-based conflict and of building peace in its aftermath. According to Minow (1990, 49), difference poses a choice between 'equal treatment' or 'special treatment' in social practice, policy and discourse, 'each of which undesirably revive[s] difference or the stigma [and] disadvantage associated with it', which makes the dilemma of difference an irresolvable challenge. By examining the case of peacebuilding in the Kyrgyz Republic after an 'inter-ethnic' conflict in 2010 against its historical background, I offer an exemplary case of the entrenchment of the 'dilemma of difference' and its utilisation by national and local authorities. I show how the current policies on minorities and administrative languages as well as peacebuilding practices in conflict-affected communities aim to establish shared spaces for exchange and peaceful coexistence but, given the wider context of these measures, they are most likely to further exclude if not stigmatise the minorities in question (Minow 1990, 20).

The article shows that productively dealing with, let alone overcoming the 'dilemma of difference' in Kyrgyzstan is unviable in light of historical legacies of social engineering and their contemporary manifestations. This is so, because, first, identity is entrenched, natur- alised and normalised as a social category and thus precludes peaceful coexistence of different ethnic and national groups in the aftermath of large-scale conflict and in the face of socio-economic inequalities. Second and relatedly, the 'dilemma of difference' is utilised by power-holders playing a double-game of 'de-emphasising' identity on the one hand (Barqués-Pedreny 2016) and benefiting from policies and social practices which create hierarchy and exclusion based on identity, on the other. I illustrate this problem and its historical dimension by tracing the Soviet and post-Soviet version of mul- ticulturalism – the so-called 'peoples' friendship' (*druzhba narodov*) – and by demonstrat- ing its instrumentalisation for a performed and 'virtual' peace. The fact that this slogan was used throughout the country's history to maintain order and unity in the face of econ- omic hardship and distribution struggles along ethnic lines (Reeves 2014, 21; Megoran 2017, 192 ff.) explains this idea's popularity as a theme for peacebuilding events. However, in light of the current state-level policies on ethnic diversity, especially in the area of language and education, such forms of multi-cultural peace appear hollow at best and, 'imperial' or cynic at worst from a critical point of view.

The well-documented perceptions of minorities in Kyrgyzstan that the only way for them to build a meaningful future is by assimilating themselves to Kyrgyzstani identity – e.g. via speaking Kyrgyz or engaging in cultural routines – draw into sharp relief the difficulty of addressing the 'dilemma of difference'. Drawing on and extending the litera- ture on this specific case, I point out the paradoxical state of affairs unfolding as authorities in Kyrgyzstan, as in other post-conflict states, can present issues of identity-based violence and injustice as addressed or non-existent in order to draw benefits in the form of donor funding and international recognition. At the same time, however, the ongoing tensions and de facto conflict is by no means solved but simply relocated into the everyday and informal realms, as I show by drawing on a number of primary and secondary analyses. The article sheds light on a case of post-conflict peacebuilding where national authorities retain the control over how peace is being built while drawing on international funding and being subject to the corresponding conditions and advice. It further presents a so far rarely conducted analysis of the nexus between historical forms of identity (re-) pro- duction and present national level policies and communal level practices in the areas of peacebuilding and inter-ethnic relations. This integrated perspective can add new insights to both literatures in peace, conflict and intervention studies and to existing analyses of peacebuilding practices and policies in Kyrgyzstan.

THE POLITICS OF PEACEBUILDING IN A DIVERSE WORLD 125

For the same reason, the article is also limited, as it prioritises breadth over depth, meaning that parts of the argument are based on literature and other analyses, while the analysis presented is focussed on identifying the 'dilemma of difference' in a heuristic manner, rather than dwelling on the deepest possible understanding, contextual details and under-researched aspects. Citations and pointers for future research are therefore provided in these regards, where scholarship has offered little insight so far. The analysis is based on the author's PhD research (Lottholz 2018b) and elaborates aspects already analysed in other follow-on publications (Lottholz 2017, 2018a). The research project included a six months-long stay in the capital Bishkek and southern city of Osh, during which 62 interviews (27 recorded, 35 non-recorded), 18 participatory observations during community-level peacebuilding events or national conferences were conducted and augmented by the analysis of available documents and observations from everyday interactions, conferences, public events, and travels through the region. The research was done through a cooperative approach that aimed at establishing a dialogue with international and Kyrgyzstani NGOs working in the areas of peacebuilding and community security. Besides closely coordinating participant observations and interviews with the respective NGOs, an important activity was sharing draft analyses and chapters with the partner organisations to receive feedback and corrections. As discussed in more depth in Lottholz (2017, 17 ff.), such a cooperative and 'dialogical' approach faces scrutiny as to its ability to critically analyse the organisations and initiatives in question. However, as argued by activist and feminist scholars (see Minow 1990, 5; Lottholz 2017, 8 ff.), the arising ethical and positionality issues do generally not fall short of the ones faced by more conventional approaches to research, as long as cooperative and dialogical approaches practice critical reflection of their own limits. Perhaps more importantly, the key aim of these approaches is to give voice to people involved in peacebuilding and security processes in a given community or organisation. Thus, documenting things the way the people in question see them cannot be seen as taking a side with them. This interpretivist and subjectivist approach differs from others in that it does not even aspire to positivist-scientific standards of 'objectivity' (Lottholz 2017, 11).

The article is structured as follows. In the next section, I trace the history of the formation of the Kyrgyzstani nation throughout the Soviet and post-Soviet periods and how identity-based claims and competitions were balanced by the concept of 'people's friendship'. Consequently, after inter-ethnic tensions erupted into large-scale clashes in 2010, the public sphere became increasingly sanitised from discussion of ethnicity. In section three, I analyse the Kyrgyz authorities' approach at dealing with this situation by analysing the institutional changes and policies they implemented, and how they continued and deepened the tension between inter-ethnic harmony and coexistence on the one hand and ambitions to strengthen the dominance of Kyrgyz culture on the other. In section four, I present a fieldwork-based analysis of 'peoples' friendship'-style peacebuilding initiatives to show how they make a sincere attempt at overcoming distrust and tensions between community members of different belonging. As I show, identity-based institutional design and social policy especially since Kyrgyzstan's independence have entrenched distrust and isolation of different ethnicities, thus entrenching the 'dilemma of difference' faced by initiatives aiming to reconcile the latter. In the conclusion, I sum up the analytical insights and link them back to the issue of historically entrenched 'ethno-essentialist' thinking and the limits it poses to attempts to forge a productive 'politics of difference'.

Social engineering, civic nationalism and ethnic conflict in (post-)Soviet Kyrgyzstan

In this section, I discuss Kyrgyzstan's social transformations in the early twentieth century and the corresponding tension between a civic, multicultural nationalism on the one hand and claims for entitlements and dominance of 'titular' ethnicities on the other. This underlying tension, which reflects the dilemma of social engineering and policy based on ethnic identities the world over, has to be understood in its historical continuity so that its significance for current social dynamics can be grasped. In Martha Minow's terms, the significance appointed to newly defined categories of national belonging and ethnicity clearly foregrounded both their recognition and emancipation, as intended by the Bolsheviks, but also set the ground for identity-based politics and competition.

Soviet modernity, ethno-territoriality and 'peoples' friendship'

The Soviet history of the Kyrgyz Republic and other Central Asian republics is often understood as synonymous with the origin of their modern form of statehood. Central Asia scholars broadly agree that it was the Bolshevik conquest of Turkestan and the social transformation campaign during Stalin's reign which led to the establishment of Central Asian nations (Simon 1991; Hirsch 2005; Reeves 2014, ch. 2; Megoran 2017, 81 ff.). The national territorial delimitation (NTD, *natsionalnoe razmezhivanie*), which was executed roughly from 1924 until 1936, is widely understood as synonymous with the founding of the Kyrgyz and other Central Asian republics – and for the territorial quarrels between them in the contemporary period (Megoran 2017, Introduction). The people of Central Asia had lived in different dynastic, religious and other pre-modern territorial arrangements or Tsarist protectorates (Haugen 2003, ch. 2). With the national territorial delimitation, ethnicity, which had hitherto been largely insignificant, situational and inconsistently practiced, was elevated to a key category for discerning the people, or rather nations (Russian *etnos*), of the five new republics (Hirsch 2005; Reeves 2014, 66 ff.). The idea underlying this 'nationalisation' (Ru. *korenizatsiia*) was that of ethnogenesis, according to which nations are formed on the basis of a common history, language, heritage and ancestral lines. This process was understood to be linked to and malleable through the steering of economic conditions, education and political engineering (Laruelle 2008). The division of Central Asia into republics along ethno-national lines was thus supposed to 'accelerate history' (Haugen 2003, 169) and consolidate the nations of the Soviet Union by appointing them the territory and the rights that they were entitled to (Reeves 2014, 74). This way, ethnographic research, census data and cartography were used to, in Reeves' words, 'define the precise spatial correlates of any particular national group' (ibid.; Hirsch 2005, 10 ff.). This process was painstaking and often led to inevitably inappropriate border arrangements given the far-flung scattering of different groups across the mountainous regions of Central Asia, especially the Ferghana Valley basin, which necessitated a lot of swapping of territory between the newly-formed republics (Reeves 2014, 50).

THE POLITICS OF PEACEBUILDING IN A DIVERSE WORLD   127

To mitigate the competition for economically valuable territory and other assets among the national republics, the ethno-nationalist and primordialist discourse was constantly balanced with an internationalist rhetoric of 'peoples' friendship' (*druzhba narodov*), emphasising solidarity and brotherhood between nations (Edgar 2007; Megoran 2017, 227). According to the evolutionary logics of ethnogenesis discussed above, with the consolidation of Communism and equality among people, ethnic belonging would gradually lose its meaning and, thanks to intermarriage of people from different ethnicities, finally fade away (Simon 1991, 307; Edgar 2007, 585). The idea of 'peoples' friendship' in a multi-ethnic and multicultural Soviet society thus served as a mobilising vehicle against the adverse effects of many Soviet policies. Most importantly, it was used to mitigate people's grievances over being cut off from their 'home' national republics[1], which was presented as inevitable given the central authorities' attempt to take into account both the ethnic composition and economic and industrial production concerns in the delimitation (Haugen 2003, 181). While the running of political affairs and administration was dominated by the respective 'titular ethnicities', the status of minority groups was secured through so-called 'positive discrimination', meaning that they were granted cultural and linguistic rights as well as certain kinds of benefits and welfare provision (Brubaker 2011, 1787). In this sense, '[e]xclusive categories of ethnic identification' were made 'the vehicle for articulating claims and demanding rights' (Reeves 2014, 80) in Soviet Central Asia and lie at the heart of the 'dilemma of difference' faced by policy-makers in the region ever since.

The nationality policy of toeing a thin line between the reification of ethnic identity on the one hand, and a civic nationalist emphasis on Soviet citizenship on the other, was fairly successful in forging a peaceful coexistence among Central Asian peoples, especially until the Soviet economy came under increasing strain in the 1980s (see Lottholz 2017, 15). However, with the often violently super-imposed territorialisation of ethnicity and ethnicity-based administrative and welfare systems, the Soviet leadership also sowed the seeds of territorial and identity-based conflict following the empire's collapse.

From ethno-nationalist sentiments to ethnic conflict

Several analyses attest to the crucial role of ethnicity in life during the Soviet Union and the institutional racism and chauvinism experienced by Central Asians living outside of their 'home republic' and especially in relation to their 'European' counterparts (Hirsch 2005, 248; Megoran 2017, 94). In Kyrgyzstan, dynamics of social change and restructuring of urban space gave rise to particular ethno-political rivalries which were contained by the 'peoples' friendship' discourse in much – although not all – of the Soviet and post-Soviet periods (Megoran 2017, ch. 4). With the increased urbanisation and industrial restructuring of Osh – among other large and middle-sized southern towns like Jalal-Abad or Bazar-Korgon – from the 1960s onwards, more Kyrgyz started moving to urban areas. The city administration decided to restructure Osh into a modern industrial town, in which the traditional Uzbek *mahalla* neighbourhoods had to give way to multi-storey residential buildings and urban infrastructures such as parks, boulevards and squares (Megoran 2017, 193). Another change was the increased staffing of administrative and intellectual posts with Kyrgyz at the expense of Uzbeks, who had been strongly represented in this area due to their high educational attainments (Megoran 2013). Despite this marginalisation forcing them to retreat into trade, crafts, farming and other professions in the private sector, Uzbeks managed to maintain their relative wellbeing as perceived by large swathes of poor and needy Kyrgyz coming to Osh from the countryside (ibid.). Especially when the Soviet economic model came under increasing strain in the 1980s and yet more people from rural Kyrgyzstan migrated to the urban centres, tensions in the competition for jobs, state-provided housing and scarce land erupted into deadly clashes in and around Osh and Uzgen in the year 1990 (Tishkov 1995). Since Kyrgyzstan gained independence in 1991, the marginalisation of Uzbeks and other national minorities intensified due the increasingly precarious economic situation and given the perception that Uzbeks, traditionally more successful in trade and business thanks to their links to trade networks in Uzbekistan and other CIS countries, were generally better off than Kyrgyz (Megoran 2017, 202).

The first post-independence president, Askar Akaev, attempted to fight such sentiments by promoting interethnic unity or *mezhdunarodnoe soglasie* (lit. international, meaning between different nationalities, i.e. ethnicities) and diversity and tolerance under the slogan 'Kyrgyzstan is our common home' (*Kyrgyzstan – nash obshii dom*) (Marat 2008, 14). His efforts included the creation of an 'Assembly of the Peoples of Kyrgyzstan' (*Assambleia narodov Kyrgyzstana*) as a forum for the representation of minorities (ibid., 15). However, the emphasis on the country's cultural heritage and traditions paved the way for a resurgence of ethno-nationalist sentiments. Akaev's revival of the epos of Manas, one of the world's longest oral narrations on an ancient hero and supposed forefather of the Kyrgyz people, was made a bedrock of Kyrgyz national identity, as its poems and narrations became a mandatory part of school teaching and cultural life (ibid.). With it, however, Akaev also started to embrace the idea of ethnogenesis. By invoking the theories used in Soviet times, he drew connections between the Manas epic and the ethnogenesis of the Kyrgyz (Laruelle 2008). Akaev's claim that the legacy of Manas could be claimed regardless of one's origin, making Manas a hero for Kyrgyzstanis of all ethnicities, appeared to be far-fetched and was insufficient for rallying more conservative and ethno-nationalistically inclined groups, especially from rural and southern districts of Kyrgyzstan (Laruelle 2012, 2008). Ironically, the continuation of the 'people's friendship' discourse thus did not mitigate identity-based tensions but further intensified them.

With the deterioration of the economic situation and especially after the 2005 revolution leading to Akaev's replacement by Kurmanbek Bakiev, ethno-nationalist discourses emerged and gained currency – especially among opposition politicians (Laruelle 2012). Some politicians went as far as to say that the Kyrgyz, being the majority or 'titular' ethnic group of the country, 'are the masters of the house, the other nations and peoples [are] tenants [*Kyrgyzy v strane khoziaeva doma, a ostalnye narody i natsii kvartiranty*]' (cited in Gullette and Heathershaw 2015, 132–133). Different authors have argued that the 2010 clashes in southern Kyrgyzstan, which disproportionately led to the destruction of Uzbek properties, businesses and loss of Uzbek lives, have to be seen as expression of such sentiment and the feeling of Kyrgyz that their sovereignty as 'titular' ethnic group and majority was being 'imperilled' (Laruelle 2012; Gullette and Heathershaw 2015). Things were certainly more complex than this sketch conveys, as ethnicity-based political mobilisation was arguably driven by a few key figures such as the mayor of Osh Melis Myrzakmatov (Isakova 2013) and was further aggravated by rivalries within the Kyrgyzstani political establishment. Key works in political science and political anthropology have

THE POLITICS OF PEACEBUILDING IN A DIVERSE WORLD   129

shown how networks of 'subversive clientelism' (Radnitz 2010) were built up through the 2000s and generated significant potential of discontent and elite-led mass mobilisation across class boundaries, and perhaps more importantly, on the basis of geographical belonging, kinship and identity (Ismailbekova 2017). Against this background, the 'Osh events' and their aftermath, indicate the fatal failure of the attempts of the Soviet and post-Soviet leaderships to balance identity-based claims and political sentiments with calls for unity and peaceful coexistence. Instead of being appreciated and celebrated, 'difference' became, in Megoran's words (2017, 189) 'a matter of life and death' in a battle to secure the territorial and otherwise integrity of the Kyrgyz state, as some perceived it.

The taboo of identity after the 'Osh events'

Unpacking the contestations around the role of inter-ethnic tensions in the conflict, complicity of law enforcement and political leadership and issues of post-conflict justice is beyond the confines of this analysis. Other authors have shown that, to defend its line of argument, the Kyrgyz government does not shy away from declaring senior policy makers such as the international 'Kyrgyzstan Inquiry Commission' head Kimo Kiljunen persona non grata (Gullette and Heathershaw 2015, 126) or revoking cooperation with the OSCE and the US over quarrels on human rights issues in the aftermath of the '2010 events'. Gullette and Heathershaw (2015) have termed this behaviour an 'affective politics of sovereignty', which is enacted when- and wherever international actors try to interfere and influence the conduct in domestic issues pertaining to inter-ethnic relations and human rights. It has also been argued that the fears and frustrations underlying this discourse, as well the mechanisms making them a legitimate political sentiment, have to be understood in their own right instead of being dismissed as irrational and uncivilised (e.g. Megoran 2017, 2013). On the other hand, it is important to point out that while calling for 'more balanced' or less intrusive reporting, authorities effectively tried to silence the issue of identity-based conflict and its continuation since the end of the June 2010 violence – in the form of discrimination, irregularities in police investigations or lack of post-conflict justice (Bennett 2016; Ismailbekova and Karimova 2018).

The challenge for current research is that the topic of inter-ethnic relations and ethnonationalist sentiments is virtually banned from public discourse in Kyrgyzstan. Attempting to declare the issue of identity-based conflict as solved or sufficiently addressed, authorities continuously argue that compensation, re-construction and reconciliation efforts since the 'Osh events' have been largely effective. However, several authors have noted the ongoing discrimination and marginalisation of Uzbeks especially in the city of Osh (Ismailbekova 2013; Isakova 2015, 2013; Megoran 2017, 2013; Ismailbekova and Karimova 2018). Such critical accounts are not only denied or relativised; but researchers and journalists trying to inquire such topics have recently been targeted by state security. For instance, both the US freelance journalist Umar Farooq in 2015 and Dan Church Aid's Conor Prasad in 2013, were detained and questioned by the local branch of the State Committee for National Security (Ru. *GKNB*) under suspicion of breaking article 299 of the Kyrgyzstani criminal code ('instigation of religious or interethnic hatred') as they had conducted interviews with Uzbek community representatives and human rights organisations (Mets 2015; see Bekmurzaev, Lottholz, and Meyer 2018, 104). While both cases were dropped but led to extradition and fines, a court trial against the international NGO Freedom House and a local partner sparked further debate, as authorities argued that a pilot survey conducted by them had included inappropriate questions about minority rights and that the organisation had not sought approval for the survey from the State Agency for Local Self-Governance and Interethnic Relations (*Gamsumo*) (Beishenbek kyzy 2014). Although this case was dropped as well, it appears that authorities aimed at monopolising the discourse on inter-ethnic relations in order to maintain the argument that identity, specifically ethnic, did not play a significant role in the post-conflict environment, and to keep foreign researchers and organisations from contesting this view (Bekmurzaev, Lottholz, and Meyer 2018, 105).

As I show in the next section, peacebuilding projects reflect this hegemonic discourse, which aims to sanitise the post-Osh reality of Kyrgyzstan from critical references to inter-ethnic relations and minority or human rights. Peacebuilding after the Osh events thus continued and reinforced the approach to managing inter-ethnic relations that prevailed in the Soviet and early post-Soviet periods, which, as I have shown, preached 'people's friendship' and unity in the hope to mitigate identity-based competition and tensions and, in Minow's taxonomy, the disadvantages and stigma stemming from non-mainstream identities. This clearly demonstrates the analytical value of the 'dilemma of difference' and the pitfalls of building peace in diverse societies: The very act of claiming to attempt to maintain harmony and a public discourse that does not stigmatise the victims of past conflict, authorities effectively silenced and brushed over the sufferings of people who might have hoped to have their cases addressed (see Minow 1990, 20).

Solve things 'on the spot': interethnic harmony in post-2010 Kyrgyzstan

In this section I examine public documents, corroborated with interviews and other perspectives from the literature, to show how historical ideas of 'people's friendship' and interethnic harmony informed state-led and internationally supported peacebuilding policies in the aftermath of the 2010 'inter-ethnic' clashes in the south of Kyrgyzstan. Shocked by the scale and speed of violent outbreaks, international and inter-governmental organisations, including the Organisation for Security and Co-Operation in Europe (OSCE), various UN agencies, international NGOs and bilateral donors initiated large scale humanitarian relief, post-conflict reconstruction, peacebuilding, conflict prevention and community security programmes. Kyrgyzstan was thus arguably made another 'Peaceland' where international consultants and aid played a crucial role in shaping the way identity and difference were addressed in peacebuilding (Lottholz 2017, 21). However, beyond the politically straightforward humanitarian and infrastructural aid and compensation payments, programmes and practices were often contested by authorities and supposed beneficiaries. Many argued that international organisations were not sufficiently competent to understand and address the complex reasons for conflict and tensions (Ismailbekova and Sultanaliev 2012; Megoran et al. 2014, 8). Therefore, and given the absence of a UN mandate for Kyrgyzstan, the Kyrgyz authorities were the main actor in overseeing, steering and implementing post-conflict peacebuilding programmes. Most of the internationally-supported projects were carried out by national or municipal NGOs, often funded and guided by larger international NGOs. The latter normally received bilateral donor and UN funding, but still had to secure government approval for their actions.

Kyrgyzstani authorities drew on well-established tools in post-conflict reconstruction and peacebuilding to convince donors and the international community at large that peacebuilding was making good progress. Such portrayal relied, however, on a narrow set of statistic indicators and exemplary initiatives which helped to build a peace that did not transcend the underlying tensions and conflicts in society but, as Heathershaw (2009) demonstrated in the case of Tajikistan, was of a rather 'performative' or even 'virtual' nature.

A major priority in the immediate aftermath of the 2010 clashes was humanitarian relief and reconstruction of damaged properties and infrastructure.[2] A new 'State Directorate for Reconstruction and Development in Osh and Jalal-Abad' was tasked to allocate the governmental and international aid to those in need. The reconstruction process did neither run smoothly nor had it the desired reconciling effects, however. For instance, the flats allocated in new apartment blocks built by the State Directorate were often rejected by the victims of the 2010 events. Especially the policy of systematically allocating Kyrgyz and Uzbeks together in these buildings faced incomprehension given the prospect that victims and perpetrators were bound to live side by side (Isakova 2013, 22). Overall, it appears that the relief measures devised by the government and Osh and Jalal-Abad city administrations – with the exception of monetary compensation for victims' families – did not evoke the trust and willingness for inter-ethnic reconciliation that was intended by officials.

The government's attempt to deal systematically with the challenges of post-conflict construction and peacebuilding is documented in the 'Conception for Strengthening National Unity and Inter-Ethnic Relations', a national policy strategy adopted by the presidential administration in 2013.[3] The commitment to the restoration of interethnic trust and harmony is demonstrated in the Conception's core values of:

> **Acknowledgement of unity in diversity,** including ethnic, cultural, linguistic, age and other differences in different spheres of social life.
>
> **Appreciation of the historical-cultural heritage of the people of Kyrgyzstan,** of the history of the state, the conservation of national values developed over centuries and ideals of unity, the uniqueness of ethnicities [*etnosov*] and development of intercultural dialogue and tolerance.[4]

This clear propagation of the cosmopolitan ambition of peacebuilding stands in tension, however, with the 'Uniting role of Kyrgyz as a state language'. Thus, the idea of the Conception is to strengthen the role of Kyrgyz as an administrative language in all spheres of life in an attempt to enhance people's interactions via promotion of a unified state language.[5] This might make sense from the point of view of civic nationalist ideas of nation-building (Megoran 2012). The negative effects within society are undeniable, however, especially given the access barriers encountered by non-Kyrgyz speakers facing republican school exams in Kyrgyz, Kyrgyz language proficiency tests for civil servants and the transfer of communication in public services to Kyrgyz language (Ismailbekova 2013; Megoran 2013). Isakova (2015, n.p.) questions the possibility of using language policy to unify the Kyrgyzstani nation, especially because of the little preparation time allotted for the implementation of the initiative, which would have the effect that 'the propaganda of the state language now brings native speakers above the rest of the population' and that it 'can be misinterpreted by the ethnic majority, giving them the right to be unjust to others'. Based on reports from Kyrgyzstani human rights organisations, the UN Committee on the Elimination of Racial Discrimination (CERD) concluded its May 2018 session with the finding that current language policies in Kyrgyzstan are indeed likely to have led to discrimination of the Uzbek minority and recommended that the government 'reintroduce Uzbek language instruction at schools' and 'reconsider its decision to abolish university admission test in Uzbek language instruction at schools'.[6]

While some Uzbeks are reportedly ready to succumb to this new language policy, it appears that the majority does not see a viable basis for personal progress and wellbeing in Kyrgyzstan. Many resort to strategies such as labour migration or complete emigration to other Central Asian countries or Russia (Ismailbekova 2013; Megoran 2013, 900). Thus, the emphasis on ethnic identity made by language policy appears to off-set the unifying impetus of the civic nationalist vision of Kyrgyzstan after 2010.

To maintain a grip on the situation relating to inter-ethnic relations and potential tensions and continuities of the 2010 conflict, the government also created a new agency tasked with implementing the above Conception and monitoring and dealing with the situation. This Governmental Agency for Local Self-Governance and Interethnic Relations (Russian acronym *Gamsumo*) has a remarkably transparent and informative online presentation and offers access to all governmental decrees, laws, and strategy documents (see Illustration 1 below).

Illustration 1. Website of 'Gamsumo'. Accessed 10 October 2017.

The website also lists a helpline (*telefon doveriia*) and contact data of the secretaries of the 20 'Community Reception Centres' established across the country.[7] This web presence suggests the excellent implementation of peacebuilding and conflict prevention policies, but leaves doubts about the Agency's impact on the ground. Isakova (2015, n.p.), for instance, has argued that Community Reception Centres were mainly opened in ethnically mixed communities and that in practice people, who on average do not or rarely use the internet, are not always aware that these offices exist. Furthermore, incidents of ethnicity- or identity-based conflict are analysed by the officers themselves before being submitted to regional level offices and the national register (ibid.). A peacebuilding consultant working for an intergovernmental organisation noted how local authorities usually say they always deal with conflicts 'on the spot [*na meste*]' by telling the involved parties to settle their difference in peaceful ways and not to be aggravated by 'irrational' inter- ethnic animosities.[8] The statistics on inter-ethnic conflicts reported to Reception Centres are subject only to internal review by *Gamsumo*, with no reports or other outputs being published or subject to national level debate.[9] Therefore, a facts-based discussion on the current state of inter-ethnic relations is precluded from the public, which is only pre- sented vague and aggregate numbers on the efforts undertaken – for instance 4,000 events on conflict prevention overall between 2013 and 2017 – and pronouncements on the importance of 'the unity of the people'.[10]

These insights suggest that tensions, discrimination and marginalisation, as they have been documented by different authors (Ismailbekova 2013; Isakova 2015, 2013; Bennett 2016; Ismailbekova and Karimova 2018), are entrenched in their hidden, everyday forms and rarely lead to outright conflict, which in turn is unlikely to be reported. The different policies, practices and discourses reviewed above reflect a dual strategy of pro- moting interethnic harmony through the 'peoples' friendship' peacebuilding imaginary – and in sync with international conditions and advice on institutional and policy arrange- ments – while instantaneously drawing on the registers of governmental sovereignty and ethno-national identity politics, such as language policies and law enforcement at expense of Uzbek livelihoods (Isakova 2013; Megoran 2013). This form of hegemonic 'conflict management' illustrates peacebuilding's 'dilemma of difference': The potentially negative effects of difference in social life and its conflict potential are denied and silenced by the presentation of structures created and efforts undertaken. At the same time, every- day identity-based exclusion and marginalisation continue to be reported and have no space to be discussed in public given the sanitisation of public discourse. The idea of 'de-emphasising' and dealing with ethnic grievances is turned on its head in justifying a social order, where continued conflict, discrimination and exclusion is silenced and brushed over in the name of harmony. The next section turns to the analysis of concrete peacebuilding initiatives against this background.

Performing peace: 'Peoples' friendship'-style peacebuilding and its limits

As I have discussed above, contradictions between official policies and institutional arrangements on the one hand and the discourse of 'people's friendship' and 'Kyrgyzstan is our common home' on the other appear to be an inherent feature of Soviet and post-- Soviet Kyrgyzstan. Not surprisingly, then, 'people's friendship' (*druzhba narodov*) has become the core idea behind numerous peacebuilding events and programmes, which try to call people and communities to unity, harmony and peaceful relations in the face of the violence in June 2010 and the continued impunity of perpetrators, persisting tensions and everyday forms of violence and marginalisation (Lottholz 2017, 16). This dilemma of unifying and making people relate to one another peacefully across difference while difference has been the basis for past violence or current discrimination is faced by peacebuilders and administrators in communities across southern Kyrgyzstan.

One good example is the town of Bazar-Korgon, west of Jalal-Abad and about 20 kilometres north of the Kyrgyz-Uzbek border, which was gravely affected by the violent clashes in June 2010 (McBrien 2013). Here, as part of my PhD project (see Introduction), I conducted research on the work of a Local Crime Prevention Centre (LCPC), a body tasked with the coordination of different social institutions such as courts of elders (*aksakals*, lit. 'white beard'), youth and women's councils, religious and traditional leaders.[11] In previous years, the UK-based International NGO Saferworld had approached people in this and other localities to form security working groups which would start from scratch or re-invigorate the activity of largely inactive LCPCs. As part of my fieldwork, I accompanied a contracted consultant in visiting LCPCs in the south of Kyrgyzstan to conduct interviews and write them up into profiles for a brochure of LCPC 'Success stories [*istorii uspekha*]' (Saferworld 2016) to be presented to stakeholders including the Ministry of Internal Affairs, whose structure the LCPCs are a part of. Although the output of the initial research was aimed at a public audience and the authorities, LCPC representatives were fairly open and (self-) critical in telling their stories for the brochure, and in providing further background during a follow-up visit. Therefore, the cooperation with Saferworld, and thus indirectly with authorities, yielded access to the LCPCs and useful insights into their work, but also necessitated their agreement with the contents and message of the research. This did not, however, lead to limitations as the material co-generated by the consultant and myself was integrated into the brochure without significant alterations and my later research outputs (Lottholz 2017, 2018a) were deemed appropriate as well (see Lottholz 2017, 17–18; 2018b, 14 ff. for more reflections on such cooperative research).

As two representatives of the LCPC Bazar-Korgon told during an initial interview[12], the conflict in June 2010 had been waged not only between different communities, but also involved the police, whose inaction or complicity with the violence against Uzbeks led to the killing of one policeman. The post-violence period was characterised by continued tensions and confusion in law enforcement and judicial procedures, as many, especially young people were detained to extort payments, sometimes targeting families of the fled perpetrators of crimes during the conflict, sometimes in an arbitrary manner. The feeling of insecurity and vulnerability people after the conflict was so grave that many would send their kids to relatives or to work in Russia and in some cases entire families were leaving their homes behind (see McBrien 2013). Although it was hard to give voice to the issues underlying this exodus and suffering of the town's inhabitants, it was clear that these things would need to be addressed when Saferworld and its Kyrgyzstani partner initiated conversations and the foundation of a 'Community Security Working Group' in 2011.

Besides trying to restore trust in the local police, the LCPC undertook comprehensive measures to mitigate ethnic tension and encourage a spirit of reconciliation and peaceful coexistence. An indicative list of peacebuilding events carried out by the LCPC between

2013 and 2015 reveals a consistent attempt to promote peace through the 'people's friendship' discourse (Saferworld 2016, 18):

- 'Festival of friendship' (*Festival druzhby*) with music and dance performances;
- Sport events series titles 'Sport – a messenger of peace' (*Sport – Poslannik mira*);
- Dialogue events 'Park of friendship' (*Park druzhby*) and 'Avenue of friendship' (*Aleia druzhby*);
- Setting up of a new seating area (*besedka*) on the school courtyard (see Illustration 1 below).

As the two LCPC representatives explained, these events and the construction of the new seating area (Illustration 2), financed by Saferworld, a national NGO and USAID,

Top left: 'Avenue of friendship'

Top right: 'Friendship square' with seating area

Bottom: A map of Kyrgyzstan held by hands in which local pupils wrote their peace messages; the hand on the right reads 'We wish Kyrgyzstan peace, unity, harmony, welfare, justice and friendship!' [Kyrgyz: *Kyrgyzstanga kaaloorubuz tynchtyk, birimdik, yntymak, beypildik, adilettik, dostuk!*]

Illustration 2. Peacebuilding based on the 'peoples' friendship' discourse, Bazar-Korgon, Source: Author.

were intended to create open spaces where people would be able to spend time with each other and forge harmonic relations. Furthermore, the winners of an arts competition created a painting symbolising a peaceful Kyrgyzstan with space for messages of the pupils of the local school (Illustration 2).[13]

The different 'friendship'-themed events and the new *besedka* (seating area) in the local school-yard present ways of creating space for interaction and coexistence, which clearly resonate with the idea of 'people's friendship' and 'unity in diversity' discussed above. Having grown up with these maxims, for most adults in Kyrgyzstan it is the frame of reference for appropriate positioning on inter-ethnic relations: For former Soviet, and now Kyrgyzstani citizens, a multi-ethnic and peaceful Kyrgyzstan should not be disrupted by conflicts and divisions. The painting on the local school's wall further shows how discourses of peace, harmony and unity are reproduced by young people. The message written by one young person clearly resonates with the discourses of peacebuilding proffered in peacebuilding events: 'We wish Kyrgyzstan peace, unity, harmony, welfare, justice and friendship!' At the same time, the choice of the map of Kyrgyzstan as a basis to accommodate the different wishes and hopes of the local pupils also symbolises the important role of territory, nation and state for a peaceful future.

When thinking about the effects of these peacebuilding initiatives, the most obvious question concerns the audience of these events and new infrastructures: Who attends and makes use of these spaces? It appears likely that they are utilised by those who already have a basic readiness to interact with people beyond their own immediate social circle (and possibly from other ethnicities). However, whether people from economically and culturally marginalised parts of the communities would also seize these opportunities to reach out and build new bridges appears more than doubtful. This was confirmed by one LCPC representative, who pointed to the history of inter-ethnic tensions during Soviet times, with clashes having happened in the 50s, 60s, and 1990s (see Tishkov 1995) and explained how the policies on urban structuring and education system after the fall of the Soviet Union gave rise to new separations along ethnic lines:

> The problem is this: In the past, Uzbeks and Kyrgyz were going together to school. Class 'a', that was Kyrgyz, the 'b' classes were Uzbeks, and the 'v' classes [the third letter of the Cyrillic alphabet] were Russians. Here in our school they learnt three languages, more than 40 years ago and they would always live and work together in a friendly way. Just when the Union broke up, they divided up schools, divided up the territorial administrative units [*uchastki*], told the Uzbeks to go there and the Kyrgyz to go here, even though they had lived together. So they created Kyrgyz and Uzbek mono-ethnic communities [*naselennye punkty*].

This re-ordering of urban space after Kyrgyzstan's independence presents a significant 're-materialisation' of ethno-territorial thinking, which was closely associated with the materialisation and, in 1999, closing of the Uzbek-Kyrgyz border after incursions of Islamist fighters into Uzbekistan (Megoran 2017, 19 ff.). While such compartmentalisation is to the benefit of few, if any, the adverse effects have been most painfully felt during the '2010 events' and their aftermath. The LCPC representative concluded:

> … people wouldn't be the way they are now if they worked together, went to school together, played together on sports events and if they knew each other. But now they do not want to be involved in such events, they are scared [*oni boiatsa*]. And the authorities are also afraid and do not let us go to them, we're not invited into the other school, 'it's not necessary', they say, 'don't do it'. But let them mix with each other whether it's a sports event, a festival or

something else! Whether it's at work or in a holiday camp [*v lagere*], that's it, you have to mix them and they will live, they will develop a positive view [*u nikh poiavliautsa khoroshie positivy*].

Although there is little information available on the exact process of re-ordering of Bazar-Korgon into districts relatively isolated from one another, a Saferworld report discussing this same case study also emphasises the issue of mono-ethnic communities and the distrust between people of different ethnicities (Saferworld 2015, 3). This, the report continues, required the local security working group to develop a work routine between its Uzbek and Kyrgyz members before tackling issues of inter-ethnic relations in the first place (ibid.). This makes the challenges of peacebuilding and inter-ethnic reconciliation and trust-building abundantly clear: With ethnicised territorial, labour market and welfare policies and provisioning already nurturing tensions during the Soviet period, authorities knew no better than creating mono-lingual schools and mono-ethnic communities (*naselennye punkty*) to strengthen national languages, cultures and traditions (Brubaker 2011, 1802 ff.). As new generations grew up in separation from one another, hardening stereotypes and deepening distrust were compounded by the perceptions of different wellbeing. Most importantly, the relative wealth of Uzbeks, some of whom sported an affluent lifestyle thanks to their bazar businesses and networks with close-by Uzbekistan, stood in contrast to the dwindling livelihood opportunities of rural and urban poor Kyrgyz, who increasingly depended on connections with the local administration or labour migration to the CIS and had accumulated frustration and envy by 2010 (McBrien 2013, 261).

The 'peoples' friendship' also foregrounded a host of peacebuilding events across the rest of the country, such as feasts, sport events, and cultural food and costume exhibitions and performances, e.g. 'festival of friendship' or 'garden of friendship', and focused on specific neighbourhoods or uniting people from entire cities on different holidays or anniversaries (Ismailbekova 2013, 115; Isakova 2013, 24). In participatory observation of such an event, the 'Day of the city of Osh [*Den goroda*]' celebrating the anniversary of the city's founding in late October 2015, I witnessed how local pupils performed ancient legends, hip hop sets and other dances during the official ceremony on Lenin square, how guests from other municipalities from Osh province presented their agricultural produce and other specialties on a farmers market, and how municipal workers from all districts and schools of the city demonstrated their art of baking *borsok*, the local fried dough specialty (see Illustration 3 below).

These events and performances, like many other friendship festivals throughout Kyrgyzstan, presented sincere portrayals of tolerance towards the diverse interests, cultural heritage and traditions of different ethnicities and (sub-)cultures in Kyrgyzstan. They equally pointed to the things and practices that bring together and unite people of diverse origins and belonging, whether it is a traditional culinary specialty going back hundreds of years into the pre-modern epoch or modern dances and other arts performances. The events and their ethos of celebrating the things that unite people, including their differences, however, still exhibited a sense of the spectacular and extraordinary. They might have served to balance the changes the city is undergoing and the frictions and tensions its inhabitants are experiencing, but more temporarily so than in a substantial and sustainable way. Peacebuilding in both in Bazar-Korgon and Osh appeared strikingly

Top left: Pupils from different schools perform on Lenin square, Day of the city of Osh ceremony
Bottom left: Picture from the farmer's market on Lenin avenue
Right: Picture from the *borsok* festival in front of the Kyrgyz drama theatre

Illustration 3. Peacebuilding on the 'Day of the City of Osh', Osh; Source: Author.

similar to portrayals from the Ferghana Valley border region (Reeves 2014, ch. 6) and Tajikistan (Heathershaw 2009): it seems that the ideas of ethnicity and identity had been internalised as a category of everyday practice in ethnically divided schools and communities, and districts divided by national borders which became increasingly impermeable throughout the past 25 years (Megoran 2017). Such experiences of everyday practice render attempts to build a peace that embraces differences in a constructive way performative and shallow in the eyes of people whose main concerns were economic survival and redress after the injustices they had suffered. Therefore, peacebuilding did not serve to overcome the 'dilemma of difference' posed by the wider context and government policies on inter-ethnic relations and reconciliation, which arguably entrenched the potential stigma and disadvantage faced by non-Kyrgyz.

Conclusion

The main goal of this article was to exemplify the limits and pitfalls of an approach to peacebuilding which is aimed at is transcending the significance of identities and belonging as ordering mechanisms in social life. I have analysed current efforts of inter-ethnic peacebuilding overseen, and partly implemented by, authorities in Kyrgyzstan against the historical background of social engineering and a policy of defining and

THE POLITICS OF PEACEBUILDING IN A DIVERSE WORLD

territorialising new nations and ethnic groups in Central Asia. The claims, competition and grievances between different nationalities were balanced with the concept of 'peoples' friendship', a slogan used to mobilise all Soviet nations to live together peacefully and brotherly, strive towards the realisation of Communism, and to eventually see the significance of their national identity fading away. With the dissolution of the Soviet Union and constitution of the Kyrgyz Republic as an independent state, established patterns of ethnicised competition were deepened and eventually led to large-scale violent clashes in 2010.

I have demonstrated how ideas and concepts stemming from the 'peoples' friendship' imaginary have informed authorities' attempts to tackle and manage the situation according to international standards and policy templates on the one hand, and to still fortify their position by strengthening Kyrgyz cultural dominance, on the other. The propagation of interethnic harmony thus stands in contradiction to language policy and security imperatives that appear to instate a 'leading culture' based on Kyrgyz traditions. Based on multi-sited fieldwork, I have shown how the myriad peacebuilding events invoking 'people's friendship' and 'unity in diversity' face inherent limitations given the current political context and history of urban planning and education policies. This was most obvious in Bazar-Korgon, where the mono-ethnic territorial division of the town's residential districts and the organisation of schooling according to language and ethnicity have produced significant cleavages and mistrust between different population groups.

According to Minow (1990), dealing with difference is problematic as it is easily underappreciated and ignored or, on the other hand, can be essentialised, distorted and stigmatised by attempts to take it into account. I have demonstrated two problems with overcoming this 'dilemma of difference'. First, I have shown how identity can be simply too entrenched, naturalised and normalised as a social category. This point is not only valid for Kyrgyzstan or other post-Soviet states, but presents an entry point for analysis in other post-imperial and nation states the world over. This is further substantiated by Behr's critique (2014, ch. 2) of the exclusionary and pervasive nature of the ontological thinking of the nation-state framework. The second issue I have demonstrated is the utilisation of the dilemma by power-holders, who play a double-game of 'de-emphasising' identity on the one hand, and benefiting from social policies and practices which create hierarchy and exclusion based on identity, on the other. This Janus-faced strategy of Kyrgyzstani authorities is well documented (Isakova 2015; Megoran 2017, 2013) and is defended as a legitimate and contextually appropriate approach with references to the international sovereignty of the country (Gullette and Heathershaw 2015).

The analysis throws up the question as to how to deal with situations where national and ethnic identity and belonging are and continue to be key to social life, and where, furthermore, the strengthening of identitarian politics and policy is claimed as a basic right by sovereign power-holders. As Bargues-Pedreny has indicated, attempts to effectively address such situations appear condemned to an endless extension of intervention mandates in light of the lack of progress and impossibility of resolving the dilemma of difference, as in the case of peacebuilding in Kosovo (2016, 234). To remain realistic about the prospects of overcoming identity-based grievances, then, it appears necessary to devote attention to studying historical legacies of identitarian social engineering, policy and politics and the way in which they foreground a deep entrenchment of identitarian and ethno-

140 THE POLITICS OF PEACEBUILDING IN A DIVERSE WORLD

essentialist thinking in contemporary societies. Besides inquiring the issue in a more holistic way that engages more with the perspectives of people concerned, such research can also point to new entry points for overcoming the 'dilemma of difference' in peacebuilding interventions.

Notes

1. As a result of the NTD, Tajiks in Bukhara (Uzbek SSR), Uzbeks in Osh (Kyrgyz SSR) and Kyrgyz living in the environs of Andijan (Uzbek SSR) became minority groups in the respective republics (Haugen 2003, ch. 8).
2. Estimates of the damaged caused by the 'June events' revolve around 470 deaths, 400,000 internally displaced persons and 110,000 who (temporarily) left the country; as well as 9,500 properties partly or completely destroyed. See Megoran et al. (2014).
3. Available under http://www.president.kg/ru/news/ukazy/1878_utverjdena_kontseptsiya_ukrepleniya_edinstva_naroda_i_mejetnicheskih_otnosheniy_v_kyirgyizskoy_respublike/
4. Ibid., 3-4; emphasis in original.
5. Ibid., page 5.
6. CERD, 'Concluding observations on the combined eighth to tenth periodic reports of Kyrgyzstan', CERD/C/KGZ/CO/8-10, 11 May 2018, p. 7, http://tbinternet.ohchr.org/ Treaties/CERD/Shared%20Documents/KGZ/INT_CERD_COC_KGZ_31206_E.pdf
7. http://gamsumo.gov.kg/ru/inter-ethnic-relations/public-reception/
8. Interview with peacebuilding consultant of an intergovernmental agency; Bishkek/Plovdiv, 2 December 2016.
9. 'A monitoring centre has been established under Gamsumo, 13 October 2014, http://www.gamsumo.gov.kg/ru/news/full/71.html. The site of the Monitoring Centre only presents the decree ordering its creation and job description but no reports: http://gamsumo.gov.kg/ru/inter-ethnic-relations/monitoring-center/
10. See report on the meeting of Gamsumo head Saliev with president Atambaev: 'A. Atambaev: The unity of the people of Kyrgyzstan is the most important condition for the stabile and successful development of the country', 13 November 2017, http://kg.akipress.org/news:1415371
11. For more details see http://www.saferworld.org.uk/news-and-views/case-study/57-enhancing-existing-security-structures-in-kyrgyzstan
12. This profiling visit to Bazar-Korgon took place on 13 July 2015.
13. Interview with LCPC representative during follow-up visit, 30 October 2015.

Disclosure statement

No potential conflict of interest was reported by the author.

Funding

This work was supported by an International Development Department Fieldwork Bursary and the School of Government and Society at the University of Birmingham.

ORCID

Philipp Lottholz ⓘ http://orcid.org/0000-0002-6616-269X

References

Bargués-Pedreny, P. 2016. "From Promoting to De-Emphasizing 'Ethnicity': Rethinking the Endless Supervision of Kosovo." *Journal of Intervention and Statebuilding* 10 (2): 222–240.

Bargués-Pedreny, Pol, and Xavier Mathieu. 2018. "Beyond Silence, Obstacle and Stigma: Revisiting the 'Problem' of Difference in Peacebuilding." *Journal of Intervention and Statebuilding* 12 (3): 283–299.

Behr, H. 2014. *Politics of Difference: Epistemologies of Peace*. London: Routledge.

Beishenbek kyzy, E. 2014. "V Oshe priostanovlena deiatelnost Freedom House [Freedom House's work is suspended in Osh]", *Radio Azattyk*, October 7. http://rus.azattyk.org/a/26624129.html.

Bekmurzaev, N., P. Lottholz, and J. R. Meyer. 2018. "Navigating the Security Implications of Doing Research and Being Researched: Cooperation, Networks, Framing." *Central Asian Survey* 37 (1): 100–118.

Bennett, W. 2016. *Everything Can Be Tolerated – Except Injustice*. Osh: Saferworld. http://www.saferworld.org.uk/resources/view-resource/1050-ldquoeverything-can-be-tolerated-ndash-except-injusticerdquo.

Brubaker, R. 2011. "Nationalizing States Revisited: Projects and Processes of Nationalization in Post-Soviet States." *Ethnic and Racial Studies* 34 (11): 1785–1814.

Edgar, A. L. 2007. "Marriage, Modernity, and the 'Friendship of Nations': Interethnic Intimacy in Post-War Central Asia in Comparative Perspective." *Central Asian Survey* 26 (4): 581–599.

Gullette, D., and J. Heathershaw. 2015. "The Affective Politics of Sovereignty: Reflecting on the 2010 Conflict in Kyrgyzstan." *Nationalities Papers* 43 (1): 122–139.

Haugen, A. 2003. *The Establishment of National Republics in Soviet Central Asia*. Basingstoke: Palgrave.

Heathershaw, J. 2009. *Post-Conflict Tajikistan: The Politics of Peacebuilding and the Emergence of Legitimate Order*. London: Routledge.

Hirsch, F. 2005. *Empire of Nations: Ethnographic Knowledge and the Making of the Soviet Union*. Ithaca: Cornell University Press.

Isakova, Z. 2013. "Understanding Peace Processes in the Aftermath of Ethnic Violence in the South of Kyrgyzstan: The Kyrgyz and Uzbeks Happily Ever After?" MA Diss., Bishkek: OSCE Academy. http://osce-academy.net/upload/file/ Master_Thesis_Zamira_Isakova.pdf.

Isakova, Z. 2015. "The Consolidation of Peace in Southern Kyrgyzstan: The Effectiveness of the Strategy After Five Years." Cabar. Accessed June 15, 2015. http://cabar.asia/en/the-consolidation-of-peace-in-southern-kyrgyzstan-the-effectiveness-of-the-strategy-after-five-years/.

Ismailbekova, A. 2013. "Coping Strategies: Public Avoidance, Migration, and Marriage in the Aftermath of the Osh Conflict, Fergana Valley." *Nationalities Papers* 41 (1): 109–127.

Ismailbekova, A. 2017. *Blood Ties and the Native Son: Poetics of Patronage in Kyrgyzstan*. Bloomington: Indiana University Press.

Ismailbekova, A., and B. Karimova. 2018. "Ethnic Differentiation and Conflict Dynamics: Uzbeks Marginalization and Non-Marginalization in Southern Kyrgyzstan." In *Understanding the City Through Its Margins: Pluridisciplinary Perspectives From Case Studies in Africa, Asia and the Middle East*, edited by A. Chappatte, U. Freitag, and N. Lafi, 161–184. London: Routledge.

Ismailbekova, A., and R. Sultanaliev. 2012. "The role of NGOs in conflict management and resolution in post-conflict Osh, Kyrgyzstan." Norwegian Institute of International Affairs.

Laruelle, M. 2008. "The Concept of Ethnogenesis in Central Asia: Political Context and Institutional Mediators (1940–50)." *Kritika: Explorations in Russian and Eurasian History* 9 (1): 169–188.

Laruelle, M. 2012. "The Paradigm of Nationalism in Kyrgyzstan. Evolving Narrative, the Sovereignty Issue, and Political Agenda." *Communist and Post-Communist Studies* 45: 39–49.

Lottholz, P. 2017. "Critiquing Anthropological Imagination in Peace and Conflict Studies: From Empiricist Positivism to a Dialogical Approach in Ethnographic Peace Research." *International Peacekeeping*. Online First.

Lottholz, P. 2018a. "A Negative Post-Liberal Peace? Inquiring the Embeddedness of Everyday Forms of Peace in Central Asia." In *Interrogating Illiberal Peace in Eurasia – Critical Perspectives on Peace and Conflict*, edited by C. Owen, S. Juraev, D. Lewis, N. Megoran, and J. Heathershaw, 97–119. New York: Rowman & Littlefield.

Lottholz, P. 2018b. "Post-liberal Statebuilding in Central Asia: A Decolonial Perspective on Community Security Practices and Imaginaries of Social Order in Kyrgyzstan." PhD diss., University of Birmingham.

Marat, E. 2008. "Imagined Past, Uncertain Future: The Creation of National Ideologies in Kyrgyzstan and Tajikistan." *Problems of Post-Communism* 55 (1): 12–24.

McBrien, J. 2013. "Afterword: In the Aftermath of Doubt." In *Ethnographies of Doubt: Faith and Uncertainty in Contemporary Societies*, edited by M. Pelkmans, 251–268. London: IB Tauris.

Megoran, N. 2012. "Averting Violence in Kyrgyzstan: Understanding and Responding to Nationalism." *Russia and Eurasia Programme Paper* 3: 971–986. London: Chatham House.

Megoran, N. 2013. "Shared Space, Divided Space: Narrating Ethnic Histories of Osh." *Environment and Planning A* 45 (4): 892–907.

Megoran, N. 2017. *Nationalism in Central Asia: A Biography of the Uzbekistan-Kyrgyzstan Boundary*. Pittsburgh: University of Pittsburgh Press.

Megoran, N., E. Satybaldieva, D. Lewis, and J. Heathershaw. 2014. "Peacebuilding and Reconciliation Projects in Southern Kyrgyzstan." Stockholm International Peace Research Institute and Open Society Foundations Working Paper. http://www.sipri.org/research/security/afghanistan/central-asia-security/publications/sipri-osf-working-paper-megoran-et-al-june-2014.

Mets, S. 2015. "Umar Farooq i kirgizskoe "delo pravozashitnikov": glavnoe - iziat' dokumenty i deportirovat [Umar Farooq and the Kyrgyz "Case of Human Rights Activists": The Main Goal - To Confiscate Documents and Deport]." Fergana.ru. Accessed March 30, 2015. http://www.fergananews.com/articles/8471.

Minow, M. 1990. *Making All the Difference: Inclusion, Exclusion, and American Law*. Ithaca: Cornell University Press.

Radnitz, S. 2010. *Weapons of the Wealthy: Predatory Regimes and Elite-Led Protests in Central Asia*. Ithaca: Cornell University Press.

Reeves, M. 2014. *Border Work: Spatial Lives of the State in Rural Central Asia*. Ithaca: Cornell University Press.

Saferworld. 2015. *Saferworld in Kyrgyzstan: Preventing Violent Conflicts. Building Safer Lives*. Osh: Saferworld.

Saferworld. 2016. *Istorii uspekha. Obshestvenno-profilakticheskie tsentry Oshskoi, Jalal-Abadskoi i Batkenskoi oblastei [Success Stories. Local Crime Prevention Centres in Osh, Jalal-Abad and Batken Provinces]*. Osh: Saferworld.

Simon, G. 1991. *Nationalism and Policy Toward the Nationalities in the Soviet Union*. Boulder: Westview Press.

Tishkov, V. 1995. "'Don't Kill Me, I'm a Kyrgyz!': An Anthropological Analysis of Violence in the Osh Ethnic Conflict." *Journal of Peace Research* 32 (2): 133–149.

Beyond Relationalism in Peacebuilding

Jonathan Joseph

ABSTRACT

This conclusion notes the rise of relationalism in theorizing peacebuilding and the advantages of this approach as evident in the contributions to this special issue. Nevertheless, it cautions against such a move and in particular, some of the ontological and epistemological consequences of the relational turn as evident in recent poststructuralism, postcolonial approaches and practice theory. It contrasts this with the critical realist approach – whose relationalism has been ignored by the current turn – allowing both relationalism and a belief in objectivity and preference for certain knowledge claims.

Introduction

The argument set out in the introduction and pursued through this special issue is that international peacebuilding is embroiled in the 'problem' of difference. While recent scholarship, as well as recent practice, now attempts to account for the problem of difference, rather than denying or suppressing it, these attempts to engage with it are deeply problematic. As the editors Pol Bargués-Pedreny and Xavier Mathieu (2018) note, the three errors are to either silence, problematize or stigmatize difference with recent attempts failing to engage with the conditions of its emergence. In particular, peacebuilders have assumed that countries would, with the right international support, transition to liberal democracy. In reaction to this, scholars started to emphasize the role of culture, a greater concern with political contestation and the role of psychosocial factors.

Hence the first error silences difference through the imposition of universalist frameworks that neglect the different roles and identities of the actors involved. In response, peacebuilding approaches sought to draw attention to difference and investigate local history and understandings. The context for intervention was broadened to include social and cultural processes (Lederach 1997). However, the second error is to treat difference as a problem to be solved, effectively essentializing difference as belonging to distinct and homogenous groups. The danger then is to contribute to the legitimization of ethno-nationalist perspectives (Campbell 1998). The role of the peacebuilder is to manage and regulate these perceived differences through top-down interventions mainly focused on liberal institution building as a means of ameliorating the effects of certain socio-cultural pathologies (Fukuyama 2004 ; Ghani and Lockhard 2008; Paris and Sisk 2009).

The third approach is to see difference not as a problem to be solved but as having a potentially positive role to play in building peace. Rather than seeing differences as an obstacle to be managed through better peacebuilding, scholars adopting this approach seek a more genuine engagement with difference (Mac Ginty 2015; Mac Ginty and Richmond 2016). This approach is critical of the imposition of liberal norms, seeking instead more local or hybrid forms of peace based on bottom-up dynamics (Donais 2009; Richmond 2009; Mac Ginty and Richmond 2016). The error identified with this third approach is that in order to respect difference, it is necessary to decide what this difference is, thus maintaining some form of stigmatization of difference as somehow deviant from the normal. Local culture and traditions are understood through a Western frame of reference from which these diverge. As the authors say in the introduction 'emphasising difference (even as something to be celebrated or as a space to cultivate bottom-up peace initiatives) does not remove the stigma attached to it insofar as what passes for "normal" is not questioned nor made explicit'.

In short, all these approaches are seen as ending up essentializing difference either through silencing, problematizing or stigmatizing it. The arguments of this special issue are therefore refreshing in bringing in an understanding of difference that is non-essentialist and relational. I have summarized the main points here in order to show my agreement. The various contributions emphasize the role of cultural difference and reject the imposition of universalism and fixed identities. Peacebuilding is to be seen as a process which constantly evades any conclusive settlement. Differences are performed realities that arise in specific social and historical contexts. Moreover, differences are intrinsically linked to power relations. Such arguments are uncontestably a good thing. They are all consistent with the critical realist framework that I support.

However, I want to take issue with the radical relationality of this position which flows from the excesses of poststructuralism and postcolonialism. In the rest of this piece, I will discuss some of the ontological and epistemological assumptions behind some of the main arguments for a relational approach to difference. This is not to reject relationality, but to ask what type of relationality? Using critical realism I will investigate the philosophical foundations of some of the main arguments on this. In particular, I will use Bhaskar and Bourdieu to argue that social structure also needs to be brought in alongside the focus on practice and performance.

Difference as a relation of power

To summarize from the introduction to this issue, the contributors draw on a combination of philosophy, anthropology and feminist/queer theory in order to make three arguments for relationality. They argue that it is non-essentialist, link it to power relations and suggest that it is performative, taking place in multiple contexts. A later section will look at the issue of performativity, while this section looks as difference understood as a power relation. It agrees with the need to see difference as relational, but sees some limitations in the reliance on particular forms of philosophy, anthropology and feminist/queer theory, arguing for a more realist approach to power based on arguments from Bhaskar (1989, 1993) and Isaac (1987). I take up here the editors' call to explore the ways in which difference can be understood in its political context of emergence and suggest that this is best understood through the critical realist lens of social stratification and embeddedness in social structure.

Such arguments are built on the realist assumption that there exists a social reality that is structured and relatively enduring over time and is, for this reason, open to scientific investigation. The social world is complexly stratified, with different emergent processes that arise in specific historical contexts. Emergence, in a critical realist sense, means that processes have both underlying and necessary conditions of possibility, and emergent and irreducible outcomes. What produces social phenomena are underlying structures and causes which are irreducible to the conceptions that social agents might have of them (Dean, Joseph, Roberts and Wight 2006, 8–9). This is quite distinct from a positivist approach which reduces the world to our empirical observation of supposedly predictable events. Yet the 'problem of difference' presented in this special issue assumes the positivist understanding of science in making its case for rejecting the idea that difference is empirically discoverable, identifiable and thus 'out there'. In response to the contributors, I would ask whether there must surely be some element of difference that is 'out there' and identifiable for this whole discussion to be meaningful in the first place? It might be correct to suggest that the three strands of peacebuilding understand difference in an essentialist way as an attribute of different people while ignoring that difference presupposes relations of power. However, are these relations of power not 'out there' and in some way identifiable? If not, how can have a meaningful discussion about them? Even if we follow current trends and say that our job is not to analyse but to let these relations 'speak to us', this is still an 'object oriented ontology'. The issue is not to abandon either the ontological claim of a reality 'out there' or the epistemological aim of meaningful identification, but to ask what sort of reality (difference) is 'out there' and what are the problems and limitations in our understanding of this reality (difference)? Contra positivism, the social world is indeed relational in the sense that it is made up of social relations rather than 'things'. However, this is different from the relational views presented here which tend to focus on relations between people (anthropological fieldwork), elements of discourse (poststructuralism/postmarxism) or between ideas and world views (phenomenology).

There are two problematic responses to this challenge present in this volume that I think realist work on power and social structure can help clarify. One is to argue for the importance of power relations in the vaguest poststructuralist sense of power being everywhere. The other is to reduce power to relations between people, or to take an intersubjective view of these relations that reduce them to world views. This is the result of the philosophical assumptions behind the largely poststructuralist or phenomenological arguments that inform the contributions to this Special Issue.

The first problem is one of vagueness. By following poststructuralism, the danger is that power becomes the primary social relation that explains all others. But if power is everywhere, and behind everything, we lose sight of anything outside of the play of power. This does not really help in the identification of the dynamics behind power. Considering anything outside of power relations themselves is said to be essentialist – discussion of things like capitalism or colonialism will themselves be considered a return to essentialism.

The other issue with relationality as articulated in the special issue is the tendency to see social relations in terms of something between people. This is well illustrated in the references to Minow's work where she sees difference lying in the relations *between* people rather than *within* them (Minow 1990, 79). This is certainly preferable to the essentialist positions being critiqued where difference is located in some people's essential and discrete characteristics. But this is only one aspect of the picture since power and difference are also positional in the sense that people's characters, dispositions, powers, capacities, understandings and so on derive from their social positioning, or their relation to social relations. This social positioning, as Bhaskar (1993, 160) argues, is more than just relations between people, but is 'four planar', consisting of material transactions with nature, inter-intra subjective personal relations, the plane of social relations and the plane of the subjectivity of the agent. There is a multiplicity of potentially disjoint rhythmics conceived of as a tense socio-spatializing process where elements of each plane are subject to multiple and conflicting determinations.

Jeffrey Isaac's well-known intervention on power also helps clarify the question of social positioning and context. It makes the argument that social power refers to the capacities to act possessed by agents. This is by virtue of their participation within enduring social relations which distribute the power to act in certain ways to different people. Hence it is these social relations rather than the behaviour – or interaction – which they shape, which are the conditions of possibility for interaction (Isaac 1987, 22–23).

In contrast, some of the contributors are keen to promote an overly-intersubjective view of social relations that downplays or ignores these other social aspects. Brigg, in particular, argues for power being seen in relation to worldviews that powerful actors promote and their particular conceptions of truth and reality (Brigg 2008, 11). World views are said to be what constitute difference because these promote notions of normal and deviant.

This view, while undeniable, is also only partial because it neglects other areas identified in the four planar model. Power here is rooted in the relation between subjects and their worldview, rather than being rooted in their four planar social situation. In particular, there is a danger here of turning the question of power into an epistemological question, effectively turning the complexity of our social situation into the socially constructed understandings we have of it. While this goes some way in identifying the social production of difference, it does not tell us the whole story of its social-structural conditions of possibility. Instead, these are turned into subjective, discursive or phenomenological concerns. The editors' introduction makes the useful corrective that linking difference to worldviews transforms the issue from questions such as what difference is and where it resides to ones of how it is constructed. However, even to address the question of its construction requires a wider social ontology than the one provided by a focus on worldviews or the intersubjective dimension of the exercise of power.

Recent approaches to relationality

Much of the discussion of relationality in IR today is monopolized by poststructuralist and now new materialist thinking with a few notable dissenting voices such as Behr (2018, this issue) who draws on older phenomenological traditions. Certainly, older, materialist or philosophically realist accounts of relationality are ignored. This section will, therefore, address some of the new developments in relationality by taking a more established, if currently less fashionable, point of view.

Most of the relevant recent issues are expertly raised (although not always satisfactorily addressed) by the arguments of Morgan Brigg – here, and in previous work. In this forum, he tries to steer a middle ground by presenting a relational approach, but also criticizing some of the philosophy underlying recent versions of this. While the earlier approaches to difference in peacebuilding presented an *identitarian* logic that foregrounds fixed, coherent entities, the relational approach of recent years takes a non-essentialist approach that conceptualizes difference as contestable, fluid and ephemeral. Brigg (2018, this issue) rightly highlights some concerns with these approaches.

While ignoring the large body of relational work present in Marxism, dialectical thinking, 'Eastern' philosophy, philosophical realism, existentialism and phenomenology, recent International Relations has followed the trend of portraying the dominant system of thought as a form of Newtonian physics based on 'things' and discrete entities rather than processes and relations. The new trend – which can certainly be found in the recent interest in such things as resilience – is to argue for complexity, emergence, non-linearity, multiple states, adaptive systems and so on. As Brigg says, these new arguments seek to render everything a little more unstable than previously thought, a little more uncertain and unpredictable, with outcomes that are more contingent and accidental.

Brigg (2018, this issue) agrees with de-essentializing approaches insofar as they see differences as fluid, contested and contestable. But he also sees that anti-essentialist arguments tend to embrace a flat ontology which is so pluralistic that difference can lose its meaningful purchase (p. 6 of online version). As he says, the consequence of this is to undermine 'the grounds upon which people may claim difference and resist dominance, including the framing and control of their lives' (p. 6 of online version). This is absolutely correct and is a criticism that postcolonial theorists often raise against new materialists and others who suggest, following Latour (2005, 16), that we render social relations as ontologically flat. Nevertheless, Brigg remains committed to an interactional ontology which in my view makes it difficult to see where dominance or hierarchy comes from. He writes that this approach challenges us to stop thinking over and above the world (another example of setting up 'modernist' science) and to place knowing the world inside the world of interaction, making knowledge dependent upon people's ways of being (p. 10 of online version).

Epistemologically this runs the danger of what Bhaskar calls the epistemic fallacy, reducing the way that the world is, to the knowledge we have of it (Bhaskar 1989). In this sense, despite its concerns, it stands alongside other 'insider' approaches including constructivism, phenomenology and recent practice theory. It still relates difference to interaction itself rather than what might provide the conditions of possibility for this interaction to take place and what might thus be responsible for the unequal positions that the actors occupy. How else might we address why hierarchies exist and are evident in this interaction? Interaction and performance sustains them, but what produces them in the first place?

In his earlier work, Brigg sees difference in terms of systems of signification which again raises the ontological question of why signification occurs in the way it does, with unequal positions of power? He draws on Laclau's work on the 'empty signifier' to demonstrate the incompleteness of representation and difference. The empty signifier refers to the 'structural impossibility in signification' (Brigg and Muller 2009, 406), yet this impossibility remains 'an integral part of a system of signification' (Brigg and Muller 2009, 405). It is something that is real yet unable to be represented. The emphasis, therefore, falls upon the impossibility of representation. This should be embraced since, contrary to the earlier 'essentialist' conceptions of peacebuilding, these are not problems to be solved, but real and positive impossibilities (Brigg and Muller 2009, 408). Accepting this helps us to better respect cultural difference. However, embracing Laclau's approach also involves clear attempts to avoid the idea that social relations and hierarchies might somehow preexist the process of articulation. Let us be clear what this position entails. As Laclau says,

> In my perspective, there is no beyond the play of differences, no ground which would a priori privilege some elements of the whole over the others. Whatever centrality an element acquires, it has to be explained by the play of differences as such. (Laclau 2002, 69)

The criticisms Brigg raises in his contribution to this special issue and in particular, his warning not to embrace pluralism to the point where difference can lose its meaningful purchase, should therefore be applied more widely to Laclau and others who deny that anything meaningful exists outside the play of difference and moment of articulation.

In a different approach, Hirblinger and Landau (2018, this issue) wish to stress the fluid, multi-layered and context-dependent nature of ethnic identity through a turn to recent IR practice theory. They argue that ethnicity is more a political category than a scientific one and that it can be known through its tangible effects. To this end, they draw on Adler and Pouliot's understanding of practices as socially meaningful action which acts out background knowledge and discourse and forms the 'dynamic material and ideational processes that enable structures to be stable or to evolve, and agents to reproduce or to transform structures' (Adler and Pouliot 2011, 4). The problem with this argument is that Adler and Pouliot invoke the notion of social structures but never spell out what this means (see Joseph and Kurki 2018). The terminology here is close to critical realism, but it is clear, looking at the rest of their arguments that it is on the notion of practice that most of the explanatory power falls. By contrast, a critical realist notion of 'positioned practices' that locates the day to day actions of people within the context of deeper social structures that these practices reproduce and occasionally transform – for example how work practices reproduce deeper capitalist social relations or how development practices reproduce deep inequalities in the international system – offers more promise of capturing the notion of hierarchical relations and inequalities of power.

Performativity and practice

An important part of the 'practice turn' is a new emphasis on performativity. As noted in the introduction, this position emphasizes how actors perform their identities through various discourses and practices. It avoids 'essentialism' by suggesting that subjects come into being through (self) enactment. This is good insofar as it rejects the idea of actors having some essential identity but it also has the effect of wiping out such notions as history, modernity, traditions, as well as science, thus reducing or limiting our ability to discuss the importance of social relations. Instead, everything is the product of discourses and practices. There is nothing meaningful outside of these. We are back to the problems which are evident in Laclau's philosophy.

There are important arguments in this special issue which usefully engage with performativity approaches, but which would benefit from setting this in the context of a deeper social ontology in order to avoid the pitfalls of radical relationalism. Róisín Read's article in this issue (2018) highlights the struggle faced by female aid workers to perform 'authenticity' in the field of humanitarian intervention. Difference operates through juxtaposition of roles – the roles of the women are contrasted with the men around them and in particular, in relation to the more experienced, more 'real' aid workers. Noticeable again is the critique of objectivity present in Read's argument about the practices of intervention where the accounts of the participants are not seen as 'objective truth' but examples of 'flesh witnessing'.

Martin de Almagro (2018, this issue) develops the concept of 'hybrid clubs' to emphasize the non-essential character of difference. This draws on performativity to show how actors can belong to different clubs and perform in a certain way while not being essentially attached to them. As she says:

> I propose the concept of the 'hybrid club' as a cluster of local and international actors that join forces to develop a series of peacebuilding and development initiatives. The club can be considered as a diagnostic site for studying complex processes of differentiation and identification in post-conflict settings. First, I argue that hybrid clubs constitute spaces where difference is crafted and performed through the sharing of knowledge and practices with and only with the members of the club. (P.2 of version sent)

This is an important argument that could be taken in a number of directions, much like Hirblinger and Landau's discussion of how difference is 'scaled'. However, it is a performative account rather than a structural one – difference is made through the complex performances of individual and collective bodies. A relational account, rather than being based on the four interactions discussed earlier, is taken to mean a focus on the 'dynamic and ever-changing relationship amongst agents ... [who] acquire meaning through and are constituted by their transactions, connections and relations with other actors' (P.3 of version sent).

The editors rightly argue that drawing attention to the performativity of difference also means examining how differences are situated in particular social and historical contexts. This means that difference cannot be understood simply by looking at performance alone, as if identity is produced only at the moment of interaction between people. If Hirblinger and Landau are correct, then the 'scaling' of difference implies that people belong to a variety of different groups at different levels with, as Martín de Almagro suggests, actors being 'local' in some situations, and 'international' in others. This is also a part of the process of claiming legitimacy at that particular scale, while power operates to deny this, or to exercise strategic selectivity over agents and their strategies. If peacebuilding strategies operate to select particular types of identity and difference, then the realist implications of this need to be developed. The situation is not simply the product of interaction, but is already 'out there' (in the sense of Bourdieu's realist notion of field) if differences depend on time and context. Indeed, the choice might be between the flat ontology offered by Latour and many of the current trends in IR, and that offered by Bourdieu and his more realist interpreters who suggest that habitus cannot be determined solely in relation to other groups and their worldviews and that the field is indeed 'out there'.

Latour believes that we need a flat ontology in order to render the social world more clearly visible (2005, 16). We should talk only of those things and processes that we observe in social interactions, avoiding talk of underlying structures. The latter would require us to engage in abstract explanations that impose themselves on what we are trying to observe (Latour 2005). He believes that such approaches end up reproducing dominant relations of power because they appeal to some higher authority and some of these sentiments are evident in this special issue. By contrast, my argument would be that by refusing to put experience and difference in this wider context we fail to fully understand the practices we are trying to describe. As Bhaskar argues, this is an onto-logical question where

> By secreting an ontology based on the category of experience, the domains of reality (the domains of the real, the actual, and the empirical) are collapsed into one. This prevents the crucial question of the conditions under which experience is, in fact, significant in science from being posed. (Bhaskar 1989, 15)

Thus to talk of the experience or performance of difference in peacebuilding still requires us to talk of underlying social structures that, in a sense, make experience and performance possible as well as imposing constraints upon it. Despite recent practice theory claiming Bourdieu as an influence, he himself is clear that to account for practices and performances, we need to relate these to the 'objective structure defining the social conditions for the pro-duction of the habitus' (1977, 78). Colin Wight's realist reading of Bourdieu suggests that habitus can be understood through the notion of positioned practices as a mediating link between agents and the socio-cultural world that they share (Wight 2006, 49). This is inspired by Bhaskar's argument that we need to understand the 'point of contact' between human agency and social structures by examining a mediating system of positions – places, functions, rules, tasks, duties, etc., and practices, activities etc., which are engaged in by virtue of agents' occupancy of social positions. Crucially, this position-practice system is to be understood relationally (Bhaskar 1989, 40–41). I thus offer this understanding of rela-tionality in contrast with that outlined in the Special Issue.

As Milja Kurki and I have argued elsewhere (Joseph and Kurki 2018), some notion of struc-ture is necessary in order to make sense of some of Bourdieu's key notions such as misre-cognition, habitual reproduction and the largely unconscious nature of habitus. Social practices and performances act as the means of mediation between structures and agents and it is through the routines and everyday practices (highlighted in this special issue) that objective social structures are reproduced. Bourdieu sees these activities of the habitus as largely unconscious, unreflective or at least based on limited understanding of the wider context. Indeed, Bourdieu's key notion of misrecognition depends upon this understanding of structure, agency and practice whereby practical taxonomies are under-stood as 'a transformed, misrecognizable form of the real divisions of the social order … [that] contribute to the reproduction of that order by producing objectively orchestrated practices (Bourdieu 1977, 163). This makes the realist point that such practices produce mis-recognition of a real situation. By rendering the world as ontologically flat and eschewing discussion of anything other than practices, it is Latour and those who follow his example who, in fact, contribute to the reproduction of existing social orders by refusing to examine its conditions of possibility and the hierarchies that lie behind it.

Conclusion

Firstly, the strengths of the contributions present in this special issue were outlined. In par-ticular, they identify and seek to rectify the errors of previous approaches to peacebuilding

THE POLITICS OF PEACEBUILDING IN A DIVERSE WORLD

where difference is either discarded, identified as a problem to be overcome, or stigmatized as a reality at odds with our normal frames of reference. The arguments present in this special issue problematize, deconstruct and interrogate the ways that difference comes into being in order to provide a better understanding of the peacebuilding process. In doing so, I believe the contributions collected here offer important insights.

However, I also argue that there are some limitations to such approaches due to their distance from realism, their scepticism about objectivity, their critique of knowledge claims and, in particular, the absence of a strong notion of social structure. In my view, this limits some of the important insights contained here. These are not problems specific to this volume, but are characteristic more generally of the current 'practice turn' and arguments for poststructuralism, new materialism and current arguments for non-essentialist relationality.

With the practice turn as well as other recent developments, the focus falls upon that which is observable, the everyday, the common place, the 'ontic', what goes on at the surface level (Kustermans 2016, 191). The effect of this, I have argued, is the neglect of the structural. The significance of this, I suggest, is that we are then denied the opportunity to adequately explain the context within which difference occurs, the hierarchies that underpin difference and the means for enacting the sort of social change that might overcome some of the more problematic elements of difference.

In its place, I suggested that rather than trying to avoid the structure–agency relationship, we should adopt an approach to practices and difference that seeks to 'position' practices (Bhaskar 1993) in their appropriate context, recognizing not only intersubjective relations, but the inter-intra, material and social character of these relations. These exist in a complex multiplicity of tense socio-spatializing processes. Yet, despite this complexity, analytical attention can be paid to the capacities possessed by agents by virtue of the positions they occupy, their capacities to act and their relation to enduring social structures that enable and constrain (Isaac 1987).

In short, a relational approach to difference is more important than ever, but not without an analysis of the social and material relations that contribute to the production of difference.

Disclosure statement

No potential conflict of interest was reported by the author.

References

Adler, Emanuel, and Vincent Pouliot. 2011. "International Practices." International Theory 3(1):1–36.
Bargués-Pedreny, Pol, and Xavier Mathieu. 2018. "Beyond Silence, Obstacle and Stigma: Revisiting the 'Problem' of Difference in Peacebuilding." *Journal of Intervention and Statebuilding* 12 (3): 283–299.

Behr, H. 2018. "Peace-in-Difference: A Phenomenological Approach to Peace Through Difference." *Journal of Intervention and Statebuilding* 12 (3): 335–351.

Bhaskar. 1978. *The Possibility of Naturalism*. Hassocks: Harvester Press.

Bhaskar, Roy. 1989. The Possibility of Naturalism, 2nd ed. Hemel Hempstead: Harvester Wheatsheaf.

Bhaskar, R. 1993. *Dialectic: The Pulse of Freedom*. London: Verso.

Bourdieu, P. 1977. *Outline of a Theory of Practice*. Cambridge: Cambridge University Press.

Brigg, M. 2008. *The New Politics of Conflict Resolution Responding to Difference*. Basingstoke: Palgrave Macmillan.

Brigg, M. 2018. "Relational and Essential: Theorizing Difference for Peacebuilding." *Journal of Intervention and Statebuilding* 12 (3): 352–366.

Brigg, M., and K. Muller. 2009. "Conceptualising Culture in Conflict Resolution." *Journal of Intercultural Studies* 30 (2): 121–140.

Campbell, D. 1998. *National Deconstruction: Violence, Identity and Justice in Bosnia*. Minneapolis: University of Minnesota Press.

Dean, K. J. Joseph, J. M. Roberts, and C. Wight. 2006. *Realism, Philosophy and Social Science*. Basingstoke: Palgrave.

Donais, T. 2009. "Empowerment or Imposition? Dilemmas of Local Ownership in Post-conflict Peacebuilding Processes." *Peace and Change: A Journal of Peace Research* 34 (1): 3–26.

Fukuyama, F. 2004. *Statebuilding: Governance and World Order in the 21st Century*. Ithaca: Cornell University Press.

Ghani, A., and C. Lockhard. 2008. *Fixing Failed States: A Framework for Rebuilding a Fractured World*. Oxford: Oxford University Press.

Hirblinger, A., and Dana M. Landau. 2018. "Governing Conflict: The Politics of Scaling Difference." *Journal of Intervention and Statebuilding* 12 (3): 385–404.

Isaac, G. 1987. "Beyond the Three Faces of Power: A Realist Critique." *Polity* 20 (1): 4–31.

Joseph, J., and M. Kurki. 2018. "The Limits of Practice: Why Realism Can Complement IR's Practice Turn." *International Theory* 10 (1): 71–97.

Kustermans. 2016. "Parsing the Practice Turn: Practice, Practical Knowledge, Practices." *Millennium: Journal of International Studies* 44 (2): 175–196.

Laclau, E. 2002. *On Populist Reason*. London: Verso.

Latour, B. 2005. *Reassembling the Social: Introduction to Actor Network Theory*. Oxford: Oxford University Press.

Lederach, J. P. 1997. *Building Peace*. Washington, DC: United States Institute of Peace.

Mac Ginty, R. 2015. "Where is the Local? Critical Localism and Peacebuilding." *Third World Quarterly* 36 (5): 840–856.

Mac Ginty, R., and O. P. Richmond. 2016. "The Fallacy of Constructing Hybrid Political Orders: A Reappraisal of the Hybrid Turn in Peacebuilding." *International Peacekeeping* 23 (2): 219–239.

Martin de Almagro, M. 2018. "Hybrid Clubs: A Feminist Approach to Peacebuilding in the Democratic Republic of Congo." *Journal of Intervention and Statebuilding* 12 (3): 319–334.

Minow, M. 1990. *Making all the Difference: Inclusion, Exclusion, and America Law*. Ithaca: Cornell University Press.

Paris, R., and T. D. Sisk. 2009. *The Dilemmas of Statebuilding: Confronting the Contradictions of Postwar Peace Operations*. London: Routledge.

Read, R. 2018. "Embodying Difference: Reading Gender in Women's Memoirs of Humanitarianism." *Journal of Intervention and Statebuilding* 12 (3): 300–318.

Richmond, O. P. 2009. "Becoming Liberal, Unbecoming Liberalism: Liberal-Local Hybridity via the Everyday as a Response to the Paradoxes of Liberal Peacebuilding." *Journal of Intervention and Statebuilding* 3 (3): 324–344.

Wight. 2006. *Agents Structures and International Relations*. Cambridge: Cambridge University Press.

Index

Note: Page numbers in *italics* refer to figures
Page numbers followed by 'n' refer to notes

Aboriginal Australian peoples 74, 78–81
Abu-Lughod, L. 11–12
action 58; and anticipation of future 58; intentionality, and meaning 57; Schütz on 57, 58
Addis Ababa Agreement (1972) 110
Adler, Emanuel 148
advent (Derrida) 59–60, 61
affective politics of sovereignty 129
Afghanistan 25, 30
Agier, Michel 21
Ahmed, Sara 22, 23, 26, 30
Ahtisaari, Martti 118n4
Ahtisaari Plan 114, 115, 116, 118n4
aid workers: international, lifestyle of 26; *see also* humanitarianism, reading gender in women's memoirs of
Akaev, Askar 128
Ali, Mia 24, 30
Anderson, Benedict 103
Anghie, Antony 5
anthology 19–20
anti-essentialism 3, 8, 11, 61, 63, 72, 75, 82, 147
Aristotle 72
Assembly of the Peoples of Kyrgyzstan (*Assambleia narodov Kyrgyzstana*) 128
assimilation 7, 8, 10, 88, 124
Auschwitz trials 96
Australian peoples, Aboriginal 74, 78–81
authenticity, and Field 26, 149
Avruch, Kevin 3–6

Baker, Catherine 21
Bakiev, Kurmanbek 128
Bargués-Pedreny, Pol 1, 22, 86, 103, 123, 139, 143
Bazar-Korgon (Kyrgyzstan) 134, *135*, 137, 139
becoming, process of 56, 59
Behr, Hartmut 53, 139, 146
Being and Time (Heidegger) 56, 59

Bernath, Julie 12, 85
Bhaskar, Roy 144, 146, 147, 150
Björkdahl, Annika 23–24
Blair, Tony 62
Bosnia 10
Bourdieu, P. 144, 149, 150
Boutros-Ghali, Boutros 4
Brenner, Neil 109
Brigg, Morgan 11, 12, 62, 70, 146, 147, 148
Brown, Gordon 62
Bryant, Miranda 27–28
Buber, Martin 74
Buddhism 73
Bush, George 62

Café Genre 47
Cambodia *see* Extraordinary Chambers in the Courts of Cambodia (ECCC); Khmer Rouge regime
Cambodian People's Party 92
Campbell, David 10
Case, Sue-Ellen 28
Caswell, Michelle 96
Central Asia 126
Chasing Misery: An Anthology of Essays by Women in Humanitarian Responses 18, 19–20, 23, 30, 32
civic nationalism, in (post-) Soviet Kyrgyzstan 126–130, 131
Civil Administration of the New Sudan (CANS) 111
civil society 5, 43, 92
Clinton, Bill 62
Cold War 4, 92, 104, 123
colonization/colonialism 72; and Aboriginal Australian peoples 80; and indigenous difference 78–79; and Sudan 105, 106, 110
Committee on the Elimination of Racial Discrimination (CERD), UN 132

Communist Party of Kampuchea (CPK), Cambodia 88, 89, 90
communities: imagined 103; mono-ethnic, in (post-) Soviet Kyrgyzstan 136, 137; religious, in Ottoman Empire 106; term 114
Comprehensive Peace Agreement (CPA) 106, 110, 118n1
Comprehensive Proposal for the Kosovo Status Settlement plan *see* Ahtisaari Plan
conflict: integrative approach to 76; peacebuilding, post- 4, 85; *see also* ethnic conflicts; Kyrgyzstan, (post-) Soviet
constructivism 55, 65n6
crimes against humanity 90
critical realism 144, 145, 148
cultural difference 1–2, 144, 148; and pragmatic tolerance 4; undervaluing/overvaluing 3–6
cultural recognition 72
cultural sensitivity 5, 6
'cultural turn' 5
cumulative radicalization 89

Daoism 73
Darwin, Charles 76, 77, 82
Dasein 60
decentralization 104, 111, 113–118
decentralized despotism 106
de-essentialization 54, 55, 63, 70, 71, 75, 78, 79, 81, 82, 147
democracy 4, 60, 113, 143
Democratic Kampuchea (DK) *see* Khmer Rouge regime
'democratic peace hypothesis' 62
Democratic Republic of Congo (DRC), feminist approach to peacebuilding in 37–40; differentiating gender narratives, resisting peacebuilding initiatives 42–44; hybrid clubs 44–48; implications for politics of difference 48–49; international as personal experience 46–48; local ownership 47; performing embodied sameness and difference 45–46; relational approach 39
Derrida, Jacques 55, 58, 59–61, 66n14
différance (Derrida) 61
difference, in peacebuilding 1–3; characteristic attitudes of the West towards 8; closure, deferring 10–11; critiques of liberal peace, stigma in 6–8; governing 105–107; performing multidimensional identities/differences 3, 8, 9–10; policies, field of 6; and power *see under* power; problematizing 3, 8, 86, 143; relational and open-ended interactions, longing for 10–11; silencing 3, 8, 86, 143; stigmatizing 3, 12, 61, 144; and time/context 9; undervaluing/overvaluing cultural difference 3–6
dilemma of difference 7, 123–140
Dinka (South Sudan) 110
Documentation Center of Cambodia 96

Donovan, Kevin P. 24
Doty, Roxanne Lynn 103
dress, and embodied identification 45
Duncanson, Claire 18, 20–21
dynamic of difference 5
Dyvik, Synne L. 20, 21, 24

economic liberalism 4
Edwards, Penny 99n12
egology 59
embodiment 20–23, 29, 31, 40, 41, 45–46, 48–49
emotional distance, and The Field 25, 27
'empty signifier' 147
epistemic fallacies 147
essentialism 5, 53–54, 62, 75–78, 82, 145–146, 148; anti-essentialism 3, 8, 11, 61, 63, 72, 75, 82, 147; de-essentialization 54, 55, 63, 70, 71, 75, 78, 79, 81, 82, 147; Extraordinary Chambers in the Courts of Cambodia 95–96; non-Western 64; positivist 38; in post-liberal peace concepts 63; relational–essential approach 79–81; sociobiological 76; strategic 11, 38, 66n17, 95–96, 103
ethnic conflicts 72, 75, 82; in Kosovo 114; in (post-) Soviet Kyrgyzstan 127–129; in South Sudan 111, 112
Ethnic Groups in Conflict (Horowitz) 107
ethnicity 72, 89–90, 94–95, 97, 104, 105–107, 123, 124, 148; *see also* Kosovo, politics of scaling difference in; Kyrgyzstan, (post-) Soviet; South Sudan, politics of scaling difference in
ethnocentrism 70
ethnogenesis 126–127, 128
ethno-nationalism, in (post-) Soviet Kyrgyzstan 126, 127–129
ethno-territoriality, in (post-) Soviet Kyrgyzstan 126–127
European Union (EU) 62, 116
existential philosophy 103
expatriates 27
experience 39, 40, 41; lived 20; personal, international as 46–48
exteriority 9, 58
Extraordinary Chambers in the Courts of Cambodia (ECCC) 87–88; Cham minority 87, 90, 91, 95, 96, 97; creating difference between victims of genocide and other victims 91–93; crimes against humanity 91, 92; crimes of genocide 90; dilemma of politics of difference at 93–97; exclusion from narratives of shared suffering 96–97; genocide, definition of 89–90; legal categories, ordering of difference in 89–91; potential for transformation 94–95; risks of essentializing difference 95–96; Vietnamese minority 87, 89, 90, 91, 94–95; *Yuon*-ness 94
eye witnessing 21

INDEX

Farooq, Umar 129
Feldacker, Caryl 28
female aid workers *see* humanitarianism, reading gender in women's memoirs of
feminism 18, 20, 76, 103; *see also* Democratic Republic of Congo (DRC), feminist approach to peacebuilding in; humanitarianism, reading gender in women's memoirs of
First Sudanese Civil War 110
flat ontology 147, 149–150
'flesh witnessing' 18, 19, 21, 22, 23, 24, 31–32, 149
floating zone of elite subalternity (Spivak) 38
Follett, Mary Parker 72, 75–76, 77, 78, 82
Framework for Peace, Security and Cooperation for the Democratic Republic of Congo and Region (2013) 42
Freedom House 130
free market 4
friend–enemy distinction (Schmitt) 103

Gaanderse, Miranda 29, 30
gender *see* Democratic Republic of Congo (DRC), feminist approach to peacebuilding in; humanitarianism, reading gender in women's memoirs of
genocide *see* Extraordinary Chambers in the Courts of Cambodia (ECCC); Khmer Rouge regime
Gil, Jose 74
Goffman, Erving 73
Goma declaration 42
Graham, Mary 74
Greenhalgh, Emilie J. 26, 28, 30
Grosz, Elizabeth 72, 75, 76–78, 82
Group of Experts (UN) 90
Gullette, D. 129

habitus 149, 150
Hagon, Kirsten 25
Hameiri, Shahar 108
Harari, Yuval Noah 21
Heathershaw, J. 129, 131
Heidegger, Martin 55, 56, 59
Heraclitus 74
Herb, Guntram H. 108
Hinton, Alexander 88, 93, 94
Hirblinger, Andreas T. 9, 103, 108, 148, 149
historicism 56
historiography 56
Hobsbawm, Eric John 103
Hoppe, Kelsey 19–20, 25, 26, 28, 30, 32
Horowitz, Donald L. 107, 108
Hubbard, Rachael 24
Hughes, Caroline 108
humanitarian exceptionalism 9, 21, 22, 27–29
humanitarianism, reading gender in women's memoirs of 9, 12, 18–19, 148–149; aid workers

and beneficiaries, divide between 27–28; authority of 'The Field' 23–27; *Chasing Misery* 18, 19–20; crying of women 30; difference, embodiment and passing 20–23; difference between local and international 22; 'in-group' recognition 28; motherhood 28; passing 29–31; romantic relationships 28; women as flesh witnesses 31–32
Husserl, Edmund 55, 59
hybrid clubs 11, 37–50, 149
hybridity 22, 23, 41, 49, 93, 108
hybrid peace 7
hybrid tribunal 87, 93; *see also* Extraordinary Chambers in the Courts of Cambodia (ECCC)

identitarianism 70, 71, 72, 79, 81, 147
identity(ies) 76–77, 108; collective 19; cultural, Derrida on 61; deconstruction of 10–11; ethnic *see* ethnicity; of female aid workers *see* humanitarianism, reading gender in women's memoirs of; formation 63; group 45; and hybrid clubs 38; and Khmer Rouge regime 88; Kyrgyzstani *see* Kyrgyzstan, (post-) Soviet; multidimensional 9–10; 'post-identitarian' peacebuilding 11; racial 22; reproduction, relational process of 42; and Simmel 56
identity theory 73
imagined communities 103
imperial peace 55, 59
inbetweenness 20, 26–27
indigenous difference 71, 74, 75, 78–81
infinity 58, 59
institution building 5–6
integrative approach, to conflict 76
intentionality 57, 58, 59
interactional ontology 147
International Alert 43
International Conference of the Great Lakes Region 42
International Criminal Tribunal 87
International Monetary Fund 4
Isaac, G. 144
Isaac, Jeffrey 146
Isakova, Z. 131, 133
Islamophobia 95

Jones, Lee 108
Joseph, Jonathan 12, 23, 40, 143
Judaism 74

Kaing Guek Eav 87
Kampala declaration 42
Kaplan, David H. 108
Kappler, Stefanie 23–24
Kelsall, Tim 93
Khartoum (Sudan) 106, 110
Khieu Samphan 87

Khmer Krom community 89, 90, 94
Khmer Rouge regime 87; Khmer Rouge Tribunal
see Extraordinary Chambers in the Courts of
Cambodia (ECCC); manufacturing of
difference under 88–89
Kiir Mayardit, Salva 110, 112
Kiljunen, Kimo 129
kinship system, Australian Aborigine 81
knowledge 48, 78; and embodiment 41;
indigenous 6; local 38, 63; and relationality 39;
sharing, and hybrid clubs 38; situated 20, 63;
traditions, acknowledging 79
Kokora (South Sudan) 110
Kosovo, politics of scaling difference in 104–105,
106–107, 109–110, 117–118; Assembly of
Serbian Municipalities 115; Association/
Community of Serb-Majority Municipalities
116; Bosniak community 116; communities,
term 114; decentralization 113–118; dialogue
between Belgrade and Pristina 114, 116;
Mitrovica 115; parallel structures 115;
redrawing administrative boundaries 114,
115; Serbs 114–115, 116; sub-municipal units
(SMUs) 115
Kosovo Liberation Army 113
Kurki, Milja 150
Kvinna 43
Kyrgyz language 131–132
Kyrgyzstan, (post-) Soviet 11, 124–125;
Community Reception Centres 133;
Conception for Strengthening National Unity
and Inter-Ethnic Relations 131; from ethno-
nationalist sentiments to ethnic conflict
127–129; ethno-territoriality 126–127;
interethnic harmony 130–133; interethnic
unity (*mezhdunarodnoe soglasie*) 128; Local
Crime Prevention Centres (LCPCs) 134–135;
mono-ethnic communities 136, 137; peoples'
friendship (*druzhba narodov*) 124, 125, 127,
130, 133–138, *135*, *138*; Soviet modernity
126–127; taboo of identity after 'Osh events'
129–130

Laclau, E. 147, 148
Landau, Dana M. 9, 103, 148, 149
Latour, Bruno 71, 147, 149–150
Lefebvre, Henri 41
Lentz, Carola 105
Lévinas, Emmanuel 55, 58–59, 74
liberal peace 54, 62, 63; critiques, stigma in 6–8;
and transitional justice 86
lifestyle, of international aid workers 26
liminality, in humanitarian memoirs 22
lived experiences 20
Local Crime Prevention Centres (LCPCs), in
Kyrgyzstan 134–135
Local Government Board (LGB), South
Sudan 111
local ownership 6, 47

local turn 22, 40, 41–42, 86
Lottholz, Philipp 11, 123, 125

Mac Ginty, Roger 25
McLeod, Laura 20, 48
Manas 123
manufacturing difference process (Khmer
Rouge) 88–89
Margins of Philosophy (Derrida) 61
Martin de Almagro, Maria 9, 11, 20, 37, 149
mass atrocity *see* Extraordinary Chambers in the
Courts of Cambodia (ECCC); Khmer Rouge
regime
Massey, Doreen B. 108
Massumi, Brian 73, 74, 78
Mathieu, Xavier 1, 22, 86, 103, 123, 143
Maynard, M. 11
Mead, George Herbert 73
meaning, constitution of 57
Méditaticns Cartésiennes (Husserl) 59
Megoran, N. 129
memoirs: military 20, 21; *see also*
humanitarianism, reading gender in women's
memoirs of
micropolitics 49, 88
military memoirs 20, 21
millet system, in Ottoman Empire 106
mind–body dichotomy 41
Minow, Martha 7, 11, 86, 123, 126, 139, 145
misrecognition (Bourdieu) 150
modernity, in (post-) Soviet Kyrgyzstan 126–127
modo future exacti 57
monogenealogy 60
motion, Simmel on 55–56, 66n11
multiculturalism 4, 71, 81, 124
multidimensional identities/differences,
performing 9–10
multidimensionality, of difference 3, 8
Myrzakmatov, Melis 128

nationalisation (*korenizatsiia*) 126
nationalism, in (post-) Soviet Kyrgyzstan: civic
126–130, 131; ethno- 126, 127–129
national territorial delimitation (NTD) 126,
140n1
natsionclnoe razmezhivanie see national
territorial delimitation (NTD)
natural selection (Darwin) 76, 77
new materialism 146, 147
Newtonian physics 72, 147
Nguyen, Lima 94
Nhât Hạnh, Thích 73
non-essentialism 70, 144, 147, 149
North Atlantic Treaty Organization (NATO) 113
North–South relations 103
Nuon Chea 87

objectivity 9, 125, 149
object oriented ontology 145

O'Donoghue, Lucy 25, 26, 28, 29
O'Heir, Tracy 24
ontological imperialism 59
ontology: flat 147, 149–150; interactional 147; object oriented 145; Western 58, 59
openness 58, 59, 60
'order of interbeing' 73
Organisation for Security and Co-Operation in Europe (OSCE) 130
Orjuela, C. 10–11
Osh (Kyrgyzstan): Day of the city of Osh (*Den goroda*) 137, *138*; events, taboo of identity 129–130; restructuring of 127, *128*
Other Heading, The (Derrida) 66n14
Other/Othering/Otherness 28, 62, 88; advent of 61; Derrida on 60; and Field 24, 27; and hybrid clubs 44–48; Lévinas on 59; and phenomenological approach to peace 54, 55
Ottoman Empire 104, 106

Paipais, Vassilios 10
Pari community (Sudan) 112–113
Parity Law (Congo) 43
Partis-Jennings, Hannah 20, 23, 25, 30
passing 19, 22–23, 26, 28, 29–31
peacebuilding: 'post-identitarian' 11; post-conflict 4, 85; *see also* Democratic Republic of Congo (DRC), feminist approach to peacebuilding in; difference, in peacebuilding
peace-in-difference 10, 54, 55, 59, 62–63, 64, 65n3
peace studies 62–63
'peoples' friendship' (*druzhba narodov*) 124, 125, 127, 130, 133–138, *135*, *138*
People's Republic of Kampuchea (PRK), Cambodia 92
performativity 148–150
phenomenological approach, to peace 64–65n2; early phenomenologists and temporality 55–58; from early phenomenologists to Lévinas and Derrida 58–62; peace studies and practices 62–63; problem and argument 53–54; thinking difference 55–62
Phenomenology of the Social World (Schütz) 57
Philips, Melissa 23, 29, 30
philosophy: existential 103; *see also* Western philosophy
physics, Newtonian 72, 147
pluralism 71, 75, 147, 148
political movements *see* Democratic Republic of Congo (DRC), feminist approach to peacebuilding in
politics of scaling difference 9, 103–105, 107–109, 149; counter-scaling 105, 117; governing conflict and governing difference 105–107; Kosovo 113–117; rescaling 104–105, 117; South Sudan 109–113; unravelling 104, 117
positioned practices 148, 150

'positive discrimination' 127
positivism 145
positivist essentialism 38
postcolonial thought 103
post-conflict peacebuilding 4, 85; *see also* Kyrgyzstan, (post-) Soviet
post-liberal peace approach 62, 63
poststructuralism 65n2, 108, 145, 146
Pouliot, Vincent 148
power 2; and difference 3, 8, 11–12, 22, 40, 144–146; and gender 42, 50n17; *see also* humanitarianism, reading gender in women's memoirs of; and knowledge production 41; local ownership 6; and scaling practices 104–105, 108, 118; and transitional justice 87
practice theory 148, 150
practice turn 148, 151
pragmatic tolerance, and cultural difference 4
Prasad, Conor 129

quantum physics 74

racial identity 22
Ranke, Leopold von 56
Read, Róisín 9, 12, 18, 148–149
recognition paradigm 72, 81
Reddekop, Jarrad 74
Reeves, M. 126
relational–essential approach 79–81
relationalism/relationality 12, 39, 40–42, 71, 72–75, 76, 77, 78, 81–82, 143–144; difference as relation of power 144–146; performativity and practice 148–150; recent approaches to 146–148; social relations between people 145–146; vagueness 145
religious communities, in Ottoman Empire 106
restorative justice programmes 81
Richmond, Oliver 23–24, 62
Rieff, David 21
'Rien sans les femmes [Nothing without the Women]' (RSLF) 37, 43, 44, 45, 46–48
Robinson, Amy 26
Romano, Roberta 28, 30
Roth, Silke 24

Sabaratnam, Meera 2
Saferworld 134, 137
Scarpello, Fabio 108
Schmitt, Carl 103
Schütz, Alfred 55, 57, 58
Security, Stabilization and Development Pact (2006) 42
Seeger, Helen 23, 24, 27, 30
self 12, 55, 61, 64; and experience 41; Lévinas on 59; Ojibwe 74; and relationality 74, 75
Serbia 113, 118n1
sexual and gender-based violence (SGBV) 42–43, 47
Shapiro, Michael 66n12

Sheehan, Carmen 24, 25
Sierra Leone *see* Special Court for Sierra Leone
signification, and difference 147
Simmel, Georg 55–56, 57, 58, 66n11
Simons, Claudia 108
Smirl, Lisa 22, 23, 27, 28
social engineering, in (post-) Soviet Kyrgyzstan 126–130
Socialist Federal Republic of Yugoslavia (SFRY) 118n1
social sciences 57, 72, 88
social structures 11, 12, 23, 144, 145, 148, 150
sociobiological essentialism 76
sociopolitical ordering 79, 80
South Sudan, politics of scaling difference in 104–105, 106, 109–110, 117; *bomas* 112; county mapping tool 112; demarcation of administrative boundaries 112; Pari community 112–113; *payams* 112; Second Sudanese Civil War 110; tribe/community, term 106, 110, 111, 112; Unity in Diversity policy 110–113
space/spatiality 40, 41–42; dialogical 60, 61; and racial identities 22; and RSLF movement 45–46
Special Court for Sierra Leone 93
Sperfeldt, Christoph 94
Spivak, Gayatri Chakravorty 38, 66n17
sports utility vehicles (SUVs) 24–25
Stabilization and Reconstruction Plan in Eastern DRC 42
Stalin, Joseph 126
State Agency for Local Self-Governance and Interethnic Relations (Gamsumo), Kyrgyzstan 130, 132–133, *132*
stigma of difference 6–8
stories/storytelling 39, 40–41, 42–44, 46–47, 48–49
strategic essentialism 11, 38, 66n17, 95–96, 103
structural adjustments, free-market 4
substantialism 11, 58
'subversive clientelism' 129
Sudan: Anglo-Egyptian rule over 106, 110, 118n1; postcolonial 106; Second Sudanese Civil War 110; *see also* South Sudan, politics of scaling difference in
Sudan People's Liberation Movement/Army (SPLM/A) 110–111, 112
Sylvester, Christine 20

Tajikistan 131, 138
thingness 72
'third sex' 23
Ticktin, Miriam 18, 21–22
time/temporality 61, 65n7; and action 58; and Derrida 60, 61; and difference 9; internal time-consciousness 57; and Lévinas 59; phenomenological approach to peace 55–58, 60; and racial identities 22; Schütz on 57

Tito, Josip Broz 107
Todorov, T. 8
Townley, Ruth 24–25
transformation/transformativity: and Derrida 60; and Lévinas 59; potential, Extraordinary Chambers in the Courts of Cambodia 94–95; Simmel on 55–56; and temporality 58; and understanding 56–57
transitional justice 85–88, 97–98; definition of 85; resistance to 86; *see also* Extraordinary Chambers in the Courts of Cambodia (ECCC); Khmer Rouge regime
tribes/tribalism 105, 110, 111
Turkestan 126

UN Convention on the Prevention and Punishment of the Crime of Genocide 89, 90
understanding, process of 56–57, 58
United Nations 62, 85, 87, 90, 118n1, 132
United Nations Interim Administration Mission in Kosovo (UNMIK) 113
United Nations Organization Stabilization Mission in the Democratic Republic of the Congo (MONUSCO) 43
United States 4, 62, 129
universalism 3, 7, 8, 12, 143
universal logics 4
UN Peacekeeping Forces 4
UNSC Resolution 1325 42, 44
UN Security Council (UNSC) 42
Untersuchungen über die Formen der Vergesellschaftung (Simmel) 56
UN Women 46–47, 48
Uzbekistan 128, 136
Uzbek language 132
Uzbeks, in (post-) Soviet Kyrgyzstan 127–128, 129, 132

Verstehen (understanding/hermeneutics) 57
victimhood construction, and Khmer Rouge 87, 88, 90, 91–93, 94, 95, 96–97
violence *see* sexual and gender-based violence (SGBV)

Wagner, Roy 72
Wallstrom, Margot 42
Weber, Max 107, 108
Weberian state 5
Welland, Julia 20
Wendt, Alexander 74
Western ontology 58, 59
Western philosophy 58–59, 62, 65n5; thinking difference in 55–58
Whitaker, Benjamin 90
Whitehead, Alfred North 74
Wight, Colin 150

Wilke, Christiane 96

women *see* humanitarianism, reading gender in women's memoirs of

Women, Peace, and Security Agenda (United Nations) 43, 45

World Bank 4

worldviews, and difference 12, 146

Woronka, Kati 27, 30

xenophobia 94

Yugoslavia 87, 107